WIND BELL

Monthly Newsletter of the
San Francisco Zen Center
1881 Bush Street

Dec. 2, 1961
Issue No. 1

WIND BELL

Hanging in space by his mouth
His whole body is his mouth

East, West, South and North Wind
he does not care

Always, he talks in many ways
about Prajnaparamita for others

Tsu Chin Tsui Ryan
Tsu Jin Ryan
......Dogen

Those people interested in Zen Buddhism may be glad to know that there is a
Zen Center in San Francisco which, for nearly two and a half years, has been
under the guidance of Roshi Shunryu Suzuki.

The regular and 'special events' schedules are outlined in our Newsletter and
everyone is welcome to attend, of course.

Please come.

Shunryu Suzuki came here from Japan on the afternoon of June 22, 1959.
Since then he has been on the cushion conducting Zen at Sokoji.

His associate, Dr. Kato, professor at San Jose State College, assists by
giving lectures.

WEEKLY LECTURE PROGRAM

A series of lectures by Roshi Suzuki, entitled "The Pillow Under Mt. Fuji",
are now being given every Wednesday evening at 7:30 p.m. Lectures on the
Heart Sutra and the Diamond Sutra are now being concluded, to be followed by the
Lotus Sutra, using "The Manual of Zen Buddhism" by D.T. Suzuki (Evergreen
Paperback edition) as a background text.

GUEST LECTURE PROGRAM

Dr. Douglas Burns, a Buddhist scholar, will present a series of four lectures on
the development of the Zen way. The series will be held at the Center, 7:30p.m.
friday evenings, scheduled as follows

Friday, December 1	Early Hindu Thought as a basis for Buddhism
Friday, December 8	Theravada Buddhism
Friday, December 15	Taoism
Friday, December 22	Chan (Chinese Zen)

ONE AND A HALF DAY 'SESSHIN' AND TRAINING PERIOD IN DECEMBER

From 5:45 a.m. to 8:30 p.m. on Saturday, December 16 and from 5:45 a.m. to
12 noon on Sunday, December 17, the Center will hold a one and a half day
'Sesshin'.(Sesshin is a Japanese term for a full day of meditation over an
extended period of time). Meals will be served at the Center.

The 'Sesshin' will open a two month training period of morning and evening
meditation (zazen) in accordance with the regular schedule below.

First issue of mimeograph Wind Bell, *December 1961.*

WIND BELL

Teachings
from the
San Francisco
Zen Center
1968–2001

edited by
Michael Wenger

North Atlantic Books
Berkeley, California

Published by
North Atlantic Books
P.O. Box 12327
Berkeley, California 94712

Printed in the United States of America
Cover and book design © Ayelet Maida, A/M Studios

Wind Bell: Teachings from the San Francisco Zen Center 1968–2001 is sponsored by the Society for the Study of Native Arts and Sciences, a nonprofit educational corporation whose goals are to develop an educational and crosscultural perspective linking various scientific, social, and artistic fields; to nurture a holistic view of arts, sciences, humanities, and healing; and to publish and distribute literature on the relationship of mind, body, and nature.

North Atlantic Books' publications are available through most bookstores. For further information, call 800-337-2665 or visit our website at www.northatlanticbooks.com.

Substantial discounts on bulk quantities are available to corporations, professional associations, and other organizations. For details and discount information, contact our special sales department.

LIBRARY OF CONGRESS CATALOGING-IN-PUBLICATION DATA

Wenger, Michael, 1947–
    Wind bell: teachings from the San Francisco Zen Center 1968–2001 /
    edited by Michael Wenger.
        p. cm.
    ISBN 1-55643-381-6 (alk. Paper)
        1. Religious life-Satasha.   2. Zen Buddhism-Doctrines.   3. San Francisco
Zen Center.   1. Title.

BQ9436 .W46 2001
294.3'927'097461-dc21   2001032655

1 2 3 4 5 6 7 8 9 / 06 05 04 03 02

Contents

Foreword

The first mimeographed edition of *Wind Bell* appeared forty years ago on December 2, 1961 during the auspicious week-long celebration of Rohatsu. Since then there have been forty years of lectures, talks, and writings of Buddhist teachers, monks, and lay practioners.

Forty years might sound like a long time, but the United States—and San Francisco in particular—has been welcoming Buddhist teachers for over a hundred years. Soyen Shaku was the first Zen master to come to these shores. In 1893 he gave a talk at the World Parliment of Religion in Chicago and later settled in San Francisco as a guest of the Alexander Russell family. The fascination with the spiritual and aesthetic treasures of Asia had already shown itself in the art, architecture, literature, and philosophy of Europe and America, and people hungered for more.

From one Buddhist teacher came many: Soyen was joined by Nyogen Senzaki, an orphan found crouching by the frozen corpse of his mother; he was followed by D.T. Suzuki, Soeki-an, and Sokatsu Shaku. By the early 1900s the Young Men's Buddhist Assciation had branches of the Hompa Hongwanji in San Francisco, Sacramento, Fresno and Vacaville. D.T. Suzuki, who had initially arrived by ship in 1897 to work on a translation of the *Tao Te Ching* for a publisher in La Salle, Illinois, soon published his own book in English, *Discourse on Awakening of Faith in the Mahayana,* and thus began what could be called the cultivation of "beginner's mind" in North America.

While most of the early teachers traveled back and forth between the U.S. and Japan to study, then teach, Nyogen Senzaki stayed in the Bay area, working as a "houseboy" and meditating in his free time in Golden Gate Park. He took what he called his "floating zendo" everywhere with him, "carrying Soyen's Zen" in what he called his "empty fist." From all those empty fists many seeds were sown.

More books on Buddhism began to appear in the 1930s. Wai-tao and Dwight Goddard published *The Buddhist Bible*. D.T. Suzuki published the first of his *Essays in Zen Buddhism*, a book that profoundly influenced many who went on to become practioners. It was a first taste, a first step on the path. When Suzuki lectured in London, a young man named Alan Watts came to hear him. That Dharma talk changed Watts' life... and the thread kept unravelling.

World War II altered the entire world. After Pearl Harbor over 100,000 Japanese Americans and Japanese immigrants who lived on the Pacific coast were unconstitutionally incarcerated in ten inland "relocation" camps; Nyogen Senzaki took his "floating zendo" to Heart Mountain in Wyoming.

On the other side of the world a young man named Robert Aitken who had been working construction in Guam, was imprisoned by the Japanese. During his confinement a guard lent him R.H. Blythe's *Zen and English Literature*. It became Aitken's *vade mecum*. Then Blythe himself, also taken captive, was brought to the same camp, and the two men spent the war talking Buddhism.

After his release, Aitken came to California looking for Krishnamurti but ran into Senzaki Roshi who was then ensconed in the old Miyako Hotel in Los Angeles' Japantown. Senzaki persuaded Aitken to study Zen in Japan, which he did, and he was joined by two other Americans, Philip Kapleau, and Walter Nowick. In the meantime, Alan Watts began publishing books on Zen that reflected the the old Ch'an masters' influence, and D.T. Suzuki started lecturing at Columbia University. So many auspicious coincidences, so many books and Dharma talks, like a moon being passed around.

By the mid-1950s, Allen Ginsberg, Jack Kerouac, Gary Snyder, and Philip Whalen had read, met, and talked; what had been mostly an intellectual pursuit of the Dharma began to find its footings in practice. With the arrival of Shunryu Suzuki Roshi in the spring of 1959, the whole idea of Sangha and daily practice was given a home and, in the process, made widely accessible to anyone interested.

That was the year the Chinese invaded Tibet and the diaspora of Tibetan Buddhists began. Not only did the Dalai Lama make his way to northern India, but also Dudjom Rinpoche, the Sixteenth Karmapa, Sakya Tridzin, and Chogyam Trungpa Rinpoche along with many other abbots, lamas, monks, and nuns. Trungpa Rinpoche had been abbot of the Surmong monasteries in eastern Tibet and with a large entourage, made the long and dangerous ride over the mountains without maps or any knowledge of the outside world. They had to boil their saddle leathers to make broth because they ran completely out of food.

By the 1960s Tibetan incanate lamas had begun coming to Europe and the U.S. to teach. Robert Thurman, who had studied with Geshe Wrangyal in New Jersey, and later with the Dalai Lama in Dharamsala, became the first ordained American-Tibetan Buddhist monk. What the Beats had called the Rucksack Revolution went global.

I was fortunate to meet Trungpa Rinpoche when he first came to America. He gave a three-day seminar in Los Angeles in 1970 and he asked me to live at his newly rented house in Boulder with four other students. I traveled with Rinpoche to San Francisco when he came to meet Suzuki Roshi. We sat in the upstairs hall and as I recall, both teachers gave talks. Rinpoche became an ardent admirer of Suzuki Roshi's and was so moved by him that later he told me he wanted to be reincarnated as a teacher from Japan. The morning we received news of Roshi's death, I was with Rinpoche. He was sitting naked on his bed, his crippled hand like a cup resting on his thigh. Tears flowed. He said, "Whenever we saw each other it was true love. Now, I am so lonely without him."

Dogen said that speech and silence are absolutely the same. This marvellous compendium has both. In its pages are tiny glimpses and big Dharma talks from all over the world, from lay practitioners, roshis, monks, lamas, and nuns who give voice to the amazing variety of Buddhist teachings that we have been privileged to hear. In this book, big and small mind are bound together against the same spine. You can carry it in a pocket against your heart or against your ass—actual instruction and gentle reminder.

Tsu, tsu—the sound of the wind is the sound of the Dharma going everywhere, spilling like cream into us. Tsu, tsu. The one-mouth-whole-world-practice-space-bellsound is sanding our minds, moving our feet . . . Fuel and road, cart and horse, speech and stillness . . .

May these words, like the spring winds howling as I write, penetrate everywhere.

GRETEL EHRLICH

Introduction

The whole body is a mouth
   hanging in space
Not caring which way the wind blows
   east, west, south, or north
All day long it speaks
   of *Prajna Paramita* for everyone
ting-tong   ting-tong   ting-tong

On December 2, 1961 a one page monthly newsletter of the San Francisco Zen Center called *Wind Bell* (after the poem by Rujing, Dogen's teacher) was published. It became a mimeographed one- or two-page sheet with an occasional reprint of a short talk by Zen Center's founder, Suzuki Roshi. Suzuki Roshi would help run the mimeograph machine with first Phillip Wilson, Bill Kwong, Graham Petchey and eventually Richard Baker writing and editing it.

By 1966 Zen Center had grown into a stable practicing community and Suzuki Roshi felt that the time was right to look for some land for a retreat center. Tassajara was purchased in 1967 and named Zenshinji. It became the first training temple outside Asia, and students arrived in great numbers.

With the opening of Tassajara in 1967, the purchase in 1969 of a large city center in San Francisco and in 1972 the acquisition of Green Gulch Farm, Zen Center achieved its current form as the first large, predominantly non-Asian Buddhist institution in America.

The City Center is a residential center with 40–45 practitioners, some of which work outside or go to school. It provides a large zendo open to the residents and nonresidents alike and has easy access to a Buddhist library and visiting teachers and scholars. It is often the front door of Zen Center. It is called Beginner's Mind Temple.

Tassajara is the monastic retreat center located deep in the Los Padres National Forest. For six months, except for supplies, no one leaves and a rigorous meditation/work/life schedule is in effect. From May through Labor Day, a guest season is added and the reclusive practice turns to hospitality and sharing our life with others. It is called Zen Mind/Heart Temple.

Green Gulch is a farm, garden, retreat and conference center. It encompasses both long-time, committed practitioners and those who are very new. It is known as Green Dragon Temple.

The *Wind Bell* grew, too. In the fall of 1968, it expanded to its current printed 6 x 9 inch size with information on the campaign to purchase Tassajara. Richard Baker served as editor until 1967, bringing a fresh, American spirit to the magazine. While Baker was in Japan from 1968 to 1971, Gary Snyder, Tim Buckley, Peter Schneider, and Katherine Thanas edited issues.

From 1971 to 1983, *Wind Bell* appeared infrequently. In 1971 Richard Baker, now Roshi, became Suzuki Roshi's successor as abbot of Zen Center. He continued as the major force in the magazine, but time constraints on his schedule led to sporadic publication. During this time the content of *Wind Bell* tended to be mostly about Zen Center, with a sprinkling of other news and articles about Buddhism outside the institution.

In 1983, and again in 1987, the behavior of the abbots came under close scrutiny because of charges of ethical misconduct. Both of these situations were discussed in *Wind Bell*, which attempted to present a fair and neutral description of the facts in an emotionally charged situation. The question was how to be supportive of all the parties involved while maintaining harmony and telling the truth as straightforwardly as possible.

In 1984 Michael Wenger became editor and continued until 1990. He put *Wind Bell* on a regular schedule of twice a year in the spring and fall and opened the scope to include more emphasis on general Buddhist issues.

Since 1983, *Wind Bell,* while reporting Zen Center events, has also dealt with Buddhism as a whole and with the issues of American Buddhism. Questions such as ethics, family practice, art, children, and ethnic Buddhism were addressed. Reprints of Suzuki Roshi's lectures continue to be a staple of the magazine, as is the current abbots alternating a lecture for each issue. Also included have been articles by scholars such as Carl Bielefeldt, Robert Buswell, Robert Thurman, and Masao Abe, as well as religious leaders from other traditions such as U Silananda, Thich Nhat Hahn, and Lama Govinda. Work by, and interviews with, such artists as Mayumi Oda, Kaz Tanahashi, Gordon Onslow-Ford, Natalie Goldberg, and Laurie Anderson have also been featured. Listings of Zen groups related to Zen Center throughout America have been included. The *Wind Bell* logo, which was calligraphed by the famous Japanese painter Taiji Karyokawa in the mid-1960s, remains a trademark of the publication.

Laurie Schley took over as editor in 1991 and continued to widen the scope with issues featuring art, children growing up at Zen Center, and Mitsu Suzuki, tea teacher and widow of Suzuki Roshi.

Ed Brown served as editor from 1995–97 and added a more personal voice as well as articles about related Zen groups. Since then Michael Wenger and Wendy Lewis have served as editors building on the past while keeping open to innovation.

Wind Bell has had two major designers. From the late 60s until his death in 1990, Peter Bailey (Red Dog Pie Face) set a free professional yet informal layout and design. Rosalie Curtis ably replaced him with a polished and up-to-date style.

Wind Bell is clearly both the publication of San Francisco Zen Center as well as a national Buddhist subscription magazine. The question of balance between how much of the magazine should be devoted to Zen Center and how much to Buddhism in a wide sense is ongoing. Covering a formative time in American Buddhism, it is both a historical document and a repository of Buddhist thought.

In choosing what to include in this book I was left with the problem of what to print. With so much good material this was difficult. While I consulted widely, I still had to personally step off the 100-foot pole and choose. I picked what I felt stood the test of time and what was of wider interest not limited to a certain time in the Bay Area.

I tried different organizing schemes but finally settled for five sections: Suzuki Roshi lectures, Zen Center Teachers, Visiting Teachers, Traditional Practice, Everyday Zen. I organized each section in chronological order of printing in *Wind Bell*, earliest first.

First was the Suzuki Roshi section. I picked four selections, each representing a different teaching style to show the variety of ways he taught. The first selection was actually six lectures on the Trikaya or the three bodies of Buddha, a key teaching of Mahayana Buddhism. It shows Suzuki Roshi elucidating a difficult topic of Mahayana Buddhist doctrines. The second, "One Particle of Dust," is an exploration of a Chinese Sung Dynasty koan, relating it to the problems of creating a Buddhist practice center in the twentieth century. The third talk is "The True Dragon" a *teisho* or Zen master's personal feeling about Zen to both encourage and demonstrate the teaching. The last lecture, "Zazen, Rituals and Precepts" ties together many aspects of Zen training. Students sometimes understand the need for meditation but not for other practices. This talk addresses that attitude.

The next section on San Francisco Zen Center teachers represents the developing teaching strand at SF Zen Center. It includes lectures from all the former and current abbots and abbesses plus two significant teachers, Yvonne Rand and Katherine Thanas. It embodies the Dharma as it has been and is currently expressed at SF Zen Center.

Visiting teachers have enriched our practice. Lama Govinda is first with "On Right Translation of Buddhist Terms." Since so much of what we know of the Buddhist tradition is mediated by translations, this topic is an important one. Bob Thurman is next with his lion roar teaching on the *Vimalakirti Sutra*. He is an excellent translator as well as expounder of Tibetan Buddhism, profound and yet immensely entertaining. The eminent Vietnamese Zen teacher Thich Nhat Hahn follows with a heartfelt talk on how

Buddhism is being planted in America. Robert Buswell began as a practitioner first, studying in Thailand, Korea and Taiwan, going on to academic study and a PhD from Berkeley. His article combines this experience of Buddhist practice and scholarship. "Meditating with Anger" by Rita Gross explores Buddhism, feminism, anger, and compassion. Kaz Tanahashi closes this section by talking about Dogen (our Japanese Zen founder) and the adventure of translating him into English.

The fourth section is titled "Traditional Practice: Warm Hand to Warm Hand." It opens with the First Memorial Service lecture for Suzuki Roshi by Baker Roshi at the City Center in 1972. A zazen or meditation instruction by Pat Phelan follows. Reb Anderson comments on the Lay Bodhisattva Initiation Ceremony, opening the ceremony and the vows to the reader. Last in this section are selections from lineage holders on Dharma Transmission.

The last section titled "Everyday Zen" is the most varied as is life itself. Ranging from a Yurok Indian teaching story by Harry Roberts to an article on Buddhist psychotherapy, from the challenge of parenting in "Karma, Dharma and Diapers" to a recipe for Apple Crisp. There are articles on healing ("Buddhism and Self-Healing"), painting ("Creation in an Instant: Gordon Onslow-Ford"), Hospice ("Letting Go, Falling to Rest") and political reconciliation ("Agony of Hate"). There is Suzuki Roshi's wife at seventy-seven looking back on her life, and news reports such as fire at Tassajara, an Indian ceremony on Chews Ridge, and the fate of the Coastal Oak tree in front of the Green Gulch office.

It is difficult to do justice to such a wide and varied journal but whatever its description, *Wind Bell* speaks in many ways.

ting-tong   ting-tong   ting-tong *

MICHAEL DAI RYU WENGER
Beginner's Mind Temple
BUDDHA'S BIRTHDAY, 8 APRIL 2001

* The sound of the bell.

Suzuki-Roshi
Lectures

The one consistent touchstone in the Wind Bell *since its beginning is Suzuki Roshi's lectures. Originally a series of six talks given at Tassajara in the Fall of 1968 on the three bodies of Buddha, this article was edited and published as a complete issue of* Wind Bell. *The subject, though difficult, is well worth the effort. Who or What is Buddha?* –M.W.

The Trikaya

Suzuki Roshi

SPRING 1969

An unsurpassed, penetrating and perfect Dharma
Is rarely met with even in a hundred thousand million kalpas.
Having it to see and listen to, to remember and accept,
I vow to taste the truth of the Tathagata's words.

The Historical Buddha and the Lotus Sutra

There are several points I want to make. One is that when we read Buddhist scriptures it is necessary for us to know on what kind of historical stage they were told. In other words, *who told the scripture?* For instance, when Westerners started to study Buddhist scriptures they thought that these scriptures were a kind of myth. Scriptures may seem like nothing but myths if someone studies them literally, without knowing what kind of background they have. Or, when someone describes or compiles a scripture in a very visionary way the scripture itself may seem to be very strange, or very mysterious. So we should know what kind of people compiled the scripture; whether it is based on Mahayana teachings or on Hinayana teachings. I am not comparing or saying which is better, just that we should know with what feeling, in what kind of attitude, the scripture was told, or else we will not understand what it is.

It is the same with things and with people. Without knowing who a person is, we cannot help him. When we know who made this tea bowl (picking up his cup), and what kind of history it has, then we can treat it properly. So it is necessary to know how the tea bowl appeared here, in front of me. Without knowing who made the tea bowl and what kind of tradition it has it will be just a bowl. At the same time it is necessary to know whether it is suitable for the guest and for the season. Even though it is a very traditional, valuable one, a summer tea bowl cannot be used in the winter-time. In this way you should choose the tea bowl. We should also arrange the teachings in this way, and choose which one to use according to the time and occasion. You should know the history, the tradition, of each teaching; then you can use the teaching in its true sense and develop the teaching forever. That is the Four Vows,[1] and this kind of effort will be continued forever. I am not forcing you to observe our Japanese way at all, but you should know how Buddhism is extended from Buddha to us. This is one very important point. The other point is to know, to understand, whether a certain kind of teaching is effective to use right now, like a tea bowl. So, to arrange the teachings just horizontally is not good, and to arrange the teachings just vertically is not good enough either. When you arrange the teachings *both* horizontally and vertically, both historically and spiritually, and understand the characteristic nature of the various teachings, then you will find which kind of teaching you should apply.

This Sutra, the *Saddharma-Pundarika Sutra,* was supposed to have been told by Buddha himself, but actually it appeared about seven hundred years after Buddha passed away. So, historically, we cannot say that Buddha told this Sutra. If we ask who told it, or if you ask if all of the Sutra was told by Buddha, the answer may be "Only a part of it was told by Buddha." But it will not be exactly the same as he told it. Even the Hinayana Sutras, or Suttas, were not handed down by Buddha's disciples exactly as he told them; even they were not told by Buddha. But we say Buddha because this Sutra was not told by the Nirmanakaya Buddha, or historical Buddha, but by the Sambhogakaya Buddha. It was told a long, long, long time ago—a long time before Buddha, who knew that there was this kind of Sutra before him and told about the Sutra which was told by the Sambhogakaya Buddha, or Vairocana Buddha. We can say that Vairocana Buddha told the Sutra a long, long time before. The Sutra is constructed accordingly; it does not say that it was attributed to the historical Buddha.

So it is necessary for us to know, first of all, how an understanding of Buddha, in all aspects, developed from the historical Buddha to the Dharmakaya Buddha. Without this understanding this Sutra does not mean much. If you do not have this kind of understanding, this Sutra is just a fable, maybe like a fairy tale—very interesting, but actually it doesn't have much to do with our lives. Accordingly, I have to explain what the Nirmanakaya Buddha is, and what the Sambhogakaya Buddha is, and what the Dharmakaya Buddha is; and how Buddhism which was told by the Nirmanakaya Buddha developed to Mahayana Buddhism which was told by the Sambhogakaya Buddha.

Some people may be disappointed to hear that the *Lotus Sutra* is not a Sutra which was told by the historical Buddha, but this is the characteristic of Buddhism; Buddhism had a long history before a complete understanding of the historical Buddha came about. It took a pretty long time. At first his teaching was transmitted by the so-called Hinayana Buddhists, or Uravakas, who were the disciples, or the followers, who tried to preserve his teaching in their memory, through discussions, and at meetings. No one is sure when these meetings were held, but it is said that soon after Buddha's death they had a meeting—a Rajagriha—where they chose various disciples to compile Buddha's teachings.[2] Ananda was head of the group, and he recited what Buddha had said. Then this was discussed. In that way they set up some teaching: "This is what Buddha told us and these are the precepts Buddha set up." Naturally they became very attached to the teaching, rigidly so. Those who knew this kind of teaching, who studied this kind of teaching, of course had a special position among Buddhists, and the distinction between the four classes of Buddha's disciples, between layman and laywoman, priest and nun, became more and more strict.

It is said that a second meeting was held at Vaisali in a big cave, perhaps seventy-five or one hundred years after the first one. Buddhism had become already by that time a religion of priests, not of usual, ordinary people or laymen. They say that when this second meeting was held there were many people who did not join in. That group, and there were many good disciples and followers among the people who did not come, naturally got together and formed a separate group. So Buddha's followers divided into the *Joza Bu,* in Japanese, or *Mahastahavirah,* the "Great Elders," and the common followers, the so-called *Mahasamghikas,* or *Daishubu* in Japanese. (*Daishu* means great assembly, people, or followers; *bu* means group.) Among them there were many good teachers. And this group, about one hundred years after Buddha passed away, established another kind of understanding of Buddha and of his teaching which was very important in the origins of the Mahayana School.

Buddhism seems to have developed from Uravakas to the Mahayana, yet in reality it was not changed and did not develop. Rather, Buddhists have always tried to regain the original way, the original understanding of Buddha. This effort makes it seem like Buddhism has changed from its original form to some different teaching, but it is not so. Actually, true Mahayana Buddhism resumed the traditional and fundamental teaching of Buddha. So, the effort we have to make in these lectures is towards knowing who this Buddha is, and what his purpose was in teaching. Do you understand this point? That is why I am telling you what kind of nature this Sutra has and who told this scripture. The point is not whether the *Lotus Sutra* was told by the historical Buddha or by some other person. That is not the point. As long as you get attached to the historical Buddha you cannot understand Buddhism. Buddha was great because he understood things in this way.

How did pre-Buddhistic thought become Hinayana teaching which is a completely different current of thought? It is impossible for pre-Buddhistic teaching to be the Hinayana teaching; what was the bridge? The bridge was the Buddha who told the teaching that was the source of all the currents of Buddhist thought. When we realize this point, we see that even the Hinayana understanding was not perfect enough. The Hinayana Buddhists rejected the broader implications of Buddha's teaching and understood Buddha as a pre-Buddhistic person.[3] He was pushed backwards into having a pre-Buddhistic character. Mahayana students found that the Hinayana scriptures could not be recognized as the true, main current of Buddhist thought. How should we understand the Truth and how should we accept the Truth in the situation of each age? Because of this question we have the various schools. It is necessary to have schools, but we should not stop developing the true spirit, the main current of Buddhism.

When you have a cup of coffee on the freeway, that is very good, but no one will stay in the coffee shop—you must go on to San Francisco. We like, emotionally, that coffee shop and a big banana split, but even though it is good, we should go on with our trip. That is the Mahayana way—on and on and on. If it is not the main current it will die, eventually; only the main current will continue. That is our way, so we have no time to stay at the coffee shop so long. We must have some coffee once in awhile when we get sleepy. That is our way. With this attitude we should continue our trip. And if we want to continue our trip the Four Vows are necessary. We should continue our trip as long as our car goes, anyway; this is our being, and our attitude, and our practice.

The Nirmanakaya Buddha

Do you know of the Nirmanakaya Buddha and Sambhogakaya Buddha and Dharmakaya Buddha? The Nirmanakaya Buddha is the historical Buddha. But the Nirmanakaya Buddha has two elements. One is that of an historical human being and the other is that of a super-human being. Historically such a character existed. Buddha was, as you know, a human being. When he attained enlightenment he reached to the bottom of our human nature, True Nature, through his human nature which is universal to everyone and to every being; he subdued all the emotions and the thinking mind; conquering all of this and all of the world he became the World Honoured One. He was confident of this after he attained enlightenment, and his followers listened to him as a teacher who is also the Perfect One. So, in this way he was a super-human being even when he was alive and, at the same time, since he was their teacher, or master, there was no need for them

Suzuki Roshi lecturing at Tassajara.

to have some special super-human god. But after he passed away, because his character was so great, the disciples thought of him more as a super-human being. This idea of a super-human being was very important in promoting an understanding of Buddha as the Perfect One. So the Nirmanakaya Buddha has two elements. The most important, the vital element for the idea of Buddha, was the super-human element. If Buddha was just an historical person, or one of the great sages, then Buddhism could not have survived for so long.

The idea of Buddha as a super-human being was supported by the teaching he told. One of the most important teachings of Buddha is the teaching of cause and effect, the teaching of causality. According to the teaching Buddha told then, if you do something good you will have a good result; if you practice hard you will acquire good character; that was what he told his disciples. How could the disciples acquire such a lofty and good character as Buddha's? He told them that his good character was a result of his long practice, and they thought that since his character was so profound and deep, his former practice must have been an incredibly hard and long one. When Buddha's disciples' adoration was limitless they felt that the practice he had before attaining enlightenment, or Buddha-hood, should be limitless. Here Buddha is not just a human being; his former lives must have been endless, so the idea of "absolute"—limitless limitlessness—came to his disciples' minds. In this way the historical Buddha became more like an absolute being.

It is the same thing with us. We appeared in this world, but *how* did we appear in this world? We had a limitless background. We do not appear all of a sudden from nothing. There is something, there must be something before we appear in this world and before Buddha also. That Buddha was so great was because he had a limitless background, a limitless practice. This point is very important in the development of the idea of Buddha.

As a super-human being Buddha was described in various ways. He had eighteen characteristics which were completely different from the usual person's, and he had eighteen virtues which were also different from the usual person's. And he had, physically, the thirty-two marks of a great man. They say this is just a description, just a big adjective for the Buddha. Maybe so, but there was some reason behind using such a big adjective for Buddha so that this kind of thing was described even in the Hinayana Sutras. But actually Buddha was a human being and when he was eighty years old he passed away. At this point he was not a super-natural or super-human being. How should we understand his death in terms of his being super-human? If he was a super-human being there would not have been any need to take Nirvana. When we say "to take Nirvana" this means it was his choice to die or to remain alive. For other people it is not possible to have this kind of choice. Buddha took Nirvana because he had given people the chance to attain enlightenment; he had completed giving the full teaching for attaining enlightenment so there was no need for him to live anymore. That is why he took Nirvana, and his disciples understood his death in this way.

Usual people appear in this world, according to Buddhism, because of karma, and because of karma they die. This is usual for a person. But Buddha appeared in this world because of his vow to save all human beings. With this vow, instead of karma, he appeared in the world. Here we have the teaching of vow instead of karma. Actually karma and vow are the same thing, but our attitude changes when our understanding changes; karma changes into vow and instead of living by karma we live by the vow to help people who live in karma. That is Buddha's teaching. And this kind of teaching was supported by the teaching which was actually told by Buddha when he was alive and this is the actual teaching we see through Buddha. This kind of Buddha, who started his limitless training as a Bodhisattva and finally appeared in this world as a Buddha, as a Perfect One, is called an incarnated body or Nirmanakaya Buddha.

So far, all of this kind of teaching is called Hinayana Buddhism. But if you see these teachings closely you see that there is already Mahayanistic theory and understanding in them—it is difficult to say which is Mahayana teaching and which is Hinayana teaching. But I said "incarnated body." So there must be an essential body, too, the mother of the incarnated body. When our understanding reaches this point, the more profound teaching will be understood.

The Sambhogakaya Buddha

I started this kind of talk to explain who told the *Lotus Sutra*. This Sutra was supposed to have been told by the historical Buddha, but actually, what is told here was told by the Sambhogakaya Buddha, not the historical Buddha. It is valuable *because* it was told by the Sambhogakaya Buddha instead of the historical Buddha. Shakyamuni Buddha, as I told you in the last lecture, has two elements: Buddha as a human being and Buddha as a super-human being. The idea of a super-human nature of Buddha is the result of the more emotional attachment to his character and his teaching, which the Uravakas, or Hinayana Buddhists, had. This Buddha, Shakyamuni Buddha, who has two natures, or two elements—that of the historical Buddha and that of the idealized Buddha—is called the Nirmanakaya Buddha. Actually, who *is* the historical Buddha? If we arrive at the concept of just the Nirmanakaya Buddha we have already lost Buddha himself. The reason that the historical Buddha was Buddha is because he attained enlightenment. He changed. Starting as a Bodhisattva, he became Buddha; he is always changing. So he is not a true historical Buddha.

Who is changing should be the next thing we ask when we really want to know who Buddha was. When we want not just an emotional or romantic observation of Buddha, but, more sincerely, deeply, want to accept him as our teacher, it is necessary for us to know why he is Buddha. If we come to this point we must have a fuller idea than just that of an incarnated Buddha, or Shakyamuni Buddha, or Nirmanakaya Buddha. That is, we must know that Buddha is the Sambhogakaya Buddha and that the Sambhogakaya Buddha is the Perfect One, or Truth Itself. Truth Itself, when it is observed by people as a truth, may be a teacher; but even plants and animals, mountains and rivers, can be our teachers when we really have eyes to see them. When the idea of the historical Buddha has this kind of background, he will be accepted as our teacher in its true sense. Not just in an emotional way, but whole-heartedly we can accept the historical Buddha as our teacher, because he is the one who teaches us, who is enlightened in the Eternal Truth, who is the strong background of Truth. He became the Buddha because he was enlightened in the Truth, and he is the one who teaches us the Truth he found. For the Buddhist, Buddha is not just an historical person, he is Truth Itself. An historical Buddha cannot be perfect, but the background of the historical Buddha should be Truth and, if so, Truth Itself should be the real Buddha for us. Without this kind of background, Buddha would not have been remembered by human beings for such a long time. When Buddha is acknowledged as Truth Itself, then, as long as Truth exists, and as long as we care for the Truth, we can remain as Buddhists. This Buddha is the Sambhogakaya Buddha.

The true Buddha is the Sambhogakaya Buddha, and when the Sambhogakaya Buddha takes some activity, or is observed by someone, he may be called the Nirmanakaya Buddha. So before the Nirmanakaya Buddha there must be the Sambhogakaya Buddha, and before a Bodhisattva appears to save others, there must be the Sambhogakaya Buddha as a background. Bodhisattvas, Buddhas, and their activity of helping others come from this source, from this origin in Sambhogakaya Buddha, who is Truth Itself.

Buddha's teaching is not the written teaching, or something told by the historical Buddha. When the Sambhogakaya Buddha tells the teaching, it is the true Buddha's teaching, very much so. But when we read, trying to figure out what he told us, what the true teaching was, and who the historical Shakyamuni Buddha was, we are deeply attached to someone else, forgetting all about the ultimate fact that "we are here." As long as we try to understand the real Buddha in this way, we cannot understand who he was. To help others and to help ourselves, is the same thing; to realize the truth myself and to make you realize it, too, is the same thing. To be enlightened does not mean to be aware of it, or to observe oneself objectively. Of course when Buddha attained enlightenment he was aware of himself, but not objectively. He had confidence in himself, and accepted himself as he was. He knew that "I am here" and accepted that. When you do not care for anything, you know "I am here" already.[4] That is the most important point. To stand on your own feet *before* you observe yourself objectively, that is the true way. When you ask "Who am I?" or "What kind of enlightenment did I have yesterday?" that is not true. To realize oneself is a deeper experience than this kind of superficial observation. To be one with ourselves *before* we objectively observe ourselves, that is enlightenment.

Buddha attained this enlightenment when he found his true nature and knew exactly who he was. At that time he became the Sambhogakaya Buddha; he became Truth Itself, one with himself, and one with the whole universe. He was completely satisfied with himself, and when he became one with himself and with everything else, he saw that everything had the same nature as himself. As he existed under the Bodhi tree as an Enlightened One, as a Perfect One, so everything existed. That is why the Buddha said, "It is wonderful to see. Everything has Buddha Nature."

"As he is so everything is Buddha," we say; but when we say so, in its true sense, it means "I am Buddha." Only when we have this view, when we stand on our own legs, can we help others. Before this, when you observe yourself with ideas like "Who am I?" "Have I attained enlightenment or not?" "Am I able to help others?" you cannot help others. When you become just you yourself, without comparing yourself to others, just "I am I," "I am here," and when you have difficulty, just "I can manage myself pretty well," that is Buddha.

But we should be this kind of Buddha, the Sambhogakaya Buddha, even before we attain Enlightenment, and without this confidence, you cannot even practice zazen. How can you practice zazen when you doubt, or when you are observing yourself objectively without having any subjectivity? Only when you accept yourself, when you really know that *you exist here,* that you cannot escape from yourself, can you practice zazen. This is the ultimate fact: "I am here." This is very true. Don't you think so? But still you doubt, and still you make a separation from yourself and observe yourself from outside: "Who am I?" "What am I doing?" Zazen practice is not this kind of practice. Someone else is practicing zazen, not *you.* *You* should practice zazen. That is *shikan taza,*[5] and that is Sambhogakaya Buddha.

Sambhogakaya Buddha is, figuratively speaking, like the sun; instead of observing things objectively, he understands his Buddha Nature in activity within himself. So, like the sun, although he is not trying to shine on everything objectively, to illuminate everything objectively, he is actually illuminating everything; he is actually helping others without trying to help. He can illuminate everything because he has, originally, that kind of power or potentiality. For Sambhogakaya Buddha the most important thing is to see, to attain enlightenment inwardly; his way is to illuminate himself, or to acquire enlightenment, instead of trying to illuminate the objective world. His purpose is, instead of observing things respectively, one by one, to observe his nature within himself.

When he, as the sun, observes his inner world he finds himself as the earth. That earth nature will be universal. This earth is earth and the sun will also be earth. Everything is earth, so there is no difference between the objective world and the subjective world. The Sambhogakaya Buddha is the Omniscient One who knows everything within himself. To be enlightened in his inward nature is to be enlightened outside, too, in the objective world. For him the whole world is his inside world, or subjective world. When he reaches this kind of world, we call him the Sambhogakaya Buddha.

His world is limitless; it includes the sun and stars and everything. His virtue is limitless, and his wisdom is also limitless. So, for Buddha, to save others and to be enlightened himself is the same thing. To help others and to help himself is the same thing. For him there is nothing without. That is the Sambhogakaya Buddha.

The Sixth Patriarch said, "When we are in delusion, the *Lotus Sutra* will turn us, but when our mind is clear we will turn the *Lotus Sutra*." When the *Lotus Sutra* is understood by us as a Sutra which was told by the Sambhogakaya Buddha, then it makes sense to us, and if we lose this point we will turn it. I say "I am reading," but actually, I am *telling* the *Lotus Sutra*. We will tell the *Lotus Sutra* for Buddha. So to read and to study the *Lotus Sutra*, to listen to it and to tell it are not two different things; to read it and to tell it are the same thing. Whenever we talk we tell the *Lotus Sutra*. Now I've come to the conclusion already but let us think more calmly, and understand clearly what we have been studying in these lectures.

The Dharmakaya Buddha

There is, you know, Nature. When we say Nature, Nature is, of course, Truth; but Nature includes what we see, and Truth is not, in its strict sense, something which we can see. Because many people may ask us, "What is Dharma?" or "What is the Dharma Body?" we must say something about it. What can we say about it? If *I* don't say anything people may think, "He doesn't know anything about it, he is not a good teacher." I must make some narrow escape. I must talk about some truth. There's no way to talk about the Dharma Body, but still, if you allow me to say something about the Dharma Body I'll call it Truth Itself, like the Sambhogakaya. There is some Truth, yet Truth is something which you cannot see; you can see the apple; you cannot see the theory of gravitation. But nothing happens just by accident. When something happens there must be some reason. In this sense the "reason" may be Dharma Nature or close to Dharma Nature. We can understand it in some way, we can figure out some rules. We call Dharma *Body* the source of all Truth, of all rules, of all Nature.

Dharmakaya Buddha, or the Dharma Body of Buddha, is called the fundamental, undeveloped Buddha Body. When we say undeveloped body or fundamental body, we mean that it is the Original Source Itself. It is another interpretation of the same thing as the Sambhogakaya, but when we understand this thing as something which is very calm, which is not in activity, we call it the Dharmakaya. Actually, the Dharmakaya does not remain calm and inactive; it is always active. We understand this reality in two ways, as activity and as non-activity; we have two understandings for one reality. In one case we call it Dharma *Nature,* meaning something in action, or Sambhogakaya, and in the other, Dharma *Body,* or Dharmakaya, meaning something which is not active, which is not developed. Rather, all Dharma Nature exists in the Dharma Body as potentiality. So we have two understandings for one reality; one is Dharmakaya, the other is Sambhogakaya. The Sambhogakaya Buddha is the Buddha who realizes this Dharma Nature in activity, and he is the Buddha that is the original source of the Nirmanakaya Buddha. The Sambhogakaya Buddha gives birth to the Nirmanakaya Buddha. So I think it is necessary to explain the Nirmanakaya Buddha and the Sambhogakaya Buddha more thoroughly. Then, naturally, you will understand what Dharmakaya Buddha is.

When we realize Dharma Nature in its true sense, we are the Sambhogakaya Buddha. When we observe things as we observe the objective world, and when we want to help people who are involved in the objective, or materialistic world, then we are the Nirmanakaya Buddha. How can we help others as Nirmanakaya Buddha? We must take various forms and give them some handy help, that is how to help others as Nirmanakaya Buddha. But as Sambhogakaya Buddha we should know our own nature, and we should realize that there is no "I" and no "you," that all is one being. When we realize this universal nature, we can help others without trying to help others because whatever we do, that is our helping activity.

When you practice zazen there is no "you" and no "others," your practice includes everything. You are a part of me, and I am a part of you. When we reach this kind of understanding we are the Sambhogakaya Buddha. Everything then takes place within yourself. For one with this understanding there is no objective world anymore. Without trying to help others, we will help others anyway; that is the Sambhogakaya Buddha, and that is the way to help others, the way to preserve our teaching, the way to practice Buddhism. There is a difference between the Nirmanakaya and the Sambhogakaya Buddha, but when we realize that our practice includes everything, Shakyamuni Buddha is included in our practice, too. Thus, when we practice zazen, all of the Nirmanakaya Buddhas which Shakyamuni Buddha spoke of all at once will attain enlightenment. Do you understand?

Spring 1969

The Sambhogakaya Buddha is not the Buddha who will attain enlightenment or who will not attain enlightenment; he is the Truth Itself and, at the same time, the Nirmanakaya Buddha. People observe the truth in many ways, but the truth is always the same. Do you understand? If we understand the Sambhogakaya Buddha and his background in this way that is also the Dharmakaya Buddha, Truth Itself.

The Nirmanakaya Buddha is within ourselves, but before we reach this kind of understanding, he is just a hero. He has no eternal life. He is just one of the great heroes in our history. But when we understand Shakyamuni Buddha as a Sambhogakaya Buddha, or a Dharmakaya Buddha, for the first time he has perpetual life. This is the traditional understanding of Buddha, and actually this kind of understanding was supported by Buddha when he was alive, although it took several hundred years before we understood who Shakyamuni Buddha was in reality. This kind of understanding, which was accomplished by his disciples, gave Buddha a new life, and made him the perpetual Buddha. So Buddha, in this sense, is called the Tathagata.[6] This is the history of how understanding of Buddha developed and, at the same time, the true understanding of his teaching.

When we understand reality in this way, as the Sambhogakaya Buddha, our understanding includes everything, and the reality which includes everything as an *undeveloped potential* is the Dharmakaya Buddha itself; Dharma itself; Being itself. For the Dharmakaya Buddha there is no need to attain Enlightenment. He is already enlightened-from beginningless beginning to endless end, he is always enlightened. Only the Nirmanakaya Buddha attains enlightenment, and becomes Buddha. This is our way of understanding things, and it is exactly the same as our zazen.

We say "just sit." What does it mean, "just sit?" When we say "just sit" it includes, actually, all of the activity, all the potential activity which we have; we remain in an inactive state, but we have infinite potentiality. In this sense our practice includes everything. When we sit we are just sitting; each one of us is sitting, and each one of us is the Dharmakaya Buddha. But, even though we are sitting, we breathe, our heart is beating, so we are, in activity, the Sambhogakaya Buddha and the Nirmanakaya Buddha too. We understand reality in this way. The Sambhogakaya Buddha and Dharmakaya Buddha are the Source of all Being. They existed before the Nirmanakaya Buddha, and so, in this sense, Sambhogakaya and Dharmakaya are eternal perpetual beings. So we call Buddha the Tathagata or, in Japanese, *Shinjyo*.

The *Lotus Sutra* describes this kind of reality, the world of the Tathagata. That is why it is told on a big, cosmic scale. In short, the *Lotus Sutra* is the Sutra which tells us what the Tathagata is and how everything exists in the realm of reality, the realm of the Tathagata, this world. Of course, it is described in a very dramatic way, but what it means is, simply, how things exist in this world, this Dharma world, this world of the Tathagata.

This point is important. The *Lotus Sutra* was told by the Sambhogakaya Buddha, in his wisdom, in a figurative, dramatic, verbal way to save all sentient beings. It puts special emphasis on Dharma Nature, instead of Dharma Body. You cannot talk about Dharma Body because it is something beyond our world, beyond our wisdom, beyond our understanding. The Dharma Body is just a *source* of activity, but not activity itself, you see? But without this source there is no activity. When there is activity there must be a source, but this source does not always expect some activity. You can have the idea of Source, or Body, without activity, of something which is not in activity, but actually there is no such thing-whatever it is, it has some activity. Even a stone has some activity. So we cannot talk about the Dharma Body itself.

What shall I do? If I *talk* about something, that already shows Dharma Nature, tells how Dharma goes and what it is like. When I say what it is like, that is already Nirmanakaya Buddha-objectively speaking that is form; more subjectively speaking it is Nature. But what is the Source of Dharma Nature? No one knows. We know it, but we cannot say anything about it. If you say something, it is not Dharma Body, it is Dharma Nature, it is an attribute of the Dharma Body. So we cannot talk about what the Dharma Body is. But we understand that there must be some source; that is the Dharma Body. Form and color of Dharma, and nature of Dharma, and Dharma itself; Nirmanakaya Buddha, Sambhogakaya Buddha, and Dharmakaya Buddha. Do you understand? Nirmanakaya Buddha is the form of Dharma, and Sambhogakaya Buddha is the Nature of Dharma, and Dharmakaya Buddha is the Dharma Body, which is beyond our words, which cannot be described. When we listen to the *Lotus Sutra* we will understand what is the Dharmakaya Buddha, and who is Nirmanakaya Shakyamuni Buddha.

The purpose of this Sutra is to describe our Dharma Nature. Buddha was Buddha because he was the Enlightened One, he was illuminated by his own nature, Dharma Nature, which is everyone's nature. He knew who he was. For him there was no disciple, and no "objective" world. So he said all sentient beings are his sons, are part of him. That was Buddha. Only when we understand Buddha in this way, as Sambhogakaya Buddha or Dharmakaya Buddha, does he become the real Buddha. When we arrive at this kind of understanding, there will be no need to talk about what is Theravada Buddhism, or what is Mahayana Buddhism. All Buddhism, whether it is Theravada or Mahayana, will just be Buddhism. This is how the teaching has been transmitted from Buddha to us.

Tassajara Creek.

Questions

STUDENT: What does understanding of the Bodhisattva's Vow have to do with understanding the Sambhogakaya Buddha?

ROSHI: Sambhogakaya Buddha is the Buddha, the Perpetual One, who exists from beginningless beginning to endless end. Like the Dharmakaya, he is Truth Itself. Secondly, as the Nirmanakaya Buddha, he is the one who exists moment after moment in various forms. So, the Sambhogakaya Buddha is the background of the Nirmanakaya Buddha, and the Nirmanakaya Buddha is called the Nirmanakaya Buddha because he is the embodiment of the Sambhogakaya Buddha. The Sambhogakaya Buddha gives birth to the Nirmanakaya Buddha who exists moment after moment in various forms. That is why "Sentient beings are numberless"; we are beginningless and endless. We exist here, but we are not permanent beings. Only in this moment do we exist like this. In the next moment I will change and tomorrow I will not be the same person. This is true. In the next moment I shall be the future Buddha. Yesterday I was the past Buddha. In this way there are many and many Buddhas.

Since we are only incarnated bodies, with some certain color and form and character, there must be some source of each being just as the Sambhogakaya Buddha was the source of Shakyamuni Buddha, who is called the Nirmanakaya Buddha. When Shakyamuni realized this point and accepted himself as the Nirmanakaya Buddha, he also knew himself to be the Sambhogakaya Buddha and the Dharmakaya Buddha. When we understand ourselves in this way we will live in this world to continuously try to express Buddha Nature, moment after moment. That is the effort we should make, instead of being caught by some certain color or form. We should make our best effort in each moment. That is a kind of attachment but this attachment is, at the same time, detachment, because in the next moment you should make your best effort also. So it means detachment from our last incarnation, a moment ago. In this way, moment after moment, we exist. This kind of understanding is expressed by our technical terms of Nirmanakaya, Sambhogakaya and Dharmakaya.

STUDENT: Can all sentient beings, then, be considered the Nirmanakaya?

ROSHI: Yes, all sentient beings are Nirmanakaya Buddha, whether they realize it or not. For them, they are not if they don't accept themselves as a Nirmanakaya Buddha. But for us who understand ourselves and others they are, all of them, Nirmanakaya Buddhas and Sambhogakaya Buddhas and Dharmakaya Buddhas.

STUDENT: What do you mean by "making your best effort in each moment?"

ROSHI: I mean don't sacrifice this moment for the future, and don't be bound by your past life, or try to escape from it either. This is the kind of effort you usually make. But there should be a more important point in your effort. What is that? To stand on your feet is the most important thing. To sacrifice this moment for your future, for your ideal even, means that you are not standing on your feet. So, the most important thing is to accept yourself, to have true subjectivity in each moment. Don't complain; accept things as they are and satisfy yourself with what you have, right now. You should think, "This is the only reality, the only Buddha I can see, I can experience, I can have, I can worship." At that time you are the Nirmanakaya Buddha, and Sambhogakaya Buddha, and Dharmakaya Buddha.

STUDENT: I didn't understand the emphasis in the *Lotus Sutra* on the future lives of the different disciples, and why or how they are valued.

ROSHI: "Future disciples" means that Buddhism is the teaching which is limitless, which has a limitless future and a beginningless beginning, which is always true. So, in the *Lotus Sutra* there are many disciples and Buddhas who will exist in the future and who existed in aeons of time before.

If your understanding does not lead to an understanding of the Sambhogakaya Buddha or the Dharmakaya Buddha the kind of description which is in the *Lotus Sutra* won't make any sense. It will look like a fable, like tales. In this Sutra, as you may see,

Buddha said that his direct disciples should survive until Maitreya Buddha appears, many many aeons into the future. You cannot understand this kind of thought without the idea of the Sambhogakaya Buddha. Now, you may say that the Sambhogakaya Buddha is just an idea, but if you have the experience of zazen you can accept it. That is why Zen Buddhism has survived.

STUDENT: Some people live by karma, you said, and some by vows.

ROSHI: By vows, yes. For people who do not understand this truth, life is karmic life. For those who know this point, life is not karmic life. But even karmic life is another version of Buddhist life. The Nirmanakaya Buddha comes into this world, not through karma, but with a vow to save all sentient beings. By a vow he appears in this world, and practices the Bodhisattva's Way, and attains enlightenment as Buddha did, to save all human beings. He is called an incarnated body. He changes his form in various ways- sometimes he's a Bodhisattva, sometimes a Buddha; to help people, he takes various forms. So, in a wide sense, everything is Nirmanakaya Buddha. And in the narrow sense, people who appear in this world because of a vow, instead of karma, are called Nirmanakaya Buddhas.

Editor's Notes

1. The fourfold Boddhisattva's Vow, or Four Vows, of Mahayana Buddhism are:

Sentient beings are numberless; I vow to save them.
Desires are inexhaustible; I vow to put an end to them.
The dharmas are boundless; I vow to master them.
The Buddha's Way is unsurpassable; I vow to attain it.

Although, in the usual view, Hinayana Buddhists do not take or follow this vow, according to the *Lotus Sutra* and to Suzuki Roshi's teaching, all Buddhists follow this vow, consciously or unconsciously. Actually, the *Agoma Sutta,* the earliest extant Buddhist scripture, is written very much in the spirit of the Bodhisattva's Vow, but later Hinayana interpreters of this Sutta neglected this point. In a deep sense Buddha became manifest as the Tathagata Shakyamuni to fulfill this vow. Thus, as Dogen Zenji, the founder of the Soto Zen School, taught, there can be no real distinction between Hinayana and Mahayana Buddhism in terms of following or not following the Boddhisattva's Vow. All Buddhism is simply Buddhism, and all Buddhists seek the salvation of all sentient beings (see below).

2. The sanskrit term for this convocation is *samgiti,* meaning the collection, fixing, or revising of the canon; the defining of terms in order to have a certain uniformity of understanding. This effort perhaps began with some specific meeting, but it certainly continued over a long period of time until the creation of the Pali Canon, long after the death of Buddha and of his direct disciples.

Because Shakyamuni Buddha spoke in the ancient dialect of Magada, and his original followers, coming from many different areas, spoke divers dialects, it was necessary to arrive at some common terminology among them. No texts appeared in *either* Pali or Sanskrit until at least two hundred years after Buddha's death when, recent scholarship has suggested, both Pali and Sanskrit arose, almost simultaneously. However, none of the texts from this early period have survived.

3. One of the fundamental teachings of Buddhism is that of the Three Marks, or Three Signs of Being. According to this doctrine all being is subject to three conditions; *anicea,* change, transience; *dukkha,* suffering, imperfection; and *anatta,* having no separate or immortal soul. In the pre-Buddhistic view permanence and immortality were possibilities, in Buddha's view they were not. Because early Buddhists misconstrued *dharmas* as static, they missed the true import of such teachings as that contained in the Three Marks—that *everything,* even the Dharma, changes. In doing so, in missing the subtle distinction between "immortal," and "eternal" or "perpetual"—the former, a static concept, the latter, fluid ones—they could not see that even Buddha and his teaching changes. In this way they cast him as a pre-Buddhistic character.

4. This is not an advocation of selfishness. On the contrary, because the Sambhogakaya Buddha includes everything, (see below), there is no-thing outside of "himself" to care for. Thus in taking care of "himself," "his" immediate situation, the Buddha cares for, and takes care of, everything.

5. *Shikan taza* is themeless meditation, and it includes the source of all themes. It is "just sitting," or "sitting quietly doing nothing." *Shikan* means "to give up illusions and attain enlightenment," *taza* means "to sit."

This type of zazen is practiced mainly by the Soto Zen sect, in contrast to the use of *koans,* or "no-sense" questions, in Rinzai Zen practice.

6. Tathagata is a title of the Buddha coming from the words *tatha,* thus, or such, and *gata,* gone (or *agata,* come). It means one who has attained unity with the Absolute, who has realized Suchness (in one sense *Sunya,* Emptiness, the Unconditioned Reality), and so neither comes nor goes. The natures of all sentient beings are the nature of the Tathagata, yet the Tathagata is eternal, always abiding. Thus the title connotes at-one-ness with the Dharmakaya; however, it is applied to Buddha in his Nirmanakaya manifestation. It implies infinite wisdom

and compassion. Shakyamuni Buddha took this title himself after his enlightenment, and it is used by Buddhists, in reference to the Buddha, as a term of the
highest respect and veneration.

May the merit of this penetrate
To all things in every place
So that we and all sentient beings
Together may realize the Buddha's Way.

Sentient beings are numberless; I vow to save them.
Desires are inexhaustible; I vow to put an end to them.
The dharmas are boundless; I vow to master them.
The Buddha's Way is unsurpassable; I vow to attain it.

This lecture on Case 61 of the Blue Cliff Record *is accessible to koan and non-koan readers alike. It examines the difficulty, hubris, and potential of creating a Buddhist practice institution. It was given in July, 1971 at Tassajara, looking at the creation of Zen Center, and was printed in* Wind Bell *in 1985 when Zen Center was undergoing growing pains and reexamining itself. It was relevant in the past and is still pertinent today.* –M.W.

One Particle of Dust

Suzuki Roshi
ZEN MOUNTAIN CENTER, 26 JULY 1971
SPRING 1984

Case 61: Fuketsu's "One Particle of Dust" *

Engo's Introduction

Setting up the Dharma banner and establishing the Dharma teaching—such is the task of the teacher of profound attainment. Distinguishing a dragon from a snake, black from white-that is what the mature master must do. Now let us put aside for a moment how to wield the life-giving sword and the death-dealing blade, and how to administer blows with the stick: tell me, what does the one who lords it over the universe say? See the following.

Main Subject

Fuketsu said to the assembled monks, "If one particle of dust is raised, the state will come into being; if no particle of dust is raised, the state will perish."

Setcho (at a later time), holding up his staff, said to his disciples, "Is there anyone among you who will live with him and die with him?"

Setcho's Verse

> Let the elders knit their brows as they will;
> For the moment, let the state be established.
> Where are the wise statesmen, the veteran generals?
> The cool breeze blows; I nod to myself.*

Whether you are a layman or a monk, there is an important point that we should make clear. The point is to put more emphasis on big mind rather than small mind. In this way, more and more, you will develop your Buddha mind which is big mind.

When you begin to practice in this way, experiencing big mind, you will feel that you are expressing it toward everything: your friend, your food, your household or your teacher. But actually, if you continue to practice, eventually you will not feel that you have big mind or are developing big mind. So that is called normal.

◉

Big mind in contrast to small mind is not real big mind. Normal is actually the great mind. The reason we have Zen Center is so that we can practice our way and develop our great mind. But if you have the idea of Zen Center too much as an organization, basically there is something wrong. This point should be carefully examined.

There is a koan about Fuketsu Ensho (who was the fourth generation descendent of Rinzai). At one time he mounted the platform and said to his students, "If you pick up one speck of dust, the nation will become prosperous. If you don't, nothing will happen." That is the first part.

Setcho, commenting on this, says, taking up a staff, "Is there anyone who will go through birth and death with you?" That is the whole story.

Fuketsu says, "If you pick up a speck of dust, the nation will become prosperous. If you do not, nothing will happen." That is what Fuketsu said. Later when Fuketsu died, Setcho Zenji, taking up his staff said, "Is there anyone who will go through birth and death with you?" There is an appreciatory remark by the same Zen Master Setcho, but I want to explain the first part first.

To pick up a speck of dust means to do something like start a monastery or to start a Zen group or zendo somewhere. But he didn't say it just that way. He said just to pick up a speck of dust. In the great universe or in great Buddha land, to start a zendo is just to pick up a speck of dust. Not a big thing. It may be just a small thing; but, nevertheless, if you don't do it, nothing will happen. When he says the nation will be prosperous, he means Zen students will prosper.

Many Zen students come to Zen Center or go to some other Zen center. Is this something meaningful or not? If something good happens, at the same time something bad will happen. Most likely if one good thing happens, ten or twelve or more than twenty bad things will happen. So we should think, when we pick up a speck of dust, whether it is a good or a bad thing to do. But if you don't, nothing will happen [laughing]. This is also true. What will you do? Will you pick up a piece of dust or not pick up a piece of dust? Or will you leave everything as it is without saying anything?

Many people choose to let beings suffer, let them go in the wrong direction, saying, "That is not our problem. Let them go as they go: I cannot do anything with you." That is, "We will not pick up any dust." But if you want to do something with them, or if you want to help them, at the same time many bad things will follow. That is very interesting and very real. As Dogen Zenji said, if you pick up one thing, there is birth and death, enlightenment and delusion, Buddha and sentient beings, and something good and something bad. So we call it *Genjokoan*. That is our koan to solve, the actual koan we have.

The purpose of Buddhism is not to establish Buddha's teaching, or Buddhist groups, but to help people to find their own way when they cannot find their own way. So Buddha gives them some warning: 'If you do not follow the right path, you will be lost.' That is the only reason Buddha left his teaching for human beings. So if all sentient beings follow the right path, there is no need to pick up anything. But some Buddhists will make a big mistake.

They try to establish something for the sake of Buddhism in its narrow sense.

The real purpose of Buddhism is to bring us to the point where we do not need Buddha's teaching or Zen Center even. Without a teacher we can follow our own way. That is best. That is the goal of Buddhism. The goal of Buddhism is to bring about the right human life where there is no Buddhism. So to develop our human life to the point where there is no need to pick up anything is why we make our effort. And personally, that is why the more we make effort, the more we have trouble. It is because we always try to pick up or establish something in its small sense [chuckling].

Spring 1984

If we establish something just to make more trouble, it doesn't make sense. So the most important point of our practice is to always try to do something with big mind. When you do something with big mind, if there is no need to do it, you will not do it. Only when you have to do it will you do it.

Setcho's appreciatory word for that is, "Old men will be unable to relax their eyebrows as they would otherwise." Old Zen masters with tense eyebrows will say, 'Ah, silly boys starting Zen Center at Tassajara; they shouldn't do that' [laughing]. If we do not start Zen Center, they can relax their eyebrows. They may feel better.

That is Setcho's appreciatory word, and he says, "Tentatively, I will establish the foundation for the nation even though old men may make a face; you must excuse me." Setcho continues his appreciatory word saying, "But wait a moment, where are the crafty officials and great generals now? Only the pure minds blowing over ten thousands of miles know their whereabouts."

The day may come when we no longer need any generals or *shoguns* or Zen masters, but in the meantime, to bring about that kind of peaceful situation for people, we will tentatively make some foundation. We will pick up a speck of dust.

This is the actual Genjokoan. It is the most real koan for us. This is what we are doing at Tassajara. We have already picked up something. But some old Zen master will make a face, knowing that we dare to pick up something. So again, it is good to fulfill your responsibility and help establish Zen Center; but if there is the slightest idea of self in it, you cannot see Buddha's face. It is no longer with you.

As you like Zen Center so much, you will easily be involved in a kind of self-centered idea. To think about only yourself is a self-centered idea, of course; but to think only about Zen Center is a kind of small mind. Zen Center is just a small speck of dust compared with big Buddha land. As Dogen Zenji says in his *Fukanzazengi*: "If your purpose in zazen misses the point just a little bit, then the separation will be as great as heaven and earth." Then our zazen will not make any sense. We should be able to give up Zen Center when it is not necessary. But I can't say when you can resign from Zen Center. I cannot say it so easily. But each one of us should be ready for it.

We should not be proud of our faculties or our personality or our bright smart mind. When you have good practice, that is also the enemy of Buddhism. You should not pursue the Buddha way for the sake of change, or for your own personal interest. We should not seek for some advantage in our everyday life. Whether people like what you do or not; if it is necessary, you should do it.

So if you pick up a speck of dust, people may not like it. But if you think it is necessary, you should do it. That is our spirit. You should not do it so that people will admire you or because it will help you lead a successful life in the future. What we are doing is not necessarily what we will be doing forever. It is just a tentative good means to help people. To make the best effort in our everyday life is actually Buddhist practice.

The way we extend big mind is limitless. So we say, to establish Buddha's way with defilement. Whatever we do is delusion. Knowing that it is delusion, to do something, to pick up a speck of dust is the Bodhisattva's way, and at the same time the Buddhist way. So we do not expect anything. Right now what we do seems necessary, but tomorrow we don't know.

We will be happy when people no longer want us. We will be very happy. That is real big mind. We wear robes. The reason we wear robes is maybe in order to take off robes. Unless you put on a robe, you cannot take it off. We wear a robe in the same way that we pick up a speck of dust. Even if it is a speck of dust, we must pick it up. If it is Buddha's robe, there is no reason why we should not wear it.

But Buddha's robe is a problem robe. At any time you can put on the robe. When all sentient beings realize they are Buddha, you can take off the robe. If you wear it with some idea of wearing it forever, since it is Buddha's robe, that kind of idea doesn't make any sense.

Our practice looks very rigid and formal, but the reason we observe such a rigid formal practice is to acquire absolute freedom.

People may say it might be better not to be involved in such a rigid practice. It is very difficult to discuss Buddhism with such people. They do not know Genjokoan, the koan of our everyday life. They do not know that day after day, moment after moment, we are creating bad karma. I have to accept it. Even in Tassajara, we are eating eggs, you know. They are living beings. Eggs are not dead. Each grain is a living being. You are killing them, but you have to eat them knowing they are not dead. We can do it because we choose big mind instead of small mind. Small mind will object on the ground of Buddhist precepts, but big mind will accept things as it is.

So whatever it is, according to Dogen Zenji, it is a big koan. He carefully picked out the great koan of reality, the great koan of our life. He set up a great stage for human beings. Whatever we do on the stage is Buddha's act which will continue forever. If you have a good understanding of the great koan, whatever you do makes sense. But when you are only involved in small mind, it doesn't make sense. You cannot stay on the stage of the great koan. You are not alive anymore; just moving around in your coffin; the real human being is not there. That is actually Dogen Zenji's great koan.

Suzuki Roshi in Dokusan room at 300 Page Street.

Starting from the practice of big mind, the practice will be developed in our activity together, like Zen Center or like Buddha's sangha. We will show a good example to other groups when we really follow Buddha's path and when the meaning of our life is there. In short, we shouldn't be bothered so much by the idea of good or bad. We should be concerned that our practice is sincere and supported by big mind. This is the most important point. If you have this, your mind will be constant and peaceful. By experience we know that after some ecstasy, some discouragement will follow. So if you know that, you know how important it is to have big constant mind, and you can enjoy the effort you make. That kind of mind will always keep you young and happy.

We shouldn't mind so much what will happen in the future, but we should be concerned about this moment. Whether you are happy or not is important. If you are following the right path, the quality of your life doesn't differ from the quality of Buddha's life. Of course, there is some difference in its breadth or in its lastingness or in its maturity; but the quality of practice is the same. As with a fan, whether it is large or small, a fan is a fan, same quality. So our practice may not be so good, but the quality of the practice is the same.

When we are supported by big mind and do not lose our way in small mind, small practice, that is Dogen Zenji's Genjokoan. It is koan on a big scale where everyone has great freedom from the usual small activity.

So the goal of practice is to not have any teaching or teacher or sentient beings; where there is no Buddhism and no Buddha. But if you think that without any training you can have that kind of life, that is a big mistake. You do not know what you are doing. When you say you don't need Buddhism, then you are either a great fool or a very selfish person. Don't you think so? Maybe a great fool, to be a great fool is better than to be a selfish person. Even though Buddha spoke about freedom, what Buddha meant and what you may mean is hardly comparable. You say freedom and nature, but you don't understand what freedom is and what nature is.

You say nature, but your understanding of nature is not true nature. It is a kind of home-made nature, cooked up in your kitchen [laughing]. It looks like nature, but it is not truly nature. True nature may be a nature which will ignore almost all living beings. Human beings will easily be ignored by this great nature. Whether we exist on earth or not is not a big problem.

When we realize our nature, it can be a big problem, but for someone to say that all you have to do is to follow your own narrow view of nature and that is freedom, then, in the same way, you will be ignored by the sun or the various stars in space.

If you realize that you cannot be ignored by the universe even though you are small, then you realize who you are. At the same time, you realize that you are alive because you are supported by some truth. Unless you are supported by some truth and follow that truth, you cannot be free.

Thank you very much.

*Case 61 from Katsuki Sekida, trans., *Two Zen Classics* (New York, Weather-hill, 1977), p. 314.

What you wish for is not always what you think it is. Zen and Zen practice are alluded to here. Are you ready for the true dragon? It may not be what you think it is. Each one of you will experience enlightenment and you may not like it.
—M.W.

The True Dragon
Suzuki Roshi
SPRING 1991

Dogen Zenji says, "Don't practice your way like a blind man trying to find out what is an elephant." A blind man touching an elephant may think an elephant is like a wall or a robe or a plank. But the real elephant is not any of those. And he says, "Don't be suspicious of the true dragon, like Seiko."

In China there was a man named Seiko; he loved dragons. All his scrolls were of dragons. He designed his house like a dragon-house and he had many figures of dragons. So a real dragon thought, "If I appear in his house he will be very pleased." So one day the dragon appeared in his room, and he was very scared of him, and almost drew his sword to cut him. The real dragon said, "Oh, my!" and he hurriedly escaped from the room. "Don't be like Seiko!" Dogen Zenji says.

Most of us are practicing our way like a blind man or like Seiko. That is why we have to start our practice over and over. You think you are practicing real zazen, but it may not be so. So if you notice that you haven't been practicing true zazen, you have to start the practice of true zazen again. Over and over we have to start our zazen, because we are always apt to practice zazen like a blind man, or like Seiko.

Here is another story which was told by Master Nangaku. When Baso was practicing zazen, Nangaku, who passed by, asked him, "What are you doing?" "As you see, I am practicing zazen." "Why do you practice zazen?" "I want to attain Buddhahood." And Nangaku didn't say anything but he picked up a tile and started

Dragon drawing by Karen Hamilton.

polishing it. At this, Baso started wondering what Nangaku was doing and asked him, "What are you doing?" "I am making a jewel." Baso asked, "How is it possible to make a tile into a jewel?" Nangaku replied, "How is it possible to attain Buddhahood by practicing zazen?" After this story Nangaku asked Baso, "When the cart does not go, which do you whip, the cart or the horse?"

Dogen Zenji says usually there is no person who hits the cart to make it go. Usually people hit the horse instead of the cart. But there should be a way to whip the cart. When you practice zazen almost all of you know you should whip the horse. And to whip the horse you practice zazen. You're giving the whip pretty hard to your practice, without knowing how to whip the cart. But we should know there is another way to practice: to whip the cart instead of the horse.

Horse is a symbol of mind; the cart means body. It also means zazen form—formal practice of zazen. Horse means attainment, spiritual attainment, and cart means physical practice. Usually, you know, we understand zazen practice as formal practice. Our shikantaza is formal practice and koan practice is more mental practice. But this kind of understanding is not complete. This kind of understanding is the understanding of blind men like Seiko. True practice is not formal practice or so-called shikantaza or koan practice. None of those. Those practices are just the practice to whip the horse.

This is like, Seiko loves the dragon, carved dragon, not real one. So, each one of us must think on this point. Each one of us practices zazen in his own way, with his own understanding. And he continues that kind of practice, thinking, "This is right practice." So, even though he is sitting here in the zendo he is involved in his own practice. In other words, he is carving, carefully carving his own dragon which is not real. That is what most of the people are doing. Some people may explain what zazen is in a philosophical way, or some people try to express our zazen in literature or painting or in a scientific way, without knowing that that is their own dragon, not real one.

That is not wrong. That is all right, but we should know that there must be the way to whip the cart. We should know that there is a true dragon which has no form or color, which is called nothingness or emptiness, and which includes koan practice and so-called *shikantaza,* and various Hinayana ways of practice or pre-Buddhistic practice. This is the practice transmitted from Buddha to us. But at least when we do something there must be that which is supposed to be the true dragon, real dragon. In this way, we practice zazen.

You come and practice zazen in this zendo where there should be the true dragon. But the instant you think, "This is the true dragon," that is a mistake. But knowing that, if you come to this zendo, you should practice zazen with people forgetting all about your carving or your painting. You should practice zazen with the people in this zendo, with your friends, completely involved in the atmosphere we have here. Sometimes I allow people who are sticking to an old way to do that, but strictly speaking, those who practice zazen here should be completely involved in the feeling we have in this zendo, and practice our way with people according to my instruction. That is what you should do.

But people who do not know what real emptiness is, or true dragon, may think they are being forced in this way: "Sokoji is a Soto Zen temple. I have been practicing Rinzai way." But that is not true. We are practicing the way transmitted from Buddha to us. We are Buddha's disciples. And we practice zazen with Buddha, with patriarchs.

For some people that which does not have some particular form is not true being. So they may say that it is an imaginary dragon. But for a Buddhist, there is a way to understand reality in two ways: with form and color or without form and color. That is, to whip the cart instead of the horse. If someone whips a cart, people may say he is crazy. But there is actually a transmitted way to whip the cart. To practice formal way is to whip the cart.

But for an ordinary person, to see the carved dragon is to not see the true dragon. That is so-called one pure practice—*ichigyo zammai*. Usually, ichigyo zammai is understood to mean being completely involved in some kind of practice. It is so, but at the same time, even though we are deeply involved in a kind of practice, at the same time we should have complete freedom from it. Do you understand?

Usually when you become very much attached to something, you have no freedom from it. But for us, because of complete freedom, it is possible to be involved in or to be attached to something completely. That is shikantaza, true shikantaza. So shikantaza is not even a matter of whether you practice zazen or not. Even though you do not practice our way in the cross-legged position, if you have this point you are always practicing zazen. Usually when you become very much attached to something, you have no freedom from it.

Dogen Zenji said: "Sickness does not destroy a person, but if you do not practice zazen, that no-practice will destroy a person." Do you understand? Sickness does not destroy a person. You may say: "Today I cannot practice zazen because I have a headache. If I practice zazen I shall die, so I cannot practice zazen." But Dogen Zenji says, "Sickness does not destroy a person, but no-practice will destroy you."

It is not so easy to talk about what real practice is. If we want to figure out what Dogen Zenji meant, without having this kind of experience, to talk about this point may be completely wrong. But we can figure out what he meant through our practice. His practice is something beyond formal practice or spiritual practice, or even beyond enlightenment. The more you try to figure it out, the more you feel distance from your practice and from his practice.

And yet this is a practice which we cannot escape. Actually we are practicing his way day by day, but for us there is no time to figure out what he meant completely. And even though we human beings continue his way forever, we will not be able to say: this is his way. The only thing we can say is, this is the way which has no end and no beginning, and from this way we cannot escape.

Because of this practice, various beings survive in the world, and everything is going in this way, including we human beings. So there actually is no problem for us. But as a human being who lives the Way in this world, the constant effort to keep up with the way the whole universe is going, and to practice our way is necessary, as long as this universe exists. With this feeling, with this complete calmness of mind, we should practice our way.

Spring 1991

After sitting one year, most students will actually have this quality of practice, but when you try to figure out what your practice is, there you have a problem, or you create a problem which does not belong to your practice. If you just sit, there is no problem for most of our students. But sometimes you create problems, that's all. And you fight with the problems, that's all. You are creating it, actually. In your zazen there is no problem.

When you practice your own personal practice, you have a problem. When you just sit, being absorbed in the feeling we have in our zendo, there is no problem at all.

We should make our effort on this point more, instead of carving our own dragon. In this way you have complete freedom from everything, including yourself. To talk about freedom is quite easy. But actually to have it is not so easy at all. Unless you are able to have freedom from yourself, you will never have freedom from anything. Or, if you only have freedom from yourself, you will have freedom from everything. How we attain this freedom is our practice. You should not listen to the various instructions as something forced on you. The instructions will help you only when you are ready to practice zazen according to the place where you practice, forgetting all about the old way of practice you have been making.

I am not emphasizing Soto way instead of Rinzai way, but as long as you practice zazen in Zen Center, you should practice Zen Center's way, or else you will just be involved in personal practice. You will be carving your own dragon, always, thinking: this is the true dragon. That is a silly mistake. You shouldn't create this kind of problem for your practice.

As some Zen masters say, "Our way is like taking a walk, step by step." This is our practice. When you stand on one leg, you know, you should forget the other leg. This is step by step. This is true practice. You know that if you stick to right leg or left leg, right foot or left foot, you cannot walk. This is how we practice our way. This is complete freedom.

Thank you very much.

Meditation, ceremonies and ethics: are they the same or different? This is a perennial question in the West. Some communities feel that Zen meditation is important, but not the other forms of the temple. This lecture explores this territory. –M.W.

Zazen, Rituals, and Precepts Cannot Be Separated

Suzuki Roshi

SAN FRANCISCO ZEN CENTER, 28 JULY 1970
SPRING/SUMMER 2000

I want to talk with you about some problems you may have when you come to Zen Center. I think you understand pretty well why we practice. Why we observe rituals is perhaps more difficult to understand. Actually, it is not something to explain [laughs]. If you ask me why I observe rituals, it is difficult to answer.

First, I do it because I have been doing it for a long time so there is no problem. I tend to think that because I have no problem in observing my way, then you must not have a problem [laughs]. But you are Americans, and I am Japanese, and you have not been practicing the Buddhist way for so long, therefore there must be various problems [laughs].

These problems are almost impossible to solve. But if you actually follow our way I think you will have some understanding of our rituals. What I want to talk about is the precepts.

Precepts for me includes rituals. And when we say "precepts," it is another name for our zazen practice. For us, zazen practice and observation of rituals are not two different things. How to observe the rituals is how to observe the precepts. Our practice, especially in the Soto school, puts emphasis on everyday life, including rituals, eating, and going to the restroom. All those things are included in our practice.

So the way we practice zazen, the way we practice rituals, and the way of life of a Buddhist or Zen student is fundamentally the same. But when we talk about our way of life or rituals, we come face to face with some rules. The rules of observing ceremonies are rituals, and the rules of our everyday life are our precepts.

When we say "precepts," we usually mean some rules, but that is just a superficial understanding of precepts. Precepts are actually the expression of our true nature. The way we express our true nature is always according to the place or situation in which you live. So to practice zazen is to be yourself and to observe our precepts is just to be yourself.

As you have some way of sitting on a black cushion, we have some way of observing our rituals or ceremony in the Buddha Hall. The point of our zazen practice is to be free from thinking mind and from emotional activity. In short, that is the practice of selflessness. In our observation of rituals, the point is to be free from selfish ideas. The practice of rituals is the practice of selflessness.

First you enter the room and you bow. In Japanese we say *gotai tochi*. Gotai is "our body." Tochi is "to throw away." It means to throw away our physical and mental being-in short, to practice selflessness. We offer ourselves to Buddha. That is the practice of bowing. When you bow, you lift your hands. We lift Buddha's feet, which are on your palms and you feel Buddha on your palms. So when you practice bowing, you have no idea of self. You give up everything.

When Buddha was begging, his follower spread his hair on the muddy ground and let Buddha walk over it. That is supposed to be the origin of why we bow. In ritual, you bow and work. You begin everything by some signal. That kind of thing you may not like so much [laughs]. It looks very formal, to begin everything by the sound of a bell. Whether you want to do it or not, you must do it. It looks very formal. As long as you are in the Buddha Hall, you should observe our way according to the rules we have there. We do it to forget ourselves and to become one. To be a Zen student in this Buddha Hall is why we observe our rituals.

Opening ceremony of Tassajara Zen Mountain Center.

This is a very important point. To feel your being, here, in this moment, is a very important practice. That is the point of observing precepts and observing rituals and practicing zazen. To feel or to be yourself at a certain time, in a certain place. That is why we practice our way.

So the actual feeling of rituals cannot be understood without observing them. When you observe them, you have the actual feeling of rituals. As long as you try to know what it means or why you do it, it is difficult to feel your actual being in this place.

Only when you do it will you feel your being. To be a Buddhist is to do things like Buddha. That is actually how to be a Buddhist [laughs]. It does not mean that when you are able to observe our rituals as your friends do, that you will have no problem in your everyday life. This ritual feeling, or practice, will extend into your everyday life.

You will find yourself in various situations, and you will intuitively know what you should do. You will have the right response to someone's activity. When you are not able to respond to another without wondering what he has on his mind, you will force something. Most of the time I don't think you will give the most intuitive response.

I want you to do rituals until you are quite sure about your response to other people. How one responds to others is very important. When we teachers observe our students, they may be trying to act right, and trying to understand people, but most of the time it is rather difficult for them to have some kind of intuition. If you start to have this kind of intuition, you will have big confidence in yourself, and you will trust people, and you will trust yourself. And so, all the problems which you created for yourself will be no more. You will have no more problem. That is why we have training or practice.

Spring/Summer 2000

My master, Gyokujun So-on, used to say: "Stay with me for several years. If you become a priest, you will be a good priest, and if you remain a layman, you will be a good layman or good citizen, and you will have no problem in your life."

I think that was very true. I was the sixth youngest disciple when I became my master's disciple. Two of us became priests, the rest of the disciples remained laymen. They are very good actually. When they came to my teacher [laughs], they had some trouble. Except for one disciple who passed away, the rest of them have done pretty well, although they are not priests. So I think what he said is very true.

This is very good practice for you. You may think our practice is like army practice [laughs], but actually it is not so. The idea is quite different. I think the Japanese army copied our practice. It looks like it, but they couldn't copy our spirit.

You should trust your innate nature, your Buddha Nature. That is the most important point. If you trust your true nature, you should be able to trust your teacher, too. That is very important. Not because your teacher is perfect, but because his innate nature is the same as yours. The point of practice between teacher and disciple is to get rid of selfish ideas as much as possible and to trust each other. Only when you trust your teacher can you practice zazen, can you practice rituals, and can you act as a Zen Center student.

To remain always a Zen Center student is a very important point. You become a Zen Center student by trusting your true nature, and trusting your teacher, and trusting your zazen practice without saying why [laughs]. I think you should do it, as long as you come here. And if you don't want to do so, I think you shouldn't come here. As long as you come here, you should follow our way, or else maybe you will waste your time and you will regret it.

So in this way, we can carry on our schedule. The way we carry on our schedule is the way we observe our precepts. Precepts were initiated by Buddha when he said "Don't do this, or don't behave like that." That was the origin of precepts. In India, in Buddha's time, there were Buddha's precepts. And in China, they have precepts which are based on the Chinese way of life. We have sixteen precepts, and these precepts are the essential precepts which we should observe as a Japanese, as an American, or as an Indian priest or layman.

These precepts are the precepts which you can apply to your everyday life. We say, "Don't kill," but "don't kill" does not just mean don't kill flies or insects. Actually it is too late [laughs]. If you say, "Here is a fly, should I kill it or not?" it is too late! Before we see the fly, we have this kind of problem. When we eat, we say: "Seventy-two labors brought us this rice." When we say "seventy-two labors" this includes protecting grains from various insects.

It is not just-not to kill insects. When you eat, and you chant "Seventy-two labors brought us this rice," it includes already the precept of "not to kill." After making a great effort to protect the corn from insects, we can eat. When you chant, "seventy-two labors," you should be relating to the precept "not to kill." So "not to kill," is not any special precept.

108 manzanita beads from Tassajara.

To exist here in this way is the result of sacrificing many animals and plants. You are always sacrificing something. So as long as you are involved in dualistic concepts, it is not possible for you to observe our precepts.

So how to get out of dualistic concepts and fill our being with gratitude is the point of practice. Actually it is very foolish to say "not to kill." But why we say "not to kill" is to point out or to understand our life from various angles. Not to kill, not to steal, not to speak ill of others. Each of these precepts includes the other precepts. And each practice or ritual we observe includes the others. So if you have the actual feeling of being here, that is the way to observe precepts and the way to practice zazen.

If you understand how you observe even one precept, you can observe the rest of the precepts and you can practice zazen, you can observe rituals. Zazen practice and observation of rituals or precepts cannot be separated. How to experience this kind of feeling is how you understand our precepts.

If you say it is difficult, it may be very difficult. But it will not be so difficult a thing if you say, "I will do it." That is how you observe precepts, even without thinking whether you can observe them or not. "I will do it" means "don't kill animals." You may say so, because originally it is not possible to kill anything [laughs]. You think you killed, but actually, you cannot. Even though you think you killed, they are still alive [laughs]. Even though you eat something, it is still alive in your body. If something leaves your body, it is still alive.

It is not possible for anything to be killed. The only way is to be grateful for everything you have [laughs]. That is how we keep our precepts without having a dualistic understanding of precepts.

Then you may say, "If so, there will not be any need to have precepts." But unless you are sure, you cannot feel your presence or your being. You do not feel you are alive. You do not have the joy of life or gratitude for everything. You can easily say: "No, I wouldn't kill anything." But it means that you will not sacrifice yourself for anything. You will be just you. You will not be caught by a dualistic understanding of yourself, and you will feel yourself, as you feel yourself in zazen.

It is rather difficult to explain, but that is actually how we observe precepts. Dogen-zenji says: "Even though we do not try to observe precepts, like a scarecrow [laughs] more evil comes to you." It is strange, when you feel your being in its true sense right here, no evil comes. You cannot violate any precepts, and whatever you do, that is the expression of your true nature.

You will not say: "I shouldn't say so," [laughs] or "I shouldn't do that." You will be quite free from that kind of regret or arrogance of observing some special precepts. That is how to observe precepts.

To repeat, precepts is to chew your brown rice [laughs]. Without chewing your brown rice, you cannot eat it. Only when you chew it for a pretty long time will you appreciate the taste of brown rice. When you say, "Oh this is awful! [laughs] How many times should I chew it before I swallow it down?" that is a very foolish way of chewing brown rice or eating brown rice. If you say, "Oh, sixteen precepts! Awful to be a Buddhist!" [laughs, laughter] Then you have no chance to have a real taste of the Buddhist way. If you observe them one by one, that is how you chew brown rice and how you practice our way.

Zen Center
Teachers

Zentatsu Baker Roshi's contributions to Zen Center and Wind Bell have been extraordinary. He succeeded Suzuki Roshi as Abbot in 1971, and created much of the mandala of Zen Center. The three practice places, economic support, and to some extent the teaching style were shaped by him. His stepping down in 1983 lead to changes and a maturing of Zen Center. This lecture, edited from a talk given during a sesshin (seven-day retreat) at Green Gulch Farm, is about practicing wholeheartedly with your body and mind.

Awakening the Will-Body

Richard Baker

SUMMER 1975

Suzuki Roshi felt that Buddhism needed some fresh opportunity, some place where people's minds weren't made up about Buddhism. So after he finished his first stages of training, he asked his teacher if he could go to America. His teacher said no, so he asked if he could go to Hokkaido. Hokkaido is rather like the Japanese frontier; it was only really settled in the last century, about the same time as much of the U.S. His teacher got very angry, so Suzuki Roshi had to stay. But he never gave up his idea of coming to America.

Although when he did finally come here, he felt he had not studied widely enough for us. At the same time, he felt he had come to America too late and too old. But he was convinced his successors could do it, could study Buddhism more widely and more freely. So he instructed us to do just this, to study Buddhism widely and freely-and he taught us how to do it. First of all he emphasized our sitting posture, our yogic posture. This makes sense of course because Zen is the school of Buddhism which emphasizes yoga, the body itself, and the yogic postures of mind and body. But it is also because body-rooted practice is central to Suzuki Roshi's understanding and unfolding of practice.

We don't use many aids, many rituals. Our own body is our vajra. Because of this, Zen starts with the body. We start with what

Baker Roshi lecturing at Green Gulch Farm.

we have. We experience some divided nature from childhood, some suffering divided nature. We have two parents and various ways of looking at things. So we have to begin our practice with our various parts agreeing on something, finding how our mind and body can come to some agreement. For this we have zazen. It's the feeling of "Let's sit down and see what happens."

So Zen Buddhism creates various provisional ways of practice that emphasize the body or the mind or both or all three together with phenomena. We could call these body-only teachings and practices, or mind only, or all-things-at-once. They are Zen's way of putting together the teachings of the Yogacara, Madhyamaka, and Hwa Yen schools.

Now we are doing a sesshin here at Green Gulch. And if you're going to practice with your body, of course you have to trust it. You have to give up your ideas of it as being separate from you. As Linda Ruth pointed out to me once the absurdity of feeling that our foot is "way down there." We have many such mistaken images of our body, thought-sheathes, that we have to begin to notice and free ourselves from.

The vehicle of the Tathagata can be characterized in various ways. What I am emphasizing now is that there is no separate reality behind this immediate actuality. This itself has aspects. This immediate actuality is not "real," but an "actuality" which is not repeatable. There's no way to simulate it or make it permanent. It is only itself. A second aspect is that everything is everywhere present. A third aspect is that everything is absolutely independent, infolded and outfolded in its own time. A fourth aspect is that everything is timeless and nongraspable. A fifth is that the Tathagata Vehicle is truth-bearing and thus we are capable of an immediate, ongoing perception of truth in ourself. We can call this Buddha's will, or Buddha's Will-Body, because it carries us and decisively knows the fullness of each occasion.

Most of us explicitly, or at least implicitly, assume and act on the view that reality is repeating-and hence effectually permanent. It's natural, we want the tree to be on our front lawn each morning. Although, we know it could be cut down or lost in a storm, still we expect it to be there, and the rest of the world, in an habitual way that reinforces the sense of a permanent self. Our language is based on similar assumptions: "it" rains. We have an unexamined and continuously reinforced assumption of repeatability that trains our senses to notice repeatability, which means we don't trust the independence of our senses and the nonrepeating world they can reveal.

One of the easiest things in the world to do is to bring our attention to our breath for a short time, but, as those of us who meditate and practice mindfulness know, it is very difficult to keep our attention and mind on our breath continuously. The main reason for this is our implicit need for a continuity of self that we find through thinking. This is a subtle form of permanence. It's this very effort to make reality repeatable that Buddhism calls suffering.

An existential need for permanence is the foundation of the delusively sense of an "outside" on which we can depend: an outside world and thus an "inside" too, which is separate and different from the outside world. If you have an operative idea of an "outside," then your senses will always be off base. Thus one of the teachings, one of the aids to penetration, to entering Buddha's Way and Buddha's body, is to see everything as your own mind. It's a fact. It is a practice to continuously, to simultaneously, remind yourself. To understand everything that comes to you as you, as your mind and karma, not as some different or even hostile thing. Knowing this in actuality, allows us to develop an even mind toward everyone. We know how we feel and we feel embodied and liberated within each occasion.

To practice this is one the bases for some of the things I would like to come to in this sesshin. So during these days, please emphasize an even mind, an even effort, an even, steady awareness throughout sitting and kinhin and meals and work and sleeping. And if you can give up any idea or image of your body in your zazen practice, or of outside and inside, you can become strong enough to accept anything. More and more, we accept just what comes to us, accept some hearing completely, accept some seeing, without editing and monitoring. Try practicing—repeating on each occasion, on each perception—the phrase: "Always Unfamiliar!"

Our hearing can take us, can open us up to so many things, if we just trust our hearing. What we hear just now is enough. We don't have to average it and see if it's going to occur again. In Buddhism our feeling is: only once will we hear that. Only once will we see that. By the time we go get our camera, it's different. By the time we try to base our life on it, it's different. Our life is already based in it.

By zazen we're trying to develop our strength and ability to be one with our activity. We notice the finality of each thing, that it happens only once. That it is not repeatable, or graspable, or regainable, or re-doable. If you're not there, not present, it's too late. This recognition, and at the same time, not taking it too seriously, gives our life some seriousness. You know, by the time you wish or think, it's already too late. It's delusive and all too serious when you think the outside world is there-and perhaps saving up to get you or saving up to save you.

Sesshin is also to settle down with this kind of idea, to try it on, to hold it, to live it. To practice Buddhism requires an enormous amount of confidence—confidence in yourself and your teacher and Buddha Nature, a sense that you can do it. In Zen sesshin and monastic life, we practice many "have-to's." By "have-to's" I mean the way a mother or father change their baby's diapers, because they "have to," not because at a particular moment they necessarily want to. They just do it! They don't say, "Oh boy, am I ever dying to change these diapers." They may actually enjoy it—and the baby might too, but their action is not based on wanting to or not wanting to. Someone must change the baby's diapers, so you change your baby's diapers, that's all. We actually need such things. We need such "have-to's." If we do not have wise, realistic, and integrating "have-to's," then we often make them neurotically and delusive. Zen practice is partially based on "have-to's" which are not in the realm of likes or dislikes. We come to service and chant, not because we like to or dislike to, but because it is a part of the wisdom of this practice. How-

Summer 1975

ever, if we are concerned with ideas like "When will I get to like chanting?" we're missing the point. If we get to like chanting too much, we should add something else that is rather a nuisance to do. We should be able to do basic things without much problem, things which don't harm anyone or harm the world. As Suzuki Roshi said, through such strictures or "have-to's," we can study our desires and discover our tendencies. We can deeply plumb our desires and strengths through such strictures and can discover the depths of the mind when it is not caught in the pendulum of likes and dislikes. This is the mind of equanimity. Suzuki Roshi's favorite story was about Mazu and the tile. Mazu was doing zazen, study-ing zazen to attain Buddhahood, so Nanyue picked up a tile and began rubbing it. Mazu asked, "What are you doing?" Nanyue said, "I'm turning this tile into a jewel." Mazu asked, "How can you make a tile into a jewel?" Nanyue said, "How can you make yourself into a Buddha?" Then he said, "If you want to make a cart go, do you hit the horse or the cart?" Many sayings reflect this kind of feeling. When it's nighttime, dawn is here. Before win-ter is over, spring is here. Even if you don't understand it, or accept it completely, if you are practicing you should have this kind of confidence; you should try to accept it. Can you accept it? Can you just do zazen completely? Can you just do this sesshin completely, as if nothing else existed, as if you would die on Friday night? Suzuki Roshi said we may starve to death at Tassajara or at Page Street. But if we just practiced zazen and took care of everything completely, he didn't think we would. There are two recognitions that we will come to when we are able to face things as they are, not wishing they were some other way. One is death. By death I don't mean just that someone's going to die, although through death we may realize this deeper finality, as Dogen did watching his mother die and the twin trail of smoke rising from the incense stick. The finality I'm talking about we may recognize when someone goes crazy, when we can't reach someone emotionally, or when we cannot reach ourself, when there is almost nothing but suffering in this world, when we can't do anything about each moment. Each thing just happens, and hopefully we find our singularity and accord with it. Another recognition is that we are corruptible. All of us are corruptible. When pushed, almost all of us have a price. I'm sorry to say so, but it's true. Governments use this to force people to do things. Many people use it to make the most of others—corruptibility for their own profit or power. The Bodhisattva recognizes in himself, herself, this suffering and corruptibility and so creates the conditions for good—let us say good, in himself, in herself, and in the world. Thus, the most basic suggestion in Buddhism for everyone is to practice good and avoid evil. The understanding of good and evil in Buddhism is pretty close to the roots in English of the words "good" and "evil." Good and God mean to unite something, to gather into a body, to recognize the larger body. And evil means to overextend, like the "eaves" of a house, to be off the mark, to set something up as real or over something else. The Bodhisattva doesn't set up anything as permanent. Likewise, we in our practice don't assume things are possessable in any permanent way. But we do try to create the conditions for people to exist beneficially. First however, we must find our own calmness, clarity, and freedom from perplexity. As Suzuki Roshi used to say, "Don't try to solve other's problems before you solve your own. Otherwise, you just cause more trouble."

PRACTITIONER: I'm perplexed in my mind between the purpose-lessness of zazen and the purposes I have.

ROSHI: This dynamic appears in every aspect of practice. Of course, we have purpose and things to do, but at a fundamental level, we can know and feel that there is nothing to do and no place to go. At this level, we can feel free from any purpose. But the resolution of similar contraries as in the *Heart Sutra:* "no eyes, no ears," or in the *Diamond Sutra* "no perception of a being to save," depend on a transformation of how we see. For example, to practice: "no perception of ill will," we must change how we conceive of each other. "No perception of ill will" doesn't mean we are repressing ill will. It means that we have come to see each being as a being for whom we cannot feel ill will. It is somewhat similar to how it is hard to feel ill will toward an infant or a person who discovers us after we have been lost in a forest for several hours. You will find out by experience that although some idea of attaining led you to sitting, when you sit with that idea, your sitting is quite dull and lifeless. Just to sit. As Suzuki Roshi always said, we must practice Buddhism just for Buddhism. You can use Buddhism for some purpose, gain or fame or something like that. But Suzuki Roshi's emphasis was for us to just practice with each other for Buddhism alone. He said that, while in five or ten years Zen Center and Buddhism in America would have many friends, we don't practice for this, or even for the improvement of society. Just to practice for Buddhism, just to sit for sitting, this is our practice—the conception of our practice. We have other reasons for practicing, but "practice"means that we don't review these gaining reasons. If we find ourself thinking of them, we let go of thinking of them. Do you understand? That is true practice. It might seem artificial to withdraw energy from some thoughts and ideas. But that only means we should go further and find out how artificial everything is anyway. How everything is based on artificial views and attitudes. Then find out how to counteract our attitudes with antidotal attitudes, until we can drop all attitudes. So please, in this sesshin, and those of you who are not in the sesshin too, become very friendly with your body and your life-situation as you yourself. Zazen is sometimes just some painful stale feeling, sometimes just some painful ecstatic feeling. Just this. Don't try to review your zazen.

As we stop averaging our life at each moment, we will find out many things. We will notice many mental and physical phenomena, many subtle things. As I said yesterday, how wonderful our skin feels after zazen during a sesshin. How the organ of our skin teaches us and shows us our state of mind. How cool the surface of our eyes feels. How our stomach feels. How when attitudes drop out of our breathing and mind and shoulders and hips, how refreshed we feel. Practice is beginning to trust these notices.

The acts of Buddha are Buddha. The acts of you are you. These tiny acts you are participating in. By our vow or participation, the color is very deep and we perceive things with full dimensions. When our vow is weak, our will-body is weak and we see things as flat and thin and colorless.

When our "Vow-Body," our "Will-Body," is strong we notice subtle manifestations of the path, of our existence, of our way beyond self, of our Buddha Nature. Then we recede from noting them. One part doesn't have to observe. Just let go. Just give all away. The first Paramita, you know—just give it away. Until nothing but space is sitting zazen. Nothing but space is living your life. Nothing but space is sitting this sesshin, which we create something in the midst of. In this sesshin, to eat, to get up, to do things in this way, we may realize what we actually are—with and without a "who" to realize how we actually exist, separately and all together. Please let's do it. Let's find out how Suzuki Roshi wanted us to practice. Some fresh new way from our own intimate and immediate experience, freely studying everything, freely realizing our way. Thank you very much.

Dainin Katagiri Roshi came to Zen Center in 1965 where he taught until leaving in 1974 to start the Minnesota Zen Mediation Center. In 1984–1985, he was Abbot of Zen Center, traveling between the three practice centers. This talk on true heart was given at Tassajara and is one of my favorites. His "nothing hits the mark" is a bull's eye for me. —M.W.

True Heart: Raising the Banner of Truth

Dainin Katagiri

TASSAJARA, 20 MARCH 1985

SUMMER 1985

When Nan-yueh ch'an shih (*ch'an shih:* Jap. *zenji*) was practicing under his teacher, his teacher asked him, "From where do you come?" Nan-yueh ch'an shih said, "I come from Mt. Sung." His teacher said, "What is it that thus comes?" Nan-yueh ch'an shih didn't know the answer, so for eight long years he pondered this question. Then one day it dawned on him, "Even to say it is something, doesn't hit the mark."

I think this is very important. Every day, in every activity we have to think, "What is it that thus comes?" What comes? What comes with what reason? What comes for what? Who comes with what reason? This is a big koan we have to meet day in and day out-otherwise, it's pretty hard to keep our boat on the right course. We slip off course immediately. We make a detour, moment after moment. "What is it that thus comes?" It's a very difficult question, but our outlook on life should be built up in the light of this teaching; then we can know what to do right in the middle of suffering, human life, human confusions. Constantly we have to reflect upon ourselves this way. If we don't, we become crazy pretty easily, we become overly infatuated with good or bad or neutral. So, even though we don't understand what it means, we must constantly ask, "What comes with what reason?"

Please return to your first motivation. Your first motivation is very vague. You don't know what it is, but you want to do it. That's why you say, "I want to know human life with a true heart." What do you mean by "true heart?" True heart is really vague. You can know the true heart, but you cannot pin down what it is that compels you to practice the Buddha Way, or to seek for the truth. What compels you is your first motivation. In that moment, that very first motivation, the Buddha, Truth, true heart can be found. But you simply cannot put any name on it. Whatever name you put on it, it becomes a blur, you don't know what it is.

Even though you come to Tassajara with your first motivation, seeking for the truth, don't you feel that you quickly lose your way? This is because the moment you are here, which is what you wanted, you forget your first motivation and you begin making detours looking for many kinds of courses to take. I want to ask you, what is the basis of why you are here? Your first motivation? If that were true, there would be no struggle. You would just be here and practice steadily. But you don't. What is it? Why do you do this? From the point of view of first motivation, all you can do here is just be as you really are. But, when you are right in the middle of this Tassajara you really wanted, something happens. You seek for peace, but when you are right in the middle of the peace you sought, you lose your way immediately. You seek for something else, and the result is violence, fighting, arguments, squabbles-invariably there are squabbles in your small world, in your small society, and in the larger society, or even within yourself. In your deep heart, in your true heart, you always seek peace, but when you have it, you don't know what it is. You completely lose the way. That's why you have to constantly come back to the first motivation. First motivation is really pure, clean, and shining. Temporarily we call it Buddha Nature. In plain language, maybe we can call it "true heart" or "sincerity" or "truthfulness."

Constantly you have to ask yourself if you are trying to just satisfy your desires. Did you come here to practice the Buddha Way, to lead the life of a priest, or to get priest ordination? That is alright, but it is already slipping off course because that is a course that you are looking for, that you are expecting to take. Basically, what you really want to do is to practice the Buddha Way at Tassajara. That is all you want to do, but then, immediately, you start looking for some new course to set out on: some so-called "priest's life," some spiritual fantasy, or "enlightenment." If you think "enlightenment," right away there is another situation: so-called "delusion." So if you see the delusion, you try to keep away from the delusion and try to keep the enlightenment, or nice spiritual fantasy. But that means you have gone off on a detour. What is real peace, real harmony? What is the Buddha Way?

By becoming a priest, by anticipating or expecting the life of a priest, can you understand the human world, can you understand the Buddha Way? There is no way to understand the Buddha Way, even though you become a priest. As a priest you become more confused and wherever you go it is pretty hard.

Are you attracted to the wonderful food at Tassajara? That's why you come here to practice. Are you attracted to the natural surroundings at Tassajara? Is that why you come here? Or are you attracted to success in life? Spiritual success in life? Or are you attracted to a lazy way of life?

Katagiri Roshi in courtyard at 300 Page Street.

Usual human society is hard, so you may practice here because it is easy-you do not have to struggle as businessmen do to be successful, you just follow the schedule. You can just be at Tassajara and practice the Buddha Way in peace and harmony. Are you attracted to this lazy way, this easy-going way? Then, for you, "just sitting" is the "just sitting" you have understood. It is not the Buddha Way. If you practice like this, it is really easy-going. Is this your first motivation? Are you attracted to hard practice, or to neutral practice? You should repeatedly ask yourself this.

Stone Buddha at Tassajara.

I don't think it is necessary to know something which you don't already know. This is not practice for us. As long as you are a human being, you are right in the middle of the situation of not understanding anything, because life is vast, because it is the truth. Truth or vastness, or emptiness, is very rich, but you cannot name it. So all you can do is to practice, receive, and accept that full richness. How do you know this? There is no way to know, but you are already there, so first accept this fact. Do not try to poke your head into something in order to know. You should confirm that you are right in the situation of not understanding anything at all. This is the point you have to know. That's why you constantly have to come back to the source.

When Dogen Zenji went to China, he was asked by a Chinese monk, "What are you doing?" Dogen Zenji replied, "I am reading the scriptures." The monk said, "For what reason?" "Because I want to learn about the ancestors' lives, sayings, and activities." The monk said, "For what?" "I just want to help human beings when I go back to Japan." The monk said, "For what?" "Because it is helpful to human beings; because everyone suffers so much." The monk said, again, "For what?" Then, Dogen Zenji said, "This is my way of life. I want to offer my life to all sentient beings. I want to help." And again the monk said, "For what?" Finally, Dogen Zenji couldn't say anything. This is very important because this monk cross-examined Dogen Zenji through returning to the source, what we are calling "first motivation," "Buddha Nature," "Truth," or "What is it that thus comes?"

For eight long years, Nan-yueh practiced, pondered thoroughly and precisely the question, "What is it that thus comes?" Then, he said, "Nothing to hit the mark in words." "In words" means in terms of your understanding, in terms of your thinking. Without words, you cannot think. Thinking and words come together and work together. By your thinking, by your words—if you try to put a name on it—nothing hits the mark. Maybe you can hit the mark sometimes, but it doesn't last for long. Sooner or later you must come back to zero and start again from the beginning. Whatever thing you pick up, whether from the Buddha's teachings (emptiness, enlightenment), or from the usual aspects of human life (love, hatred, passion, emotions), please look at it closely. You can temporarily put a name on it, but the more carefully you think, the more it becomes a blur and you don't know what it is.

When I was nineteen I listened to teishos given by Hashimoto Roshi. I didn't expect to understand what he said, but I really wanted to hear him. People called me crazy. I was young and didn't understand anything, but over and over I listened to him. What I can tell you now is only this point: at that time I felt the truth of what Hashimoto Roshi said in his lecture, but I couldn't put any names on it. He said that, in whatever situation you may be in, in whatever place you are standing right here and now, this is the place in which you have to erect the banner of truth. That's it. I felt this. Whoever I am—whether I am a stupid person or a wise man—doesn't matter. Again and again I listened to him speak, but I didn't understand or remember any of the words. I can tell you about it now, but in those days I couldn't say anything, although I felt the truth in what he said.

But what does this mean? It means that the naked reality of being is full of richness, but you cannot name it, you cannot understand it. Your whole existence is completely embraced by this full richness, just like a baby held in its mother's arms or sitting in its mother's lap. This is the naked reality of all beings. It is not the point that you should try to understand it. If you want to know, you should know the reason why you cannot know it. That is why, finally, after eight long years, Nan-yueh understood that nothing hit the mark. This means you have to come back to your first motivation.

The *Prajna Paramita* says, "Gate, gate, paragate, parasamgate, bodhi, svaha." Go beyond, far beyond. "Go beyond" means let's return to the first motivation. This is a really simple life: that is, to erect the banner of life, the banner of truth. This is Dogen's teaching, and also Buddha's teaching. Through this continuing practice, you can understand lots of different courses through the human world: lots of toys, techniques, teachings. Teachings are nothing but toys, if you misuse them. If you don't misuse them, the teachings become pretty nice. Then you can understand many toys, teachings, courses, and techniques for living in peace and harmony. If you don't practice this way, you are completely involved in the big whirl of courses, knowledges, suffering, entanglements, and human relations. You never stand up straight. It's pretty hard. This way is very vague—you don't understand it. But you feel something, because this is your first motivation. You are attracted to it, but you cannot put a name on it, or say whether it is useful or not.

So, the dialogue between Nan-yueh and his teacher continues. After Nan-yueh said that, "even to say it is something doesn't hit

Summer 1985

the mark," his teacher asked, "Do you think it is contingent upon practice and enlightenment?" If there is nothing to say which hits the mark, why do we do zazen, why do we think about enlightenment and delusion, life and death, etc.? Nan-yueh replied, "It is not that they don't exist, but that they cannot be defiled." Many things exist from moment to moment, but they don't hinder each other, because the basis of existence, total dynamic energy/form, exists before you think of it, and even if you don't think of it. This means that there is nowhere to go: no way to find directions, no way to know what it is, and if you

try to know, this is already a detour. Just do your best to take care of here and now with true heart. When practice comes, all you have to do is take care of practice with whole heartedness. Then that moment spreads into the ten directions. That is called infinity. Where are we heading for? What is the target we have to aim at? The target is infinity, or truth, or the vastness of existence, emptiness. It is right here, right now. That is why Nan-yueh said that it is not that practice, delusion, enlightenment, and existence don't exist, but rather that they don't interfere with one another.

The Sixth Patriarch, Hui-neng, said, "Only this undefiledness is kept and held by the Buddha ancestors." Yes, this is true; "this undefiledness" means right here, right now. Where there is nothing to find, no directions, no reason, no expectations—we have to be exactly there. Being present right now, right here, with whole-heartedness is completely beyond your speculation—nothing can contaminate it. The practice of undefiledness has been kept and held century after century by the Buddhas and ancestors. "So you are thus now, so I am likewise, so are all successive ancestors in India, in China likewise." Not only by Buddhas in India, China, and Japan, but wherever we follow the Buddha's Way. This is not something to speculate about. You have to be this, you have to do this. If you start to think about it, you immediately begin to dig your own grave.

Sojun Mel Weitsman, Sensei was an early student of Suzuki Roshi. He started Berkeley Zen Center at his request and was appointed Abbot there in 1985. From 1988–1997, he also served as Co-Abbot of San Francisco Zen Center. This talk on the four aspects of love and their near enemies is a gem. –M.W.

Four Views of Love

Mel Weitsman

SUMMER 1985

During sesshin, one of the topics I talked about was friendliness or relations between people. Because Zen puts so much emphasis on *prajna* or wisdom, seeing the true form through the cold eye of wisdom, we tend to neglect the warm eye of compassion, without which our practice becomes unbalanced. In Buddhism, there's a meditation practice that focuses on love in four different ways. It's not a formula, but it's a way of looking at love from a Buddhist point of view, a non-self-centered point of view. It's something I think we need to bring up frequently and remember. They are called the four *brahmaviharas*. They are four unlimited places from which we act. They're also called the Divine Abidings. They're very ancient and come from the Hindu background of Buddhism. They're highly regarded in Theravada Buddhism and considered a basis for any serious practice.

If you don't remember what they are, I'll refresh your memory. There are quite detailed meditations on each of these, but we don't have time to go into them here. The first of the four brahmaviharas is *metta* or lovingkindness. There is a *Metta Sutra* which you should know about. Metta is translated as lovingkindness; it's a way of extending yourself to everyone without partiality. When we meet people or are having some interaction, we should always be extending metta. It means good will or concern with the well-being of others. Strictly speaking, it means extending love impartially without having any desire in it or any kind of ulterior motive.

We always have to look at our motives when we do something: "Why am I doing this?" If we have a motive, we may say, "Well, I'm doing this good thing now so that maybe later something good will come to me because of it." That's a kind of motive, a kind of desire. It's okay, but it's not really pure. It's okay to have a motive, and within our relationships we do have motives: if I do this for

Sojun Mel Weitsman

you, then you'll do this for me. But strictly speaking, pure metta is to extend ourselves regardless of whether or not anything comes back. So the practice of metta is simply to extend lovingkindness. And, of course, the enemy of lovingkindness is hate or ill-will. They cannot exist simultaneously. It's easy to recognize the enemy, but it's also interesting to look at the counterfeit, what's called the near enemy.

The near enemy is something so close it looks almost the same. Selfish affection is the near enemy of metta, and it looks like love; but there's often so much desire in it that one's motives get mixed up easily. It's very easy to fool ourself, very easy to create an imaginary kind of love based on self-interest. So, to be really clear, we should know and respect a person in many ways before we decide what kind of relationship we're going to have with them. Love, we say, hides many faults. It's easy to fall in love with someone for selfish reasons and overlook what later you will observe as faults.

This can be a big problem between men and women: how as a man can you extend lovingkindness to women impartially, or as a woman, how can you extend lovingkindness to men impartially? That's a big challenge: how not to let it get mixed up with your desire or your illusions and fantasies. It's something we have to practice in a conscious way. It's especially important in relating to members of the opposite sex, where desire can easily come up, to be able to relate from a non-selfish standpoint. That has to be at the basis of the practice in order that we don't get confused in our goodwill. This is just one example. Metta is something which can be extended to all of our relationships. First to ourselves and to those to whom we are close, then to those we don't know, and finally, if possible, to those we don't like.

The next brahmavihara is *karuna* or compassion. Karuna, strictly speaking, means to identify with someone's suffering or to suffer with others. We have a sympathetic understanding with people which leads us to help them because we can identify with their suffering. Sympathy is a kind of compassion, but compassion is a little bigger than sympathy.

The near enemy of compassion is feeling sorry for people who don't get what they want in a materialistic way. If John doesn't get his Mercedes, we feel sympathy, but we don't necessarily feel compassion. But for the persecuted people in Central America and the starving people in Ethiopia, we feel compassion. And for people who don't see the underlying cause of their suffering, we feel compassion. It comes up in relation to the suffering people have because of their ignorance or because of the inability to change their lives in a wholesome way. The polar enemy of compassion is ruthlessly causing people to suffer. Anything we do that causes real suffering is the enemy of compassion.

The third one, *mudita,* is sometimes called gladness, but it's more usually called sympathetic joy. Sympathetic joy is being able to feel glad about another's happiness. Of course, its polar enemy would be jealousy or envy. So it's freedom from envy, freedom from competition. If something good happens to somebody, we can share that with them and rejoice in their good fortune, even if it's someone we don't like particularly. That's the hard part: even if it's somebody you don't like. That's hard to do.

The near enemy of sympathetic joy is joy over material wealth or something which satisfies our greed. So sympathetic joy is more the happiness you feel for people's true welfare or accomplishment in a fundamental sense. If you realize your Buddha Nature, we feel sympathetic joy with you. If you make some progress for social change in the world, we rejoice in your success. I won't begrudge you your new automobile or stereo set, but, strictly speaking, mudita applies to rejoicing in someone's success in unfolding as a human being. Its polar enemy is boredom or aversion.

The fourth one is *upekkha* or equanimity. Equanimity means observing things impartially, to maintain a balanced view; to be able to see every situation as it is and to be able to decide something from the point of view of impartiality. The near enemy of upekkha is indifference based on ignorance. Upekkha doesn't mean to be indifferent. Rather it means not being one-sided or partial, not being influenced by resentment or approval. It's the basis for seeing clearly. In our meditation, in zazen, impartiality is one of the strongest factors. But we must always be careful not to mistake indifference for impartiality or non-attachment, and be ready to respond to each situation that confronts us free from greed and resentment, the two enemies of equanimity.

Although these four factors are always present in our lives in some form, they become strong guiding principles when we focus on them as meditation. According to the Visuddhimagga, the near enemy is that which masquerades as the other, and the far enemy is its opposite. The far enemy is usually obvious. What one has to be careful about is the near enemy, which may not be so obvious.

If you know how to extend metta to everyone that you meet, you may find that people respond to your unguardedness and they in turn become unguarded. Even at some risk, you may do it, you may extend it. Walking down the street, without any motive in mind, just to say hello to somebody. You can try it—just walking down the street—some kind of greeting. Try it on someone who looks different than you do.

There are systematic meditations on these four, and the meditations are very elaborate. The meditations are pretty much the same for all four categories with minor differences. For metta you start by extending feelings and thoughts of lovingkindness toward yourself until you feel that you can accept it. And when you feel metta toward yourself, you can extend that to others.

So the first thing is to extend feelings of love or goodwill toward yourself and to be able to just settle in it. And when you've settled on that feeling, you can extend that to a friend, someone that you know and like. That's pretty easy, maybe easier than extending it to yourself. Then, when you can do that, you extend it to someone you're indifferent to, someone you don't have any

Outside the Buddha Hall at 300 Page Street.

particular feeling about. Then, when you can do that, try to extend metta to someone that you don't like, maybe someone you really can't stand. That's what's recommended: start with what is easy and work up to the difficult ones until you can completely open yourself. It's called eliminating the barriers. Then you can do the same with compassion, and with sympathetic joy and equanimity. After that you can extend these meditations to everyone, everywhere.

The brahmaviharas appear in their most elaborate form in the *Visuddhimagga*, but there are other places where the meditations are more abridged. In our daily interactions they can be practiced as an outgoing expression of zazen.

It's not necessary to practice them in a formalistic way. The underlying principle is, of course, compassion. But if you try it out, you can see your weak points and enhance your awareness.

Yvonne Rand was Zen Center Secretary in the '60s, President in the '70s, and Chair of the Board in the '80s. She holds much of Zen Center's history. After receiving Dharma Transmission from Katagiri Roshi, she founded her own place at Muir Beach, California called Goat-in-the-Road. The following talk was given down the road at Green Gulch Farm. –M.W.

Cultivating Beginner's Mind

Yvonne Rand

SPRING 1986

I want to talk about two practices which are conducive to cultivating Beginner's Mind—the mind fresh and awake to many possibilities. This mind is different from the mind one brings to a situation in which one slips into some habitual pace or activity or habitual language or ways of thinking about things. How can I be a beginner in each moment, even in those situations where I am doing something that I have done many times before?

Any of the following practices is conductive to cultivating Beginner's Mind. They will be more penetrating if you do them regularly than if you do the occasionally. Practice zazen; practice sitting down quietly once or twice a day; settle yourself; let your mind become quiet; find some physical posture which brings with it some stability and openness; let your attention be settled on your breath. I have found the practice of the half-smile conducive to cultivating Beginner's Mind, as is also the practice of taking on several points of view in a particular situation. These last two are the practices I want to consider today.

There are some practices, like the practice of the half-smile, which are for the space of one, or two, or three breaths can bring us to some experience of what I call "Buddha space." By this I mean the space that I know from sitting every day over some long period of time. It is that space that is the most open to the most possibilities and to seeing most widely. Often having a moment of

71

that space is enough to recall me to a wider mind, a bigger mind than the mind I normally have as I race around through the course of the day striving to get a lot of work done, answering the telephone, driving to an appointment-all those circumstances which are so familiar.

PUBLICATION OF ZEN CENTER
VOLUME XX, NUMBER 1 — SPRING 1986

Spring 1986

Please try the practice of the half-smile. Do it now. For the space of three breaths. It has nothing to do with feeling like smiling. For those of you who have not done this practice before, you can think of it as "mouth yoga." Just lift the corners of your mouth slightly for the space of three full breaths. Not a full smile or a grin. And let your attention be with your breath, particularly on the exhalation.

This is a practice that you can do when you first wake up in the morning. If you already do some daily mediation practice, the half-smile is a practice you can do when you first begin your regular meditation. When I first began doing the half-smile I did it whenever I found myself waiting. So I did it standing in the checkout line at the grocery store. I did it when I was on hold on the telephone. I did it when I was waiting for an appointment in the doctor's office or the dentist's office or when I was waiting for an appointment with someone coming to see me.

I found that if I had some signal to remind me to do the half-smile when I first woke up in the morning, than I could readily remember to do the half-smile. And if I did not have a signal, I usually did not remember. I would think of it some time around noon or three days later. So I took a picture of Suzuki Roshi laughing and I put the picture by the side of the bed. Now, when I wake in the morning, it is usually the first thing I see. And the agreement that I made with myself was that whenever I see that picture I will stop and do the half-smile for three breaths. This has been an easy way for me to begin doing the half-smile when I wake up and before I go to sleep at night. What I found was that in doing the practice whenever I was waiting, that after a while, after a month or so, it also occurred to me to do the practice when I

72

noticed some feeling of anger or anxiety or some tension arising; and the half-smile is, in fact, traditionally used as an antidote to negative states of mind.

Most of all I find that the half-smile is a practice which brings me to some sense of spaciousness, and in that spaciousness I notice more than I do than when I am feeling crowded by my pace or my activity, or by the expectations I hold for myself in terms of what I want to get done this morning, or today, or this week, or maybe even in this lifetime.

A practice I would like to consider this morning is that of taking on different points of view. I think that I can suggest this practice best by telling you some stories which illustrate the practice.

When you came here to this mediation hall this morning you came into the outer hall through one of the two sliding doors. They are noisy sliding doors. Furthermore, if the doors are not closed on a cold day, and if the stove there in the back area is lit, all the heat from the stove escapes out though those doors. If both doors are left open, wind tunnel results and a gale blows through. There has been colloquy for some time about what we can do to get each of us to remember to close the doors. Sometimes people are rather angry. We have all kinds of discussions about rules and punishments. We have cultivated our policeman's mind quite wonderfully.

Recently people who live in the back area of the building were standing in a circle around the stove warming themselves and fussing together about this problem. In the middle of the discussion, Sierra, the blond golden retriever who lives here at Green Gulch, came wagging happily along. She pushed open the sliding door and joined the group. Suddenly everyone realized that it was Sierra who comes in the middle of the night, opening and not closing the door. She comes in to be warm and dry and near her friends. Suddenly there was a kind of opening or spaciousness about this big problem with the unclosed doors. There may even have been some irritation with Sierra, but nothing like the irritation which some of us had felt toward each other.

Our minds are tricky. What happens in a situation where I am certain that Mary or Joe is the one who has left the door open?

And what happens, by contrast, when I imagine that it is sweet old Sierra the dog getting in out of the cold and rain? A kind of generosity may arise in my mind if I think it is the dog who is leaving the door open.

Thich Nhat Hanh wrote a poem call "Please Call Me by My True Names." I find it a moving and powerful poem. There is one verse of the poem which, one day, under trying circumstances, leapt off the wall where I had the poem hanging. This verse expresses in another way the practice of taking on more than one point of view.

> I am the twelve-year-old girl refugee on a
> small boat who throws herself into the ocean
> after being raped by a sea pirate
> and I am the pirate, my heart not yet capable
> of seeing and loving.

My tendency is to take the point of view of the twelve-year-old girl. It is much more difficult for me to be the sea pirate.

The last day I was in Delhi, just before I came home in January, I had an experience with a rickshaw driver: another example of this practice of taking another point of view. I had gone to the memorial site for Gandhi. It is the place where he was cremated after he was assassinated. I decided that I wanted to spend my last day in India at this memorial gathering. The monument is in old Delhi. I stayed until it was dusk and then discovered that there were no taxis in the midst of the traffic. I had no idea how I would get back to the guesthouse where I was staying. The only way I could find was by a bicycle rickshaw. I had ridden in a bicycle rickshaw for short distances in the more modern parts of Delhi, but never in heavy traffic. They are flimsy affairs compared to the big cars and buses and even compared to the little three-wheel taxicabs which we called mosquitoes. After standing waiting for a motor taxi for a long time, it became clear to me that I would ride in a bicycle rickshaw or nothing. I was frightened, but I decided to flag down a bicycle rickshaw and take my chances.

The previous evening the bookkeeper at the YWCA guesthouse where I was staying and I had stayed up rather late talking. He was Indian and had asked me what it was like being in India and what was I doing and what did I do in America. He wanted to know how did I like India. We talked about some of my encounters with taxi drivers because they were sometimes unhappy encounters for me. He talked to me for some time about the life of a taxi driver: what it is like for someone, whether he is a bicycle rickshaw driver, or a mosquito driver, or a driver of a funky car held together with string and gum, or the driver of an elegant taxi. In all instances, he said, these drivers have expenses they have to meet—payments, for example, to the owner of the vehicle—whether they get enough fares in a day or not. He talked to me a lot about the way a taxi driver

Yvonne Rand.

survives. He helped me to see the perspective of a taxi driver in Delhi, who saw me as a westerner, a lone woman. I became fair game. And if I were unaware enough to pay ten times the usual fare, that is all right. I could begin to see the situation from the point of view of the driver.

I had, up to the time of this conversation, felt angry sometimes at the taxi drivers who would try to charge me three or five or ten times what I came to know as the usual fare. This man helped me understand the taxi driver's point of view. That conversation came up for me that Friday afternoon as I was sitting in the bicycle rickshaw feeling uncomfortable being the passenger as a young, apparently healthy, but certainly thin young man made his way through the traffic peddling us along. I felt frightened but realized also that I might be in the rickshaw at most for an hour. The driver was spending long hours every day, perhaps his lifetime in that situation, wending his way in among trucks and buses and cars.

I developed quite a different sense of what was going on when the taxi driver and I discussed how much he wanted, and how much I wanted to pay, for him to carry me as a passenger from one place to another. I could enter into a discussion—not exactly as a game—but with a stance from which we could come to some meeting point and some respect for each other, and then continue on in our respective ways. It was very different from feeling angry at the taxi driver whom I resented for trying to take advantage of me.

What I am suggesting is that when you find yourself in a situation, especially a situation which you will be in for a while, take on the point of view of another being in that situation. If you are working in the garden taking care of tender new plants that the snails love, you might for a while be a snail. A friend recently described doing Hospice work, sitting in a hospital room with someone who is sick, with the family and friends there, and a television set turned on but with no one watching it. She sometimes takes on the point of view of the television set. And she can see all these people and things happening. And she can be there with no one noticing her, quietly.

Please try it and see what happens.

Thank you very much.

Katherine Thanas is a long time Zen Center practitioner and disciple of Tenshin Reb Anderson. She has led the Santa Cruz Zen Center and Monterey Bay Zen Center for several years. In this lecture, Zen's miraculous powers are revealed! –M.W.

Buddha's Miraculous Power

Katherine Thanas

TASSAJARA, 7 DECEMBER 1986

SPRING 1987

I want to talk about miraculous powers today, specifically the miraculous power of being here, right now, the miraculous power of being at Tassajara with a calm, settled mind, knowing that there are less than two weeks left in the practice period and holidays and vacations are just around the corner. Dogen Zenji called this power a "great miracle" in his fascicle, *Jintsu.*

That fascicle was written to differentiate Buddhist practice from the yogic practices being done then to cultivate exceptional abilities, i.e., the power to see what is not visible, hear what is inaudible, see into the minds of others, recall former states of existence, etc. Dogen called such extraordinary powers "lesser miracles" because they are conditioned by circumstance, time and place. They are different from the "great miracles" accomplished by Buddhist practice.

This fascicle includes the story of an accomplished yogi who came to Buddha and said, "You have six miraculous powers and I have five. What is the one I am missing?" Buddha answered, "What miraculous power are you asking about? What is it you need, what do you lack?" Buddha knew that even if he told the yogi something, the yogi wouldn't understand because the sixth power, the Buddhist power, is not a special power, it's an ordinary power that all of us have. And because it is so ordinary we don't notice it. The power to fly off to heavenly realms—that power doesn't free us from karma; in fact the desire for that kind of power creates more karma. Dogen quotes Zen Master Huizhao in saying the six types of miracles of a Buddha are different, from the "miracles" of sorcerers, fighting spirits and demons, which are the result of past actions or present skills. He says "A Buddha enters forms, sounds, smells, tastes, touchables, and objects of mind and is not confused by them. Thus a Buddha masters the six sense objects, which are all marked with emptiness. A Buddha is free of conditions . . . and does not depend upon anything. A Buddha practices miracles that are grounded on the earth." Buddha's special power is to be free from karmic conditions, and each of us has that power. Our practice is to realize that freedom. Freedom from karma sounds as if we're escaping something. What freedom from karma means in Buddhist terms is that we completely acknowledge our actions and the consequences of our actions. We know that "we" are not separate from our thoughts, motivations, feelings, actions—that "we" are nothing but our thoughts, impulses,

feelings, consciousness. Karma is not something outside of us. When we use the concept of karma in Buddhism we understand it to mean our action and the consequences of our action in the world. Understanding this is the true power of a Buddhist. So our miraculous power is the ability to be awake and to know circumstances and conditions as they arise. This is the power we all have, the power of being present for our lives. Because we all have it at all times, Dogen calls this a "great miracle." Another story in that fascicle makes a similar point. One day Zen Master Guishan was napping in his room. His disciple Yangshan Huiji came to visit. Guishan turned around to face the wall. Yangshan said "Please don't be so formal with me." Guishan started to get up. Yangshan rose to leave. Guishan said, "Huiji." Huiji came back and asked what Guishan wanted. Guishan said "Let me tell you about my dream." As Yangshan leaned forward, Guishan said "Would you interpret my dream for me?" In response Yangshan brought a basin of water and a towel. Guishan washed his face and sat up. Then another disciple Xiangyan came in.

Guishan said, "Huiji and I have been communicating intimately. This is no small matter." Xiangyan said, "I was next door and heard you." Guishan said "Why don't you try now?" Xiangyan made a bowl of tea and brought it to him. Guishan praised them saying, "You two have superior miraculous powers!" Suzuki Roshi's commentary on this exchange points out that the true power of the relationship between teacher and disciple was what was being expressed, i.e., the deep intimacy and friendship between teacher and student. Even

Katherine Thanas.

though Guishan was the teacher, he was not caught by the idea of being the teacher and even though they were disciples, they saw their teacher also as their friend. They knew exactly how he expressed himself and what he wanted. Suzuki Roshi said: "And that is an expression of the mirculous power of our practice: to be together so closely that we know each other intimately, without knowing how we know. And we help each other without any special idea of helping." The actual way we help others is when we have no idea that "I" am helping or that "you" need help. If when I am with you I am just doing my life, taking care of what is right in front of me, there is no one doing and no one receiving and nothing being done. That is the true power of "helping." In the Shoyuroku case fifty-four there is the story of Avalokitesvara's one thousand hands and eyes. In that story, Yunyan asked Daowu: "What does the Bodhisattva of great compassion do with so many hands and eyes?" Daowu said: "It's like someone reaching back for the pillow at night." Yunyan said, "I understand." Daowu asked "How do you understand?" Yunyan: "All over the body is hands and eyes." Daowu continued, "You said a lot there, but you got only eighty percent." Yunyan asked, "What about you, elder brother?" Daowu answered, "Throughout the body is hands and eyes." Think about being so alive and open, active and receptive, that every pore and cell of our bodies reaches out and connects, comes alive and awakens with everyone. Throughout the body, hands and eyes intensely alive. Sometimes through art we have a moment of recognition. Sometimes through a loving relationship, during a sporting event, or in zazen, some deeper response comes forth from our entire being, a response beyond habit, a movement beyond our usual self, where boundaries expand. To be this open and alive, intimate and responsive, available to the moment, like Guishan and his disciples, we have to be deeply in the moments of our lives. In touch with our own agendas. Aware of our self-clinging. Willing to question it. We may not feel we can remain our familiar self if we meet someone else completely. We may feel some challenge to our familiar form of body and mind if we are truly present for someone else. That unease, that tension in our stomach or throat or chest in the presence of someone can awaken us to the mind that is afraid to join others, to be open to phenomena, open to our own difficulties-the defending mind, the mind that praises and quarrels, the mind that believes there is an "I" to defend and protect. The mind that is self-verifying again and again. Noticing our ego's reactions to events creates the space inside to continue the work of just seeing. Physical tensions are a helpful clue in this work, an opening rather than a barrier if we turn toward them, open to them. Someone said recently "I don't trust my perceptions anymore." This is because he's caught on to the fact that his mind is giving a little twist to things when he hears sounds or sees objects. He knows there is some subtle conditioned response as his eye meets an object, as ear meets sound, as nose meets smell. To attend to our life closely enough to detect the subtle, imperceptible interpretations the habitual mind makes, we need a calm, satisfied mind. To be available to our experience that deeply is a manifestation of our true power. In Dogen's *Body and Mind Study of the Way* he says: "In this manner the mind studies the way running barefoot—who can get a glimpse of it? The mind studies the way turning somersaults—all things tumble over with it." When I think about that image of running barefoot it makes me feel vulnerable-thinking about letting the foot meet the earth directly, not knowing what will be there. Very different from meeting the earth with a foot that's laced into

View overlooking Tassajara Valley.

a shoe. Allowing ourselves to meet our experience without a shoe protecting the foot is really trusting ourselves and what we meet. Are we willing to allow our foot to mold itself to meet whatever is there, to take the shape of whatever is under it? Rock, pebble, sand, pavement? And the line "The whole world is turning somersaults with you" made me think of the gymnasts in the Olympic games, and what it must be like to throw your body into the air and do a couple of twists, not knowing exactly where you will come down. The abandon and trust it takes to be physically disoriented in that way, trusting that you will land upright. Letting things appear as they appear, letting a new mental and emotional configuration come—that's the kind of effort Dogen was talking about.

Suzuki Roshi said our way is difficult because it's too simple, it looks like nothing's happening. We get up every day and go to the zendo, and have *oryoki* meals, go to work, the same activity day after day. And even though we think nothing is happening, he said, something wonderful is happening.

I think it is true we don't know what is happening here in the deepest sense. And if we can stay with that not knowing, and trust it, enjoy it, we will be able to experience our life in some fundamentally different way. That's our miraculous power.

*Tenshin Reb Anderson was Abbot of Zen Center from
1985–1995. He has written two books* Warm Smiles from a
Cold Mountain *and* Being Upright. *This talk and its
companion by Mel Weitsman on Shikantaza (just sitting)
were given in* 1997 *at a conference on the life and teaching
of Suzuki Roshi.* –M.W.

Suzuki Roshi's Teaching of Shikantaza

Reb Anderson

SATI CONFERENCE, 31 MAY 1998

FALL/WINTER 1998

For the last two hundred years in Japanese Soto Zen, the under-standing of most teachers has been that shikantaza, literally translated as "just sitting," was Dogen Zenji's essential practice. In accord with this mainstream understanding, Suzuki Roshi estab-lished shikantaza as our essential practice as well. A great deal of his teaching was intended to help us understand what it means to practice just sitting in its true sense. He also told us that his main job as a Zen priest was to encourage people to practice just sitting.

He would often say that our practice is just to sit. Then he would say that that may sound easy, but that actually it is rather difficult to understand what it means to just sit. In order to help us understand what this just sitting really is he went on to say that it is just to be ourselves. Finally, he made it clear, at least to me, that we could not just be ourselves by ourselves alone. We can only just be ourselves and thus realize the just sitting practice of the Buddha ancestors by practicing in the same manner as the entire universe and all beings. Perhaps other Soto Zen teachers have taught just sitting in this way, but I have not heard it so clearly from anyone but Suzuki Roshi. I deeply appreciate the way he stressed this point.

Suzuki Roshi taught that in order to actualize our way of just - sitting by being ourselves, we must express ourselves fully. So

83

paradoxically, realizing the selflessness of just sitting depends on full self-expression. Full self-expression in turn can only be realized by meeting and practicing together with all living beings in the entire universe. Therefore, he taught that to realize the full function of the practice of just sitting, we must go and meet face to face with our teacher. Such meetings offer the opportunity to settle completely into the truth of just sitting. Only when we meet intimately with another person can we fully be ourselves. As the *Lotus Sutra* says, "Only a Buddha together with a Buddha can thoroughly master the Buddha-Dharma."

Reb Anderson.

My understanding of Suzuki Roshi's teaching of just sitting is that it encompasses a dynamic interdependence between two dimensions: an intrapsychic aspect and an interbeing or interpersonal aspect. According to this view, I see Shakyamuni practicing upright sitting under the bodhi tree and attaining the way as only part of the story of just sitting. Only when he met his students and they attained the way together was the full function of the selfless practice of just sitting realized.

So in our practice of just sitting we cannot actually fully be ourselves unless we go to see the teacher and the teacher cannot fully be himself unless he comes to meet us. Suzuki Roshi was a teacher who taught that sometimes we have to disagree and argue with our teacher and that sometimes we have to surrender to our teacher. Similarly, the teacher must sometimes disagree with us and must sometimes surrender to us. This interbeing aspect of just sitting generously encompasses all agreement and disagreement.

To be fully ourselves in this formal student-teacher relationship both must assert themselves completely and recognize each other fully. You will sometimes disagree with your teacher and at the same time you must surrender to your teacher. Your teacher, of course, must bring herself to meet you and must surrender to you.

The only way that you can fully be yourself is if your teacher and ultimately all beings come to meet you. When Suzuki Roshi was alive meeting with him was a very high priority in my life. I made a big effort to bring myself to meet him but often as soon as I made this strong effort to assert myself in his presence, I became aware of my anxiety and vulnerability and wanted to get away. However, when I didn't present myself strongly, if I was with him half-heartedly, I didn't feel the need to escape. It was only when I presented myself whole-heartedly to him that I felt most vulnerable. When Suzuki Roshi ordained me as a priest he gave me the name Tenshin Zenki. On that day he told me that Tenshin means "Reb is Reb," and then he said, "People may have a problem with that but there is no other way." Today the way I understand his teaching is that when Reb is fully Reb, when you are fully you, we are completely vulnerable. To what are we completely vulnerable? When we are completely ourselves we are vulnerable to the entire universe. The second part of my name, Zenki, may be translated as "the whole works." In just being fully ourselves, Tenshin, we open ourselves to the working of the entire universe, Zenki. This name describes how the entire universe works thoroughly through each person in the practice of just sitting. Over the years I gradually came to understand what a wonderful gift he gave me in that name. Tenshin Zenki is actually a gloss for shikantaza. So now I see that just sitting is not something that I can do by myself. It is not something that Suzuki Roshi could do by himself either. It is something that we do together. We practice it together when we bring ourselves completely to our meeting and completely assert ourselves while completely recognizing each other.

In discussing with a friend the various views of just sitting, he recalled that famous story of the blind men feeling the elephant. One person says the elephant is a wall, another person says the elephant is a huge leaf, another says it is a rope and another says it is a tree trunk. When he said that I thought to myself, "But in this case, there really isn't such a thing as an elephant."

There is not actually something out there that is just sitting. It is just that we may enter the reality of this wonderful practice by giving ourselves entirely into a situation where "the other" comes and meets us entirely. But since the other meets us entirely just sitting can't be a thing. What we do is not just sitting. Just sitting is the dynamic inter-dependence of what we give and what comes to meet us. That is not a thing. Nobody knows what that is. Even all the Buddhas together cannot fully measure it. However, we can throw ourselves into it. Although I say throw ourselves into it, even this is not a unilateral activity. We still need to have a significant other whom we meet face to face. Therefore, it is not so easy to throw ourselves into such a practice because we may feel anxious or afraid of the unknown possibilities of such concerted activity. Nevertheless, we still have to jump wholeheartedly into the unknown reality of just sitting. There is a story about the great master Yaoshan just sitting. His teacher Shitou, practicing together with him, asked, "What are you doing?" Yaoshan replied, "I'm not doing anything at all." Shitou said, "Then you are just idly sitting." Yaoshan replied, "If I were idly sitting I would be doing something." Finally Shitou said, "You say that you are not doing anything at all. What is it that you are not doing?" Yaoshan said, "Even the ten thousand sages don't know."

I recently saw a good example of the practice of just sitting in the form of the Olympic women's figure skating. These young women—actually fourteen to sixteen year old girls—fully expressed themselves. They asserted themselves with extraordinary energy, strength, precision and grace. What was so touching to me was, that at the very moment of their fullest self-assertion, they simultaneously surrendered to the entire universe. At the moment of most powerful self-expression—when they were flying through the air performing amazing feats of turning through time and space—at that very moment they were completely vulnerable to the whole world. They were vulnerable to falling on the ice, they were vulnerable to nineteen judges' minute and severe scrutiny, they were vulnerable to their parents and their coaches. A billion people were watching them. Right in the midst of their transcendent whole-heartedness they were completely vulnerable and open to the support and love of the entire world. It is this concerted and cooperative activity of all beings that the practice of just sitting celebrates and realizes.

After their performances these young champions were interviewed. They were shown tapes of their performances. At the point of their total impeccable self-expression and complete openness to the universe, they were asked what they were thinking at that moment. As I remember, they weren't able to say; they didn't know what it was they were "not doing." As Yaoshan said, "Even the ten thousand sages don't know what just sitting is."

Hotei in snow.

*The companion talk by Sojun Mel Weitsman on Shikantaza,
or "just sitting."* –M.W.

Suzuki Roshi's Practice of Shikantaza

Mel Weitsman
SATI CONFERENCE, 31 MAY 1998
FALL/WINTER 1998

I remember reading a description of shikantaza by a contemporary Japanese Zen master. He described shikantaza as a very special kind of practice in which you sit zazen so hard that sweat pours out of your body. You can sit for only about half an hour because it's so intense. And when I read that I thought, "Boy, that's not the shikantaza that I know anything about or ever heard anything about from Suzuki Roshi!"

I wasn't thinking that such intense zazen is a wrong practice of shikantaza. But it does seem to me that this is elitist shikantaza or Olympic-style shikantaza: trying to accomplish some great feat. Suzuki Roshi always talked about shikantaza as one's day-to-day, moment-to-moment life of selflessness.

One of the main themes of Suzuki Roshi was, "Don't be selfish." At Sokoji, when we were in the middle of a sesshin—maybe my first or second one—for some reason or another he said, "You people don't know how selfish you are." And I thought, "Is that the right word? Maybe he means selfless." So that was a turning word for me too, because I really understood that the central teaching of Suzuki Roshi was not to be selfish.

It's a very simple phrase. It's something that our mother always tells us, right? "Don't be selfish." But in Buddhism we learn to be selfless—no self. "Be selfless." But Suzuki Roshi said selfish, which has a connotation that is a little more personal and is one that we don't like so much.

Suzuki Roshi's simple day-to-day activities—the way he would sit down and stand up, eat his dinner, walk, put on his sandals—this was his expression of shikantaza. Everyday activity with no selfishness-just doing the thing for the thing-that was his shikantaza. We usually say that shikantaza means "just sitting." And that's true. Just putting on your shoes, too. But this "just" has a special meaning. It means "without going any further" or "without adding anything extra."

When we go about our daily activities we always have a

Fall/Winter 1998

purpose. If I go to the store, I want to buy something. So I have a purpose. And that purpose motivates me to go to the store. But while going to the store, I'm living my life step by step. It has something to do with going to the store and the motivation to do so, but it's totally separate at the same time. It's just this step, this step, this step, totally living the life of walking within walking.

We're always doing something, making up a story about our life. And making up this story about our life is okay. This is our dream. We've been talking about the dream. Everybody has a dream. We have a dream of going to the store. Every thought is a dream. But the shikantaza, or the "just doing," is the selfless activity of just doing within the dream. In other words, we move and then we rest. We move and then we rest. Life is a movement and a rest. But in our practice we move and rest at the same time. Within our movement is perfect stillness. Stillness and movement are the two aspects of this life.

I think about shikantaza as a state in which our thought and our activity have no gap. When an athlete is skiing in the Olympics and performing an outstanding feat [Mel is referring to Reb's immediately preceding lecture], body and mind have no gap. Thought and activity are one. The athlete isn't thinking about something. The thought is the activity and the activity is the thought.

But shikantaza doesn't require a highly motivated spectacular event like Olympic skiing. It should be our day-to-day, moment-to-moment activity. The simplest activity. And this is what we recognized in Suzuki Roshi. When we say, "This is what he was like," we mean that his shikantaza was right there for all of us to experience. It was not spectacular, yet there was something so wonderful about it. We couldn't put our finger on it. Just putting on his sandals or the simple act of standing up and sitting down. We all do that, but there was something about his putting on sandals that was exactly the same as skiing in the Olympics. It had exactly the same quality.

Shikantaza is rather undefinable. How do we practice shikantaza? It is the very simple practice of lack of selfishness, of lack of self-centered-ness, and of just doing. As Reb said, if you put yourself totally into an activity, the universe meets you and confirms you and there's no gap between you and the universe.

That's my understanding. Thank you.

Waterfall at Tassajara.

Zoketsu Norman Fischer was Abbot of Zen Center from 1995–2000. A disciple of Sojun Mel Weitsman, he is a poet, writer and currently itinerant teacher. This talk, given at City Center, is on Case 52 of the Blue Cliff Record, *Zhaozhou's Bridge. Zhaozhou is asked "What is the stone bridge?" His answer: "Asses cross, horses cross." I caution you to watch your step. –M.W.*

Sesshin Talk on *Blue Cliff Record* Case 52

Norman Fischer

CITY CENTER, 31 OCTOBER 1998
SPRING/SUMMER 1999

We are all many persons. Some of these people we know and others we don't—only someone else knows them. Some of these people we like and some of them we don't like. Some of them we long for, and others we want to run away from. All of this is music; it's the music of our lives if we could only stop to listen. Music doesn't have any meaning; you can't explain it. Eating a meal doesn't have any meaning either, but if there's no eating there's no life, and if we don't hear the music we can't dance. This is our practice—to eat our meals and clean up; to dance to the music of our lives, each one in our own way, and then die when it's time.

To live this way is very simple and also very profound. Nothing flashy is necessary. This is like master Zhaozhou in Case 52 of *The Blue Cliff Record*. Since there's no pointer to the case, this is my pointer. The case is called Zhaozhou's "Asses Cross, Horses Cross."

A monk asked Zhaozhou, "For a long time, I've heard of the stone bridge of Zhaozhou, but now that I've come here I only see a simple log bridge."

Zhaozhou said, "You just see the log bridge; you don't see the stone bridge."

The monk said, "What is the stone bridge?"
Zhaozhou replied, "Asses cross, horses cross."

This is a case about master Zhaozhou, one of the most wonderful and beloved Zen teachers in the tradition; a personal favorite
of mine. Throughout the *Blue Cliff Record,* the *Mumonkan,* the
Shoyoroku, everywhere in the tradition we find stories of
Zhaozhou. And I think why he is liked so much is that he is very
simple and ordinary. He doesn't send out firecrackers and wave
flags; he doesn't shout, doesn't beat, doesn't have beautiful words
and phrases. He just goes about his everyday business, living his
life, engaging with people as best he can, and yet there is a tremendous profundity in his teaching. Even though his words were never
startling, they say of Zhaozhou that he had a light playing around
his lips when he spoke.

Zhaozhou ordained as a boy at the local temple and when he
was about twenty years old, the time to take full ordination, he
heard about master Nanquan and went to visit him. The initial
meeting between the two of them is very well known. Nanquan
was either taking a nap or was sick when Zhaozhou went to visit
him, so he was lying down. Zhaozhou greeted him. Nanquan said,
"Where did you come from?"—a question that they always asked;
a question like many Zen questions which is very simple and ordinary and at the same time very profound. "Where do you come
from?" "San Francisco." "Where?" "I don't know." This was the
kind of question the master would ask to try to ascertain something of the practice of a young novice like Zhaozhou. So Nanquan asked, "Where did you come from?" and Zhaozhou
answered, "I came from the Holy Image Temple," which was the
name of the monastery where he had been. Nanquan said, "Did
you see the holy image?" Zhaozhou said without any hesitation,
"I didn't see the holy image but now I see a reclining Buddha."
Nanquan was impressed with that answer and Zhaozhou's spirit
and said, "Well, do you have a master?" Are you coming seeking
a teacher or are you coming sent by a teacher? Zhaozhou gave a
very famous answer, something like, "Winter days are very bright,
I hope your good health continues." Maybe some of you recog-

nize this line. This is the line that's spoken by *shusos*, head students, in the head student entering ceremony.

Zhaozhou didn't leave the monastery for forty years, until Nanquan's death. He was about sixty years old and felt it was time to test his practice, to go to the graduate school of Buddha-Dharma as the monks of those days did, traveling, going to different temples, meeting different masters; a time-tested and important practice of Zen. And this is how you do it—you spend forty years in one place and when you gradually get the hang of that, you go around to other places to try to understand more. When he embarked on this pilgrimage, Zhaozhou made the famous saying, which I admire very much, "In this pilgrimage if I meet an old person of eighty or ninety years, experienced in the Dharma, who needs to learn something from me, I will teach. And if I meet a young girl of seven years old who has something to teach me, I will sit at her feet and learn." This is a good attitude for life in general.

He went twenty years pilgrimaging in that way and when he was about eighty years old he thought, "Well, I am not quite ready but I might as well start teaching." So I think eighty years old is a good time to start. According to legend he lived to 120 years, so he still had forty years of teaching. Apparently, he taught not in a remote, large mountain monastery as many of the old Ch'an masters did but in a town called Zhaozhou. He was master of a Quanyin temple there. There was a famous bridge in the town called the Bridge of Zhaozhou, like the Golden Gate Bridge, a famous site that tourists would go to see. That's the bridge that figures in our case today. Let me tell you a few little stories about Zhaozhou just to warm you up to him. I would like it if the result of my Dharma talk would be that everybody would feel happy to have met Zhaozhou. That would be worthwhile.

Here is a very famous dialogue between Zhaozhou and Nanquan: Zhaozhou asked Nanquan, "What is the way?" Nanquan replied, "Ordinary mind is the way." Ordinary mind is the way, not a special mind, not a special thing to do, just ordinary mind is the way, every moment of mind is the way. This is a problem, because if ordinary mind is already the way, how do you practice?

Norman Fischer.

If somebody says, the way is this special mind over here, then you say, oh good, I am going to go that way and practice. But if someone says ordinary mind is the way, it's all there is, how do you get there? It's so easy it's impossible.

So Zhaozhou said, "If ordinary mind is the way, how do you approach it then?" Nanquan replied, "If you intend to approach it you are on the wrong track." Zhaozhou said, "If you can't intend to go toward it then how will you realize it?" Nanquan said, "It's not a matter of knowing or not knowing. To know is delusion, not to know is stupidity. If you really attain the way, your vision is like infinite space, free of all limits and obstacles."

In zazen, in sesshin, our job is not to accomplish something, but rather to release ourselves to the music of our lives. To stop holding onto our lives and desires and intentions and just let ourselves fall into the vastness of the way, of the ordinary mind way. This way isn't outside of ourselves, or beyond ourselves and our desires. It's right in the mysterious middle of it. And to find that out we need to let go. I would like to emphasize posture and breathing, that you make a very strong commitment to sitting up straight and to breathing in your belly, in and out, to being with each and every breath as much as possible, using your posture and breathing as your anchor point and just being there, returning over and over again to that, abandoning everything else. Abandoning everything else doesn't mean you don't pay attention to it, doesn't mean you suppress it or dislike or like it. You just let it go. We come back over and over again to the present moment of our posture and breathing. And in that way without intending anything, just by being present, we will discover our ordinary mind which is nothing flashy, nothing special, just vastness throughout.

A famous case that you all know of, I am sure, is the case of Nanquan's cat. Apparently, in Nanquan's monastery there was an East Hall and a West Hall. Maybe in the East Hall the monks were always in retreat and the West Hall housed the support monks, who did the monastery's work. The monks of both halls had often-times different points of view and different interests, so now they were arguing. They were arguing about a cat. Probably the monks on the one side who were running the monastery thought that this cat was very good because it was killing the mice in the kitchen. On the other side, monks thought this cat was killing the mice and that's against the precepts and besides, it's peeing in the zendo. This cat had to go. So they were arguing back and forth like this. I have heard about things like this. Even lately, even nearby. Any-way, somehow it all came down to this cat. And Nanquan picked up the cat and said, "All right, somebody better say a true word of Zen or I'm going to cut this cat in half, right in front of you all." Of course, no one ever does say a true word of Zen in these old stories, and no one did, so he cut the cat in half. That was the end of the argument. As it happened, Zhaozhou was not around at the time. He was in town buying supplies or something; maybe he was visiting a relative. When he came back and heard what had happened, he took off his traveling sandals and put them on his head and walked up and down. Nanquan said, "Oh, it's too bad that you were not here at that time; you would have saved that poor cat." So, that's the story. Now, I think that the reason why he put his sandals on his head was because it was a custom in China to put sandals on your head as a sign of mourning. If Zhaozhou had been there he would have put his sandals on his head and he would have walked up and down expressing the fact that the cat was already dead, even before Nanquan cut the cat in two. Just like you and I are already dead. We think later we'll be dead, but that's baloney. Actually, right now in each breath we are alive and we are dead. We don't know that and that's why we are suffering. If the monks in the East Hall and the monks in the West Hall had known that, they wouldn't have argued. Actually, every morning, every day we should be in mourning. Every moment we should be mourning.

Here's another story about Zhaozhou. Once when the new stu-dents were all coming in one by one for their interview at the begin-ning of the practice period, Zhaozhou asked each one, "Have you been here before?" And one would say, "Yes." Zhaozhou would say, "Oh, good, have a cup of tea." The next one would come and Zhaozhou would say, "Have you been here before?" "No, no, I have never been here before, this is my first visit." "Oh, have a cup of tea." This went on, yes, have a cup of tea, no, have a cup of tea. The prior of the monastery was watching all this and getting very upset. He said, "Somebody comes in and says no I haven't been here before and you say go have a cup of tea and somebody else comes and says yes I have been here before and you tell him go have a cup of tea. What is the meaning of this?" And Zhaozhou said, "Prior?" And he said, "Yes?" Zhaozhou said, "Have a cup of tea."

Once a novice said to master Zhaozhou, "I am only newly admitted into this monastery. I beseech you, reverence, to please teach and guide me." Zhaozhou said, "Have you had your breakfast yet?" The novice said, "Yes, I have." Zhaozhou said, "Please wash your bowls." A famous story of Zhaozhou.

There are many short answers of Zhaozhou's that are very famous. Of course, the most famous of all is: Once a monk asked Zhaozhou, "Does the dog have Buddha Nature?" Zhaozhou said, "No." This is the famous "mu" koan. It's less well known that another time pretty soon afterward a monk asked, "Does the dog have Buddha Nature?" and Zhaozhou said, "Yes, of course." Once someone asked, "What is the way?" and Zhaozhou replied, "The cypress tree in the courtyard." Another monk asked, "Who is Buddha?" Zhaozhou shot back, "Who are you?" A monk asked, "What is the most important principle of Zen?" Zhaozhou said, "Excuse me, but I have to pee. Just imagine, even such a trivial thing as that I have to do in person." A wonderful teacher, Zhaozhou. And if you think about all these stories, it's very ordinary stuff. It's not like master Yunmen saying, "Body exposed to the golden wind." It's not like master Rinzai with his shouts ringing in the ears of his student for days on end. It's not like master Deshan with his staff, thirty blows every day. I think master Zhaozhou must have been very much like Suzuki Roshi. As with Suzuki Roshi, I think with Zhaozhou sometimes you didn't know whether anything was going on or not. Whether there's any Zen or not. When Rinzai shouted at you, you might or might not have understood, but you knew something was going on. When Deshan reared up and whacked you, you might not have understood, but you knew, this is definitely Zen. But when Zhaozhou says, "Have a cup of tea" or "Wash your bowls," you don't really know. Well, you might think, there is nothing going on, he is just telling me to wash my bowls. But I think that at the same time those who have the eyes to see and the heart to know felt in those simple words, as with Suzuki Roshi's simple words, something is going on. The secret of this kind of practice is that Zhaozhou and Suzuki Roshi are not trying to do anything. For them, really and truly there is no such thing as Zen practice, or maybe Zen practice is just a convention, just a language. There is only one life, which means life and death. So there is no need to make a special point of something. But life moment after moment on every moment has an inexpressible depth. "I don't know" every moment. Every moment, even the simplest, most ordinary moment of our life, is vast. All ordinary moments are extraordinary because all ordinary moments are unknowable, empty and radically impermanent, gone even before they come. Every moment is like that, if you look. And Zhaozhou's and Suzuki Roshi's practice was not to think about this or marvel at it, but simply to be fully aware of it in each activity of life, whether they were speaking to a student or going to the toilet or eating a meal. So Zhaozhou is not saying anything more than have a cup of tea. It's just a cup of tea, but it's just a cup of tea. Wash out your bowls is not saying anything special, there is no trick, is there? It's just wash out your bowls, but it's just wash out your bowls. Everything is included. It's not conscious, it's not intentional, it's not Buddha-Dharma or something like that. It's just naturally living your life the way your life really is. So in sesshin we should live like that, this is the way to live, with no special intention, but simply paying attention to our lives, being there in our lives as they really are.

What prevents us from doing this? Our enormous habit of self concern. Every moment, how am I doing; is this good or bad; this is right or wrong; look at him, look at her, look at them, look at us; why is this that way; I want that this way; that was good then, what about now? We are full of self concern, we don't want to adjust, we don't want to enter the vastness of this moment. So we have to let go of our self-clinging mind, and see that. Zhaozhou is there, Suzuki Roshi is there. So you don't have to do anything; you just have to undo something, come back moment after moment, as an anchor to the fundamental thought of your being embodied, of your being in the posture of your breathing.

Finally I get around to the case! The case says: A monk asked Zhaozhou, "For a long time I've heard of a stone bridge of Zhaozhou. But now that I've come here I just see a simple log bridge." It was the famous stone bridge, of course. But also, when the monk is speaking of the stone bridge he is also speaking about Zhaozhou himself. I came all this way to see a famous master of Ch'an and I see you? This is how we know that Zhaozhou was not an impressive guy. If you are a monk walking 200 or 300 miles with your little straw sandals to get to see the storied master Zhaozhou, you are expecting something. And you arrive; here is this guy. Not much to him. This is how the Ch'an monks of old were. They were very present and forthright and they called a spade a spade. "You know you're not too impressive. I came all this way and heard all this stuff about you; there's not much here, is there?" Imagine, if you were Zhaozhou. How would you feel? What would you say? Zhaozhou said, "Oh, you see a log bridge"—just a log bridge, no important Zen master here. It was okay with him that he wasn't much. But that's only half of what he said. If that's all he said then he would be clinging to being nothing special. He added, "—you don't see a stone bridge." This is true for us, too. There is not much to us, just a log bridge. But do you see the stone bridge in your own life? Zhaozhou said, "Yes, you're right, just a log bridge, but you don't see a stone bridge. Too bad, not for me; too bad for you. I think the monk heard the master and he suddenly lost his arrogance and asked in all humility, "What is the stone bridge of Zhaozhou?" Zhaozhou said, "Horses cross, asses cross." Our attachment, our stupidity, our enlightenment, our heroism, our cowardice, our confusion, clarity, compassion, selfishness, all of that goes across the famous stone bridge of Zen and arrives safely on the other side. It is a bridge; it is a crossing point. In and of itself it's nowhere, just a bridge.

You are alive and then you're not, and that's it. It's so easy to forget that this is the case. It's very easy to forget. If you walk across the room in your house from one door knob to the next, and at one door knob you vow that between the time you walk from this door knob to the other you will stay with your practice, you will not be able to do it. By the time you get to that other door knob, you forgot already. This is the human mind. It's unbelievable when you think about it. It's an absolute marvel. And think of the centuries and generations that went into that stupidity. It's truly a marvel. This is the mystery, this is the music of humanity, unbelievable.

We need to resort to drastic measures. It's a shame. Just so that we can remember a little bit more often the simple fact that we are alive right now. It's a total situation. And it's never going to happen again. We should dance through sesshin with that spirit, trying to pay attention, that's all, to each breath in and each breath out, paying attention to eating and serving, bowing, cleaning, resting, walking, sleeping, changing clothes, coming back over and over again to where you are. And letting go of everything. Don't wish for anything, don't intend anything, just dive into the ocean of Dharma. The most important thing is that the spirit, the feeling, with which you do all this is a feeling of kindness. It's very important that you have a feeling of kindness and

Spring/Summer 1999

lightness in the doing of this. Because your tricky mind will try to make this into another form of self-clinging, and the antidote to that is simple kindness. Just being kind, to yourself, and to everyone practicing together with you, not only in the room, in the sesshin, but also in the surrounding sangha and everyone everywhere else.

Please do make your best effort to practice in the way that I am encouraging you to practice. Don't try to do anything; be gentle and kind with yourselves and every moment, let go. In the end this is the only way to find peace, to let go of suffering, and it's the only way that we will ever truly be able to benefit others. Let's help each other in that effort.

Zenkei Blanche Hartman, a disciple of Sojun Mel Weitsman, is Zen Center's first Abbess. She ascended the Mountain Seat in 1996 and is Abbess at I write this in 2001. For many years, she has concentrated on the teaching, sewing and wearing of Buddha's robe. In this talk she asks you to examine "What is this?" —M.W.

What Is This?

Blanche Hartman
16 JANUARY 1999
SPRING/SUMMER 1999

What brings us all here today? I'd like to suggest that we are all here to investigate, "What is this?"

Those of you who are here for the first time have, quite naturally, a quality which Suzuki Roshi greatly appreciated. It's called in Japanese, *shoshin* or *hoshin*—"beginner's mind." In fact, he so appreciated this quality in the people who practiced with him that he named the temple here in San Francisco, *Hoshinji*, Beginner's Mind Temple. He often spoke to us of the importance of this beginner's mind. When you're brand new to something, you naturally have this open mind. You ask: "What is it?" "What is this, I wonder?" and "I'll look into it and see what I can see." There's a very pure and fresh feeling to this kind of inquiry and it's very hard to maintain over time.

Those of you who are here for the first time don't have your minds made up. You're just kind of interested and open to what you might find out here. "Is this something that interests me or not?" "Is this something that touches me, that invites me to look further?" There's a phrase that we use in ordination ceremonies: "May your practice always be like this." Because at that time people often have the openness and freshness of beginner's mind. We say, "Please do not get caught in that place where you think you know."

You may think you know, so you say, "It's great, and I love it, and I'm going to do it, and whoopee!" Or you think you know and you say, "Well this isn't really my thing." Suzuki Roshi said in *Zen Mind, Beginner's Mind:* "For zazen students, the most important thing is not to be dualistic. Our original mind includes everything within itself. It is always rich and sufficient within itself. You should not lose your self-sufficient state of mind. This does not mean a closed mind, but actually an empty mind and a ready mind. If your mind is empty it is always ready for anything. It is open to everything. In the beginner's mind, there are many possibilities. In the expert's mind, there are few."

There are people here who are back for a second or third time. Probably there is still some freshness, curiosity and openness for you. There are also people here who are just beginning our practice period and there are people here who have been practicing for a little longer who may have decided they want to live in the temple. There are those here who have lived in the temple, or at Green Gulch, or at Tassajara for some time and are now living nearby. So this is a very big mix of people, from people who are here for the first time today to people who have been practicing for twenty or thirty years. I think it's kind of wonderful.

And we're all here to practice what Dogen Zenji says is the most important thing and what Suzuki Roshi says is the most important thing. Sitting upright. Sitting upright and being awake. Just to be awake to what is in each moment, to meet it fresh without preconception. Not intellectually but directly.

Why are we here doing this? It may be difficult for you to say why you are here today. But at some point in our life (much like the traditional story of the Buddha's life) having lived like a child with some ease and protection from knowing about difficulties, we become aware that there is suffering. We become aware of what are called in Buddhism the three marks of existence: impermanence, no-self, and *dukkha,* which is sometimes translated as suffering. It means something more like unsatisfactoriness. And we begin to wonder, in such a world where all things are impermanent and without self and there is this taste of unsatisfactoriness, how does one live? How shall I live in such a world?

And for some of us, this questioning may lead us here to Beginner's Mind Temple, to investigate what response Suzuki Roshi made to the awareness of suffering. We ask, "What was his compassionate response to suffering?" Which leads to our own questions "What is my compassionate response to suffering? How shall I discover a compassionate response to suffering?"

Because we are human this question arises in us. Compassion is not some quality that we have to look outside ourselves to find, it's something that is right here all the time. We become aware of suffering and we want to respond to it. How do we respond to it? We all try different ways. At a particular point in my life when I was very aware of suffering and very aware of the ways in which I had tried to respond to it, I felt that I had not yet discovered a way that seemed to answer my need for a compassionate response. My response up to that point was motivated by anger and resentment at what I saw as other people's noncompassionate ways rather than seeing the ways in which I was not responding skillfully.

At a certain time I would have characterized my life's work as "fighting for peace." There is a funny contradiction in this phrase "fighting for peace" which at some point I noticed. It had been going on a long time, but at some moment I happened to notice. "That's odd," I thought. I realized my response to people whose attitudes were different than mine was one of self-righteous anger or rejection or putting them down. I was not hearing them, not actually communicating with them or trying to see where they were coming from. I just knew I was right and they were wrong. Ultimately that did not feel right to me, it had a bad feeling. So I thought, there must be another way to respond to suffering.

When I met Suzuki Roshi I felt from him a complete response to my suffering. His first response was to welcome me, to encourage me to sit, to be as he was, quite still, present and available. He saw me as complete, whole and perfect just as I am. And that was startling to me. Since he said that he sat zazen, I sat zazen. But, you know, this zazen thing has been going on a long time. This cross-legged zazen posture is depicted in the earliest cave paintings which are thirty thousand years old.

In *Bendowa*, or *Wholehearted Practice of the Way*, Dogen Zenji says, "All Buddha-Tathagatas together have been simply transmitting wondrous Dharma and actualizing supreme perfect enlightenment for which there is an unsurpassable unfabricated wondrous method. This wondrous Dharma which has been transmitted only from Buddha to Buddha without deviation has as its criterion, *jijuyu zanmai* (self-fulfilling and self-enjoying samadhi). For disporting oneself freely in this samadhi, practicing zazen in an upright posture is the true gate."

Suzuki Roshi said: "Zazen practice is the direct expression of our true nature. Strictly speaking for a human being there is no other practice than this practice. There is no other way of life than this way of life."

From these two great teachers and many others you see a deep faith in this practice of sitting still, sitting upright, clearly observing the coming and going of breath, of thoughts, of sensations, of feelings. Just clearly observing, not grasping anything, not pushing anything away. Not leaning towards or not leaning away from. Just sitting upright, being present. In this practice, there is the possibility of using our open beginner's mind, just sitting with the openness of "What is this, I wonder?" In this way we may see more directly how to live our life.

In the *Mumonkan (The Gateless Barrier)* there is a story about Zhaozhou and Nanquan. It goes like this. When Zhaozhou was a young man he went to visit Nanquan. Zhaozhou was very serious about practice. He asked Nanquan, "What is the way?" Nanquan said, "Ordinary mind is the way." Zhaozhou asked, "Shall I direct myself toward it or not?" Nanquan responded, "If you direct yourself towards it, you will betray your own practice." Then Zhaozhou said, "If I don't direct myself towards it, how will I know the way?" Nanquan replied, "The way is not a matter of knowing or not knowing. If you actually reach the way, if you actually reach the Tao beyond all doubt, you will find that it's as vast and limitless and boundless as outer space. What could that have to do with affirmation or negation, with right or wrong?"

Immediately Zhaozhou had a great awakening. In his commentary, Mumon says, "Although Zhaozhou had a realization at this time, it took him thirty years to confirm it." This is what it's like. You get a glimpse of how things really are, and you say, "oh," but then you fall into your old habits. Those of us who have been practicing for twenty or thirty years are still falling into old habits and extricating ourselves and falling in again and extricating ourselves again. After twenty or thirty years we may catch ourselves a little sooner than we did ten years ago or twenty years ago, but still there is the habit of self-clinging, that habit of thinking there is some real separate thing that we call a self, something different from what we call not-self, something separate, not interconnected, interrelated or intertwined with everything. That habit is strong and we find ourselves grasping it again and again.

What we realize is that there is suffering right there, right there in the separation, right there in the grasping self. And we say, "Oh yes, now I remember." Then we can open our hand and let it go and continue. Our practice is continually letting go of the grasping, letting go of the grasping, letting go of the grasping and returning to beginner's mind, returning to the mind that says, "What is this, I wonder? How shall I respond to this?" We are continually meeting whatever arises in front of us. Continually realizing our inseparability from all that is. We continually sit upright in zazen to return to this mind which is open and ready again and again. The cultivation of beginner's mind comes through devotion to sitting—immovable upright sitting—being still, being quiet, being present and awake. It is in this state that we can actually study beginner's mind.

Why do we do this? Do we do this just so we'll feel better? I don't think so. Really what is required, before we can actually deeply enter practice, is what is called *bodhicitta*—the altruistic mind of awakening, the mind which realizes that because there is suffering I must wake up. The mind that seeks a way to live in this world of suffering for the benefit of all beings.

Dogen Zenji in *Wholehearted Practice of the Way* talks about his own path. He experienced one of his deepest insights into practice as a small boy while watching the incense smoke curl up into nothingness at his mother's funeral. This experience is expressed when he wrote, "To see into impermanence, to actually see impermanence, is *bodhicitta*, this is the mind which determines that I must wake up for the benefit of all beings." After some years of practice, going to China and meeting his root teacher in China,

Dogen had an awakening in which he said, "Body and mind dropped away." Then he knew, "To spread this Dharma and free living beings became my vow."

This I think is the result of awakening. This response of Dogen's was the echo of Buddha's awakening. At first it seemed very difficult when the Buddha realized great enlightenment. He thought nobody would understand. But then, out of compassion for living beings he began to teach what he had learned. This is also Dogen Zenji's path: "To spread this teaching, to spread this true gate of zazen became my vow for the benefit of all beings."

Continuing that teaching, Suzuki Roshi carried the same concern and interest. From the time he was a young priest, Suzuki Roshi wanted to come to the United States where he hoped he would meet people with beginner's mind. He didn't want parishioners already set in their attitudes and opinions towards the Buddha-Dharma, who saw Buddhism as just ceremonies and funerals. He wanted to come where he could meet people with beginner's mind and spread zazen as the most important thing. He didn't go out proselytizing. He just came and sat zazen and as people heard that there was this Zen master in town, they came around. He was sitting in a Japanese-American temple in San Francisco's Japantown and these people came around and they said, "Hey man, teach us about enlightenment. Teach us about Zen." They didn't ask about zazen, they asked to be taught Zen. He said, "Oh, I sit zazen every morning, and you may join me if you like." And he just hung out with the people who came there to sit.

So why did they stay? Why did I stay? Those of you who've been around a while, why have you stayed? And those of you who are here for the first time today, what will encourage you to come back? It's up to you. It's completely up to you. One of the interesting things here is that there's never been any proselytizing. I don't think this practice is something you can do because somebody else tells you it's a good idea. I don't think it's something you can do if your best friend tries to get you to do it. I think it's something you do because you have to, because you need to, because you want to. Because your life needs the support of a practice like this, a practice where you can become intimate with yourself, where you can see what is the cause of suffering in your life. Inevitably the questions arise "How does suffering arise in my life? How does suffering arise in those around me? How can I respond to this suffering in a compassionate way?"

The most compassionate response to my suffering that I have received is Suzuki Roshi's offering of this practice—of just sitting. So, when I saw this line from Dogen's *Bendowa*, "To spread this Dharma and free living beings became my vow," I thought, oh, that's my vow too. That was Suzuki Roshi's vow. That's the vow of everyone who really has deeply arrived at bodhicitta, at the mind of awakening. To spread this Dharma and free beings is the vow of the Bodhisattva. We are all Bodhisattvas. We all want to respond to suffering with compassion. We all want to offer to each one we meet, who is faced with suffering, a way to live that will ease their suffering.

Blanche Hartman.

So I commend to you these two major teachings of Suzuki Roshi. First, always return to beginner's mind. Then when you find yourself caught in duality—right or wrong, good or bad, separate or not separate—whatever duality you find yourself stuck in, let go of your ideas and return to beginner's mind by asking, "What is this, I wonder?"

The second teaching and great offering of Suzuki Roshi is to sit down, be still, breathe, wake up. Suzuki Roshi said to us: when you're sitting, each part of you should be sitting. Your *mudra,* your hand posture, should be doing zazen independently. Your chin and head should be doing zazen. Your shoulders should be doing zazen. Your back should be doing zazen. Your legs are doing their own zazen. You don't have to cross your legs for your convenience. You just cross them and there they are, sometimes painful, sometimes not. But they're doing their own zazen. Don't move them for your convenience. Just give them your kindness and compassion.

Check your mudra every now and then and see that it's open. This mudra emphasizes accepting everything as it is. It should be nice and round and open. And if you find it collapsing, wake it up again. If you find it falling apart, bring it back together. If you find it tense and tight, allow it to soften again. Let your mudra sit zazen. Let each part of you sit zazen. Find your balance, leaning neither forward nor backward. That's important, because when you lean forward or backward you become tense and tight. But when you're balanced, the weight just goes right down through your sitting bones. You should align yourself with gravity, so that from the crown of your head right through your sitting bones, your spine is exactly lined up with gravity so you won't fall in any direction. And your neck should be free. So if you notice that your neck is tense, free it up a little bit.

And breathe. Try to allow your breath to come all the way to where your strength is. Your strength is right here below your navel. Your center is right here. So try to let that be strong. Have you seen those daruma dolls, the Bodhidharma dolls or balloons? They've got a weight in the bottom and they're round. They have no legs. You push them over and they come right back up. That's what we're like. We're really weighted and sinking into the earth, and we just rise up from that base like a flower.

Katagiri Roshi said, "We sit to settle the self on the self and let the flower of our life force bloom." So let yourself be settled, still, upright and awake and when you find yourself grasping anything, just let go. Please keep your beginner's mind. "For disporting freely in this samadhi, zazen is the true gate." "Strictly speaking, for a human being there is no other practice than this practice." These are statements of Dogen's and Suzuki Roshi's great faith, offered to us out of deep compassion. Please take them to heart.

*Jiko Linda Ruth Cutts became Co-Abbess with Blanche
Hartman in 2000. She is a disciple of Tenshin Reb Anderson.
This talk is an exploration of spiritual malaise and ways
through it.* –M.W.

Acedia and the Good Friend

Linda Ruth Cutts

GREEN GULCH FARM, 12 MARCH 2000

SPRING/SUMMER 2000

Today I want to talk about friendship, envy, hate, and acedia.
Acedia, a new word I've recently learned, means spiritual torpor, ennui, apathy. There are situations that arise in monastic life
and in everyday life, that are monotonous and repetitious. The
feeling quality, quite hard to work with, is that we cannot keep
going on with the endless things we have to do. It is all too much.
Burnout. Desperation.

What are the antidotes to acedia, to spiritual torpor? How can
we help ourselves and our friends when this kind of situation
arises? And what fans the flames of acedia?

In *The Quotidian Mysteries: Laundry, Liturgy, and "Women's
Work,"* Kathleen Norris talks about acedia and quotes from the
fourth century Catholic monk Evagrius. He considers acedia to
be like what, in the Buddhist tradition, we call Mara, or the evil
one: a demon that enters your consciousness and begins to under-
mine your resolve, your state of mind and your vows. Evagrius
writes that the demon of acedia, "makes it seem that the sun hardly
moves, if at all, and that the day is fifty hours long. Then [it] con-
strains the monk to look constantly out the windows, to walk outside the cell, to gaze carefully at the sun to determine how far it
stands from the ninth hour [lunch time]."

This may sound familiar. A feeling, whether in the monastery,
at home or at your work, of looking at your watch, looking at
your computer screen, "When do I get to take that old lunch break
and get out of here?" The sun hardly moves. The clock stands still.

I remember feeling that way in high school especially. The monk (in this case, male) is distracted by this. He is supposed to be meditating or doing mindful work and instead he finds himself distractedly gazing around hoping lunch time will come soon.

Then acedia moves inward and "instills in the heart of the monk

Linda Ruth Cutts.

a hatred for the place. A hatred for his very life itself." The monk begins to think less of the other monks with whom he lives and works. We might feel less friendly towards our co-workers, or family members, or neighbors. We might spend time "brooding on the ways they have angered, offended, or merely failed to encourage us." They're ruining my practice, these people!

"This demon [then] drives the monk to desire other sites where he can more easily find work and make a real success of himself." So you reject those around you, reject what is going on with yourself, and start to pity yourself, thinking about the "memories of your dear ones and your former way of life." It used to be better in Seattle. You begin to think, gee, if I just move there, or get another job, or get a new apartment, or get a divorce, or get married, then I'd make a real success of myself, then I would be appreciated. Thinking like this we believe we can change things around, so that everything finally, once and for all, will be okay.

Evagrius reports how acedia triumphs, "[depicting] life stretching out for a long period of time, and bringing before the mind's eye the toil of the ascetic struggle and, as the saying has it, it leaves no leaf unturned to induce the monk to forsake his cell and drop out of the fight." The monk believes it is going to be terrible, in just this way, forever, if he stays where he is. Absolute bleakness. You give up on even making an effort.

The word acedia itself comes from the Greek, meaning: a lack of care, and the root of the word, care, means: to cry out, to lament. Acedia is a crying out for help that is not recognized. Can we understand this and "turn the light inward" to look at what are the causes and conditions of this feeling, rather than believing that the environment is wrong for us or that there is someone to blame? I remember my first sesshin, it was very painful. The person who sat next to me had a jaw that cracked every time she chewed. For seven days all the meals, there was this noise when she chewed: "click click." And I hated her. I really felt she was ruining my whole sesshin. She was making it so difficult. I turned outward and blamed it all on her. She was the bothersome problem. If she would just get out of the way, get another seat, then I'd be able to practice. It was hard to understand that the practice was right there in front of me, in working with the very annoyances and irritations I felt. This is the fertile ground of our practice. But, caught in acedia, we can't find the energy to make that kind of effort, to give that kind of attention to what's going on, to "study the self" in that way. We don't care anymore.

One of the antidotes to acedia is to throw yourself into your daily life, the details of your daily practice, to enter the "quotidian," the everyday. The "dian" of the word quotidian means "divine, to shine or bright sky." Doing our daily activities of laundry, dishes and grooming is an expression of our connection to life. When these simple activities are forgotten it often means there is deep trouble. Staying grounded in the quotidian is one way to address acedia. That is the mystery of the everyday. Everything is included. Continuing with our sitting practice at those times of acedia is very important. We may turn away from zazen just at the time when we need to practice more thoroughly.

Another antidote to acedia is to encourage others, to help others. Helping others is a powerful way of encouraging ourself. When you extend to someone when they are in need, or needing encouragement, you find words that really are meant for yourself as well. You are being encouraged at the same time that you're encouraging others. Dharma talks are like that: encouraging others, but encouraging myself at the same time.

Friendship and the Good Friend are important at these times. The Buddha, as the teacher of Dharma, is the quintessential Good Friend and these Bodhisattvas are thought of as Good Friends as well. The way you actually help another, the greatest gift you can give, is to expose someone to the teachings. In fact, having Good Friends is one of the main, proximate causes that are conducive to practice. We can help one another in many other ways as well, including the material realm. Our friends are those that we can trust in such a way that it feels like—this is how it's described in the Sutras—as if you're a baby putting your head down on your mother's breast. That feeling of complete reliance, trust, and faith in our friends—that is a true friend.

On the other hand, the Sutras say, if you take a wonderful stick of incense and wrap it in an old dead fish it will begin to smell like an old fish. The same with our friends. You can have great resolve, but if you are wrapped in friends who are not upholding the precepts, you will be strongly influenced by this. If you surround yourself with Good Friends, that will have an amazing positive effect on you as well. Both sides are true. I have a friend who has a chronic illness, and she has found, by carefully watching her life and taking care of her body, that there are certain people she cannot spend time with, because they drain her. She actually feels more sick after spending time with these people.

Although the Bodhisattva ideal is to go everywhere and be with anyone, sometimes the Bodhisattva herself needs protection and care, like a young flower. It is important to be aware of how strong this influence from our friends can be.

What is friendship? The root of the word "friend" means: to love, beloved, belonging to the loved ones, not in bondage, free. All these words come from the root of the word "friend." Also, dear, precious, safety. I think that's how we feel with our true friends. We feel safe to reveal ourselves and express ourselves. We feel that we are beloved, and we love.

One of the fuels of acedia is not being a friend to our own self, not being content within ourself. A dissatisfaction and a dis-ease within ourself that's not being attended. This is "the crying out for help that is not recognized." It is fed by the daily round of

Green Gulch Garden.

annoyances, irritations and sufferings of our regular everyday life, which we cannot avoid. Being human beings there is no way we can get outside, around and away from these kinds of difficulties and pains of the day. Be they an extreme form of illness, suffering, lamentation and grief, or just having someone's jaw click who sits next to you for seven days, when those things begin to irritate us, if there is a dissatisfaction or discontent that we are not examining and taking up in our life, we experience Zen annoyance. This annoyance conditions our getting angry and hateful. The slightest thing can tip us into a full-blown expression of anger.

It is a mental discomfort, not necessarily a physical pain. I think many of us know people who have physical difficulties and pain and yet they are at peace. They are not on the edge and irritated all the time. They're working with it in a way that's an example and a great inspiration to everyone. When the kind of unhappiness and dejection I'm referring to goes unattended, these are the conditions for outbursts of anger, envy, jealousy, and greed. One way of thinking of hate is as if it were an enemy who's got his or her chance to get in there and do some harm. Another traditional image of hate is a snake, ready to strike, spreading venomous poison, even to those that we love, or those we call our friends.

Again, what is the nature of friendship? What are true friends? It may get mixed up in our minds. We may feel that someone is a real friend to us, and then something will happen and we are shocked to hear that they spoke about us in an unkind way. These are the pains of our life. Or we may find ourself talking about someone in a way that may be bordering on slander. Using speech in a way that ruins another's reputation, or plants seeds for other people to think less highly of someone is slander. A true friend is love and peace and safety and relying. So are we able to be a true friend to our friends and family? Or does something unconsciously get constellated so that we strike out in such a way that we don't even know what's going on ourselves?

One of the ten qualities that is present in every wholesome state of mind is called, in Sanskrit, *prasrabdhi*. Prasrabdhi is translated as serenity, lightness, pliancy. A definition of pliancy is: "fitness for action that freely applies the full energy of body and mind for

good purposes." Pliancy. Fully applying your mind for good purposes—at will—turning freely. This ease comes from relaxing rigid-
ity in body and mind. Rigid ideas and rigid views about how things
should be, the way it used to be, and how we want it to be. Looking around and discriminating in that way, there's a rigid quality
to that. So relaxing that, allowing what is to come forward and
realize itself, and to witness it-this is a kind of ease with whatever
happens. Lightness. Serenity. Tranquility. Just saying the words.
They're beautiful words. So along with pliancy is happiness and
joyfulness, preceded by faith and clarity. When there is lightness
and fully using the body and mind toward good purposes rather
than "errant tendencies," then striking out, hatred and its deriva-
tives cease. This means freedom to move, beneficial action, and
being the Good Friend.

It reminds me of watching the Aikido black belt tests I saw
recently, at the Aikido Dojo where my son takes lessons. In the
final of these tests, the student is surrounded by five or more black
belts who come at her from all sides doing different moves, moves
not scripted ahead of time. The student just has to be ready. Totally
ready. She meets each person in whatever way he comes, turning
this way and that, throwing each one in turn. It was amazing to
see. This is pliancy. Allowing the full energy of body and mind to
meet whatever is coming. There was also a tranquil feeling, a peaceful way; no hate, no striking out venomously. Just meeting, meeting, all the way. At the end, the teacher said one student really
exemplified the peaceful way of Aikido. It was a grandmother, a
little tiny lady, perhaps in her late sixties. Her face during the test
was completely serene and unstrained as she just met each person,
all of whom, by the way, were much larger than she was, and
threw them into the air. It was just fitness for action that freely
applies the full energy of body and mind. Very beautiful.

This is a way to live in the world with pliancy. But if we are
encumbered by the unattended parts of ourself, those parts of
ourself crying out but unrecognized, then it's very hard to turn.
Various afflictive emotions may gain ground: envy, jealousy,
covetousness. "Covet" is an interesting word. I remember as a
young person never knowing what the word "covet" meant, when

Green Gulch Farm.

it was referred to in the ten commandments. It wasn't a word that was bandied about in my house. Covet and envy are "contemplating another's successes, possessions, or good qualities, and wanting those for yourself." There is a feeling of discontent and resentment around this very contemplation of others' desirable possessions. The root of the word envy is "to look out at other things," and the root of the word covet is "to smoke," "to cook," "to move violently and agitate emotionally." When you covet something you are right over the fire, on a slow rotisserie, smoking and cooking, agitating. Your mind is the one that's disturbed.

There's a prayer from Saint Teresa of Avila: "Thank God for the things that I do not own." This is the opposite of envy or covetousness. Seeing the pain that material possessions can cause someone, you are so happy that your life is simple, and that you are free to turn and help others. Envy, jealousy, covetousness: your body and mind experience these as painful and actually unhealthy. If you look at the medical literature, these kinds of emotions cause constriction of the blood vessels, high blood pressure and other problems. Very different from pliancy, serenity, freely moving and engaging with whatever arises.

In the traditional literature, it is said that a person who has a hateful temperament also has a temperament conducive to wisdom. The hate type has a disaffection for people. In wisdom however, the same type of person has a disattachment for objects of the senses, or external objects. Disaffection means the same as disattachment, but the former is disattachment in an unprofitable way, a hurtful way, an unwholesome way. The hate type and the wisdom type are the same person except one way is unprofitable, the other profitable, one way unbeneficial, the other beneficial. The hate type, when it transforms, becomes wisdom; hate has the possibility of transforming into wisdom. For all of us who deal with hateful feelings, whether momentary or of longer duration, it is important to know that this feeling can be transformed.

One antidote to hatred is, "not to see unpleasant people." This is similar to my friend's experience, realizing she can't go out to dinner with certain people because she gets sick. At certain times, this kind of practice may be necessary.

"Encouraging the pleasure that comes from association in such matters as common meals" is another antidote to hatred. This reminds me of those studies about the French, who sit at a meal for hours on end, and eat cream and butter and all those things that we are not supposed to be eating any more, and they have less heart disease. This simple practice can address the constriction associated with hatred.

And perhaps the most fundamental antidote to hatred is friendliness, rooted in prasrabdhi, rooted in the freedom to move, the freedom of beneficial action. Friendliness, *maitri,* is one of the four Brahma Viharas, or "heavenly abodes," including equanimity, compassion, and sympathetic joy, cultivated by Bodhisattvas. Though Bodhisattvas see that beings don't actually exist in a substantial way, that they have no "inherent existence," nevertheless, Bodhisattvas radiate great friendliness and compassion toward all these very same beings, and give their attention to them, thinking: "I should become a savior to all those beings. I shall release them from all their sufferings." This is the Bodhisattva's vow of saving all beings. This friendliness brightens the world.

Friendliness means to have hopes for the welfare of others, to long for it. This is the opposite of coveting, wherein you contemplate what others have and what you want of theirs for yourself and feel resentment. It means to delight in the happiness and prosperity of others. It is affection unsullied by motives of sense desire, passion, or hope of a return.

In the traditional literature, friendliness is explained as three-fold. In Bodhisattvas who first raise their hearts to enlightenment, friendliness has beings for its object. For Bodhisattvas coursing in the way, it has dharmas (defined as fundamental elements of reality) for its object. And for Bodhisattvas who have acquired "the patient acceptance of dharmas which fail to be produced," who have acquired the "intuitive tolerance for the inconceivability of all things," for these Bodhisattvas, friendliness has no object at all. These are Bodhisattvas who understand emptiness. They understand the non-production of dharmas. They have no object for their friendliness, they are just friendliness. They don't need anything to direct it toward: it is just friendliness that covers the universe.

There is a story told of the Buddha encountering a woman who had lost all her presence of mind, after enduring enormous suffering in her life. With great maitri, Buddha said to her, "Sister, regain your state of mind." A friend of mine has that on her computer screen, as a screen saver. When she is at work and the demon acedia has entered, and she is wondering when lunchtime is going to come, and pliancy and joyfulness seem far away, then, being a Good Friend to her own self, she can say, "Sister, regain your state of mind." Recover your presence of mind. We have the ability to do this.

Visiting
Teachers

Lama Govinda lived near Zen Center the last few years of his life. Born in Germany, he became a Tibetan Buddhist and writer. His autobiography, The Way of the White Clouds, *is a classic. This article on the difficulties of making translation is very useful for all readers of translations.* –M.W.

On Right Translation of Buddhist Terms

Lama Govinda
SUMMER 1985

Lama Govinda wrote the following piece shortly before he died in January, 1985. The article was originally written as a possible introduction to a proposed book on Buddhism by another author. The piece includes many of Lama's thoughts about Buddhism as he understood it at the end of his long life of study and practice of the Buddha's teachings. Lama's interest in Buddhism began when he was sixteen years old.

On Right Translation of Buddhist Terms

Religion is a form of experience, or more correctly, an expression of life. Therefore a philologically objective and correct translation is not sufficient to express the essentials of a religion. Religion is a subjective experience which becomes foreign to life if we make it into an object of intellectual observation and judgment. This does not deny that religion also has its objective aspect, but any interpretation by outsiders who belong to a different cultural background is the result of a more or less subjective attitude. And this is all the more the case when they deal with word-symbols of a foreign and probably ancient language, which, like all verbal expressions, contain not only facts, but also feelings that are closely connected with other experiences and associations, which we can detect only in poetry. Therefore it requires an extraordinary degree of sensitivity to translate ancient religious literature without identifying ourselves with the contents and the tradition of a still living religious experience. Unfortunately, this sensitivity is lacking with most translators and interpreters.

Each religion is the mirror of, and the psychological condition in which, a particular part of humanity grew up. It is not a question of what is higher or lower. Important alone is what corresponds to our various states of consciousness. Before we think ourselves in a position to judge, we first should regard all forms of religious experience with respect and we should endeavour to understand them. This is the foundation of all tolerance. The Buddha in his admonition to the Kalamas has clearly outlined what he meant by tolerance. He was the first world-teacher who made this one of the main pillars of his message.

Lama Govinda.

At the same time, we have to be conscious that every religion is subject to constant change, growth, and expansion, and to constant re-evaluation of all its values. When this process comes to an end, religion becomes dogma, philosophy becomes scholasticism, and scholasticism becomes mere tradition from which all life has fled. But if we recognize religion as a living organism, we must try to understand the necessary phases of its development which are the result of its growth.

The beginnings of Buddhism differ from those of all other religions because these beginnings were not based on revelation, or on an existing form of recognized religion, but on a general human experience. The Buddha was not interested in what people believed, or what they thought probable, but in what they did in order to relieve others' suffering as well as their own, and to find a path toward peace and happiness. He was not a reformer of Vedic tradition, as scholars at one time assumed. Instead, he rejected the main pillars of the Vedic religion, which was based on animal sacrifices and caste distinctions, rather than upon the recognition of ethical values, such as the sacredness of life *(ahimsa)* and the dignity and self-responsibility of all men, irrespective of their caste *(varna)* or the color of their skin.

The roots of early Buddhism are therefore not in the Vedic-Brahmanic tradition, but, rather, in the tradition of the Sramanas who remained outside the social order and were known as wandering ascetics who sought for truth and for deliverance from the bonds of religious institutions. The Buddha was known to his contemporaries, and to the following generation, as Mahasramana (Pali: Mahasamana), which explains his reluctance to create a monastic institution with permanent dwelling places and administrative rules and regulations, places of worship and study, etc. But, as his community of followers grew, this institutionalizing became inevitable, and he finally gave in to the requests of his disciples. Just as the Jains did, he also maintained that he belonged to an ancient (pre-Vedic) tradition, which continued to survive as an undercurrent, even during the overlordship of the Aryan invaders from the north who had conquered the greater part of India and had created the caste system in order to preserve their superiority.

Concepts like karma, causality, and rebirth, as well as ahimsa (non-violence), and *karuna* (compassion), concepts which we now think of as "Hinduism," were unknown to the Vedas and were introduced much later under the influence of Buddhism and Jainism. In fact, the word "Hindu" was coined by the Arab scholar and explorer Alberuni as a collective term for all the people beyond the river Sind (Indus). It therefore is wrong to maintain that Buddhism was derived from Hinduism. In fact, the opposite is the case! But it is difficult to overthrow this popular prejudice because previous generations of scholars regarded the Vedic religion as the foundation of all Indian tradition.

After having considered the philological foundations of the Buddhist teachings, it is time to explore the psychological and religious origins and motivations of Buddhism. The Buddha did not demand blind faith from his followers, but rather sincere effort and a selfless life for the sake of the happiness of all living beings, as well as for oneself. His teaching encouraged people "to come and see for yourself!" Open your eyes to the realities of life, be honest with yourself and do not try merely to escape suffering. Instead, try to overcome it within yourself where you will find its origins. What you believe is not important, but what you do is. You are inheritors of your deeds, thoughts, and intentions. In fact, thoughts and intentions are more important than the physical outcome of your deeds. Thoughts and intentions belong to you more than what you call your possessions.

Therefore it is said: "This six cubit body contains the origin and the dissolution of the world." The Buddha did not intend to promulgate a theory about the universe; he wanted, instead, to point out that the only world we can observe and influence is that of our own body in both its physical aspect and as a spiritual organism. He was aware that the functions of our body and our consciousness are not arbitrary phenomena, but follow universal laws, although they may be modified by our attitudes.

In the tantrism of the Vajrayana, we find this idea in an even more pronounced form when it is said that our body not only mirrors the universe, but that it is our ultimate body. Here the realm of consciousness and intuition turns into the realisation of a higher dimension in which we take part when our mind has transcended the limits of the three dimensional world.

Therefore it is said, according to the oldest Buddhist tradition: "Well proclaimed is the law (Dharma) by the Enlightened One, visible to all, timeless, profound, comprehensible only to the wise." It is a significant and characteristic feature of Buddhism that it emphasizes the value of seeing, of direct perception, as a means of intuitive knowledge. While *ditthi,* in the sense of "opinions," is to be shunned, *samma ditthi,* complete or perfect seeing (not merely a partial or one-sided vision) is the way to the highest realization. In the same way, *dhyana (jhana)* is not what some people explain as "trance"; in fact, it is visualization as a means of direct perception, as opposed to "thinking and reflecting" *(vitarka-vicara)*. The Buddha is never represented with closed eyes. Meditation is not "mystic trance," or aimless speculation, or mushy thinking. Buddhism is based on clarity of mind and thought. Tantric visualization demands clear definition, but not "visionary hallucinations," as modern mystics are apt to believe.

The simplicity of the Buddha's words and of the formulations of early Buddhism confounds the overly intellectual and is comprehensible only to the wise man who has rediscovered his inner unity. However, before we have rediscovered this unity, we follow blindly the all-pervasive force of life, which in itself is neither good nor bad, but which may become one or the other according to our attitude. It is the immanent force of our consciousness which carries us beyond the limitations of our individuality or separateness.

Therefore the first link of the Pratityasamutpada is *avidya,* ignorance of the conditions of our all-relatedness, in which nothing can be regarded as separate, or absolute, without relationship to everything else. This ignoring of reality has nothing to do with "stupidity" or lack of intelligence, as has often been assumed, for we are not concerned here with intellectual knowledge, but with subconscious formations *(sankhara)* which precede the awakening of normal human consciousness *(vijnana)* in which we do not yet realize our position in the world, but assume ourselves to be different, thus splitting the world into subject and object, mind and matter *(nama-rupa),* self and others. Out of the dualism arises the further split into the six realms of consciousness *(sadayatana),* on account of which contact *(sparsa)* of the senses with their objects becomes possible. On this basis arise feelings *(vedana),* craving *(trsna)* (literally "thirst"), clinging or the urge to possess *(upadana),* which, in turn, results in the further process of becoming *(bhava),* birth *(jati),* old age and death *(jara-marana).*

The only link of this chain of cause and effect (or in this concatenation of events) which we are able to influence or direct is our consciousness (vijnana), and this enables us to become conscious of ourselves and of our relationship to the world in general, and of our attitude towards all living beings. That, however, is why the Buddha stresses the importance of meditation, which is the realization of all-encompassing love, compassion, sympathy (sharing the happiness of others) and equanimity (maitri, karuna, *mudita,* and *upeksha*). The latter has been defined as the faculty of being able to define one's own suffering as unimportant, but it does not mean showing indifference towards the suffering of others. According to the Pali scriptures, upeksha is defined as "mental balance" *(tatramajjhattata).*

Pratityasamutpada is to be understood not only as a causal nexus, but also as a simultaneously arising concatenation of events which may be conceived either as a successive development in time or as a timeless principle of interrelated conditions. The Buddha opposed neither logical thinking nor the principle of synchronicity, but recognized both ways of thinking, as we can see from the many forms in which he referred to pratityasamutpada in his discourses, sometimes leaving out several of the consecutive links. This also corresponds to the literal meaning of the word itself, which is "dependent" (causal) and "simultaneous arising" (samutpada). Under this latter aspect, even the term *akaliko* ("timeless" or "synchronic") becomes plausible, and we understand the Buddha's exhortation when Ananda thought the formula of Dependent Origination was a matter of simple understanding and mere common sense without any deeper meaning.

As long as we are on the level of human thinking, the Buddha maintains the rules of logic. But he knows that the deepest aspects of reality are timeless, and he refuses to give in to any metaphysical speculation, so that even concepts like nirvana and karma lose their metaphysical connotation and, within the structure of Buddhist psychology, are reduced to their original meaning. By popularization of these concepts, nirvana has become a purely quietistic ideal, implying one's "dissolution into the All"; but the Buddha, by contrast, gives us a clear psychological definition, namely, the absence of greed, hatred, and infatuation. Karma is not an unqualified fatalism, in which every action and every happening becomes a fetter which binds us to our past. According to Buddhist understanding, karma means "deed," "action," in the sense of an

Tassajara Creek.

intentional act with a fully conscious resolve *(cetana)*, which creates our pattern of repeating our behavior when similar circumstances arise again.

The *Lankayatara Sutra* describes this tendency as "habit-energy," the force of habit, the tendency to repeat the same action automatically unless new motivation has been created, as happens when there is a complete "turning about in the deepest seat of our consciousness." If such a thing were not possible, no liberation would be thinkable. Therefore, the Buddha calls conversion (or the reversal of our will due to honest conviction) the only miracle that deserves the name.

In the same way, he also freed the concept of egohood (or the "I") from being an eternal, unchangeable principle, and considered it to be, instead, a psychological point of reference of the individual consciousness which changes continually according to prevailing circumstances. This inner point of relationship is the necessary precondition for every kind of balanced consciousness and every reasonable action. However, if this so-called "I" becomes an independent and automatically acting principle of uninhibited self assertion, it turns into a cancerous growth which destroys the very organism that it intended to support.

Even if Buddhist psychology rejects the concept of a soul-monad, in the popular sense, it nevertheless emphasizes all that we understand under the word "psyche," that is, all the spiritual and psychic forces of man which make us human beings. Buddhism is not the teaching of "soullessness," but of solidarity and compassion with all living beings, as expressed in the "divine states" (brahmavihara) of meditation.

Nowadays it has become a fashion, even in Buddhist circles, to translate the word "maitri" (Pali: *metta*) by "friendship," in order to exclude any connection with sex. The latter seems to have become an obsession due to the overemphasizing of this quality, and the tendency of most modern religions to outlaw sexuality. Instead of it being understood that love is a matter of the heart and not of reason or of cold calculation, and that love is a matter of inner sharing and of intimate relationship which involves the whole of our being and goes far beyond a mere friendship or a mere well-wishing, the word maitri has been robbed of its original meaning and has been replaced with a colorless (morally disinfected) expression. The Buddhist definition of "maitri" is:

"Just as a mother protects her child with her own life, in a similar way we should extend an unlimited heart to all beings."

Just as "love" has been purged from the Buddhist vocabulary, the word *sankhara* has become the source of misunderstandings and has turned Buddhism into dark pessimism. In this connection even the *Dhammapada,* the most popular Buddhist scripture, which has been translated into all the major languages of the world, has frequently been quoted as saying: "All is transiency, all is sorrow, all is unreal." The text says: *"Sabbe sankhara anicca, Sabbe sankhara dukkha, Sabbe dhamma anatta."*

First of all, Sabbe sankhara is not "all," or "the whole world," but only our subconscious formations or latent tendencies (conditioned by our past), and, secondly, the original Pali text makes it clear in the third line that all that is real in the ultimate sense (dhamma) is "non-ego." So, the word anatta (non-ego or not-self) has simply been omitted (!) and the original meaning of the text has been supplanted by the opinion of the translator (or that of the Upanishads, which were at one time thought by some to be the origin of the opinion of the Buddha). On the basis of such "translations" the whole of Buddhism has been misinterpreted. Finally, under the influence of Schopenhauer's philosophy, to which most of the early interpreters of Buddhism succumbed, the teachings of the Buddha were made into plain pessimism.

But in the same *Dhammapada* which we quoted above we find verses in the "Canto of Happiness" which give quite a different picture, one which shows us that the ancient Buddhists did not feel that their attitude had anything to do with pessimism:

"Let us be free from hatred and let us live happily among those who hate. Among men filled with hatred, let us live free from hatred." (Dhp. 197)

Here it becomes abundantly clear that it is not impermanence which is the root cause of suffering, but greed, hatred and delusion. These three factors make us imagine that we can hold on forever to what we regard as our ego or our mortal "I." Therefore it is said in the same chapter of the *Dhammapada:*

"Let us live happily, we who call nothing our own. Let us be like the shining gods *(abhassara),* who are nourished on joy (or "inspiration": *piti*)."

To make this exhortation even more justified, each of the above-mentioned root causes of our suffering is followed by the words:

"He who perceives this with a clear mind (or with "insight") will be freed from all suffering. This is the way of purity."

But even this important statement has been spoiled by some translators who have thought fit to replace the word "nibbindata" by the notion that we should get "fed up" with suffering, instead of overcoming it as the Buddha intended.

How little we can trust even our philologically correct translations becomes evident when we consider such words as *shunyata, Siddha, siddhi,* etc. The philological equivalent of shunyata is "emptiness." However, this is not identical with "nothingness," as has been frequently thought. "No-thingness" would perhaps be more adequate. Emptiness as such is unthinkable. Even what we call a vacuum does not exclude radiations of various forces like magnetism, gravity, light, etc.; it only excludes air, or any other known form of gas.

So, if we speak of emptiness, the question arises: "empty of what?" Buddhism answers: "empty of all designations or preconceived conditions and, therefore, a state of infinite potentiality or primal space." It was this idea which inspired Nagarjuna's philosophy and the subsequent growth of the movement of the Great Vehicle or Great Way (Mahayana), which freed Buddhism from a narrow orthodoxy of purely monkish institutions and opened the way for a universal fellowship comprised of men and women, monks and laymen, scholars and poets, artists and common folk. If this were not the true meaning of emptiness, how could we explain how an abstract and apparently negative term like shunyata could inspire millions of people of many races and carry Buddhism into the farthest reaches of Asia?

Something similar happened with the teachings of the Siddhas, the medieval Buddhist mystics, who lived between the sixth and the tenth centuries, who rejected any kind of orthodoxy. They were poets and philosophers, monks and laymen, princes and commoners, workers and wandering ascetics, Brahmins and outcasts. They did not recognize social conventions and used the common language in preference to Sanskrit.

Fortunately, the tales of the Siddhas became part of the religious tradition of Tibet and have been preserved in faithful Tibetan translations. The aim of the Siddhas was a realization, which would be attainable by a religious life even under the most unfavorable conditions, thereby allowing any occupation to become the means to perfection. For this reason the Siddhas were called the "Perfect Ones." Grunwedel's first translation of the Siddha stories never seems to have reached the wider public, probably because of his misleading title, which introduced the Siddhas as the eighty-four "sorcerers." Yet he would not have called Buddha, or Christ, a sorcerer, in spite of the fact that many miracles are ascribed to the latter. It is strange that everything which does not correspond to something in a translator's or interpreter's own cultural background is usually represented by him as being from a culture of a lower order.

In the same way, the Buddhist mystery plays have consistently been represented as "Devil Dances," and even the images of Dhyani-Buddhas, which depict the Buddha as the supreme physician, are labelled as "Medicine Buddhas," which creates the impression that we are dealing with something like the "medicine men" of some primitive African tribes.

The Buddha compared himself to a physician and formulated his doctrine as a diagnosis of human suffering, in which the first of his "Noble Truths" represented a fundamental analysis of universal suffering, the second the cause of suffering, the third the

Students eating at Tassajara.

remedy of our ills, and the fourth the practical way to apply the remedy. So the Buddha was not only a physician of bodily ailments, but a healer (German: *Heiland*, i.e., a "savior") of all human suffering.

In the same way we have to understand that rebirth in Buddhism has a completely different meaning from what is commonly known as the "transmigration of souls." It would be more correct to speak of a continuous transformation of psychic forces, even beyond the destruction of our material body. The same forces that built up our former body, and all its mental and spiritual faculties, now create a new body, freed from all accretions and superfluous accumulations, transferring the flame of life to the germ of a new organism that now develops according to the impulse and the direction given by the character of the past incarnation.

It is like lighting a lamp from another one. The flame does not wander from one lamp to another, by disappearing here and reappearing somewhere else: it merely transfers the impetus or impulse from one source of energy to another. The only difference is that the flame does not transfer the quality of the material on which the flame feeds, but only the heat that is necessary to ignite the new material. But as no simile is perfect, and shows only one particular side of the process one wants to illuminate, we have to bear in mind that our psychic forces are complex, and, at the same time, dependent on our past experiences and our present character, so that the impetus expresses not just the initial direction of our life force, but its qualities as well.

When the wise Nagasena was asked by King Menandros whether or not the person who is reborn is the same person who died in his previous existence, Nagasena replied, *"na ca so, na ca anno,"* "neither the same, nor another one." This is because (as Heraclitos said) "we do not enter the same river twice": not only is the river a different one in each moment, but also we ourselves are not the same in two consecutive moments. As the river flows constantly, so do we ourselves. The newly born child is not the same as the grownup person, though the grownup person has become what he is due to his childhood. Identity is one of those abstractions on which we build our logic and all our statistical values, which are merely simplifications, without which no science can exist.

But have we ever seen two identical trees or two absolutely identical human beings or animals? The relationship between childhood and old age rests not on the identity of the person concerned, but on the dependent origination of perpetually changing conditions of life which develop in the direction of their growth.

Man may strive after the blissful state of being, but just because he is striving, he is in the process of becoming. Only when he is capable of releasing the fullness of his being can he transcend the state of becoming. Therefore, the Buddha emphasizes the process of becoming as the law of all life, and the Buddhist psychology speaks of the *bhavanga-sota,* the stream of becoming.

The *Lankavatara Sutra* likewise declares:

"There is a constant stream of becoming, a momentary and uninterrupted change from one state of appearance to another."[1]

---

[1] Translated by D.T. Suzuki and quoted by Dwight Goddard in his *Buddhist Bible,* Thedford, Vermont, 1938, p. 296.

"Things are not eternal, because the marks of individuality appear and disappear, that is, the marks of self-nature are characterized by (what we call) noneternality. On the other hand, because things are unborn and are only mind-made, they are in a deep sense eternal."[2]

The overcoming of suffering was the main object of the Buddha's teaching, and the way to achieve this is the Noble Eightfold Path. But here arises the question: have we to understand this as a way of eight steps, of which each one is higher than the previous one, or as a way that is broad enough to accommodate eight individual paths side by side? Most people prefer the idea of a flight of steps. But how is one then to explain that the first step already presupposes the last and highest step? How can one, without deeper insight into the nature of the world, achieve an impartial (not ego-conditioned) "right view" *(samyag drishti),* in order to make the right resolve *(samyak samkalpa)* that leads to ethical behavior in words, deeds and livelihood *(samyak vak, s. karmanta, s. ajiva),* resulting in "right effort and mindfulness" *(samyak vyayama, samyak smriti)* and culminates in the perfect realization of *samadhi?*

The word samyak (Pali: *samma,* Tibetan: *yang-dag),* which generally is rendered as "right," has a far greater importance than that. This is because "right" and "wrong" are relative concepts, which depend merely on the view point of the observer, but have no value in themselves: what appears right to one person may be wrong to another. But samyak has a much deeper and wider meaning. It signifies a state of mind in which our whole being is involved and united.

Would it not be better to translate this word according to its original meaning, as it is revealed by the language which was used in the time in which the teaching of the Buddha was remembered and committed to writing? The term "Samyaksambuddha" shows us that the word "right" does not fit into the context, for the Buddha is not a "rightly" Enlightened One, but, rather, a perfectly or

[2] Ibid., p. 295.

completely Enlightened One. This is also confirmed by the Tibetan translation of samyak as yang-dag, which implies the idea of the Middle Way, avoiding all extremes, being unprejudiced and open minded.

It is this attitude of the Buddha which became the foundation of his teaching and which is represented as the highest step of the Eightfold Path: samadhi. It is the complete unification and integration of our being. In order to achieve this we must first attain a perfect unity of all our psychic faculties. And if we have thus established harmony within ourselves, we have to course the Eightfold Path on ever ascending higher planes of experience and realization.

In order to comprehend this we have to have a clear conception of the last steps of the Eightfold Path, namely, wholehearted mindfulness and complete one-pointedness of purpose. All these qualities have concentration as their root. But samadhi is much more than simple concentration. Every bank clerk has to have perfect concentration, but that does not mean that he is a saint. In the same way, "samadhi" is not just a state of tranquility, hypnosis, deep sleep, or a self-induced trance.

In the West, the words "concentration," "contemplation" and "meditation" have become almost synonymous. But there is a vast difference in the terminology of Buddhism. Effort is the one-pointed exertion of the will to abstain from harming others and to promote all that which is beneficial to others and to ourselves. Contemplation is the attentive observation of our thoughts and the mental visualisation of our aims. Samadhi, however, is more than what is commonly regarded as meditation, in the sense of intellectual activity, or thinking and reflecting on a given subject. It is the integration of subject and object, the becoming one of the meditator and the object of his meditation.

However, one thing remains the common basis for all these steps: they are characterized by the word samyak, which means that we are to employ all psychic and spiritual faculties. They consist not only of merely moral and intellectual motives, but are the expression of a well-balanced mind, undisturbed by momentary intentions and expectations. They are the expression of our innermost convictions. Samyak excludes any kind of one-sidedness.

Samyag Drishti, therefore, signifies more than what is commonly called "right views," or the acceptance of a certain set of recognized religious ideas. It means a perfectly open, unprejudiced attitude, which enables us to "see things as they are" *(yatnabhutam)*, i.e., not only from one side (and especially not from our own!), but from all sides, without bias, without suppressing what appears to us disagreeable. Instead of closing our eyes to all that creates suffering for ourselves and others, we have to recognize its cause. And if we realize that this cause lies also in ourselves, we shall be able to transcend it.

However, he who tries to close his eyes to this fact due to indifference, or so-called "detachment" (in the sense of cutting oneself off from all human emotions), misses the very essence of the Buddha's message. Detachment means non-possessiveness, but not callousness. The selfless but warm love which is able to share the joys and sufferings of others is what the Buddha calls *cetovimukti* and the "liberation of the heart" and the realisation of wisdom *(prajna vimukti)*.

*Robert Thurman is a Buddha jewel. Committed, creative
and learned in Tibetan Buddhism, it is a joy to be in his
presence. The* Vimalakirti Sutra, *which he has superbly
translated from Tibetan, is a repository of wisdom,
compassion and humor. The combination of Thurman and
the* Sutra *cannot be beat.* –M.W.

Vimalakirti

Robert Thurman

GREEN GULCH FARM, MARCH 1987

FALL 1987

Green Dragon Temple is a very auspicious place to talk about
the *Vimalakirti Sutra* because, as you may know, the
Mahayana Sutras, in the Buddhist account, were discovered in the
Dragon Kings' palace in the bottom of the ocean by the great
Nagarjuna. The Mahayana Sutras themselves are believed taught
by Shakyamuni Buddha, on the Vulture Peak and in other places.
This particular one was taught in Vaishali, one of the great cities—
a San Francisco or Los Angeles—of India of its day. But they were
not preserved by the human beings in India at the time, who were
not ready for the Mahayana teaching, the profound teaching of
non-duality. It seems they would have confused it with either a
nihilistic type of teaching, or a monistic type of teaching. Therefore, the dragons took these teachings away with them, down to the
bottom of the ocean where they stored them in their wonderful
palaces. Four hundred years after the Buddha's time, these dragons came to the Bodhisattva Nagarjuna, and they said, "We have
some things you'd like." Dragons can come in the world looking
like human beings, so they didn't startle the people too much. Then
Nagarjuna went down with them to the bottom of the ocean, and
he brought back this text. Western scholars of course don't believe
that, my colleague professors don't, and they worry about me! But
I tell them it's a matter of allegory; it's up to you whether you think

it's a living allegory, or a literary allegory. Then I say no more, and that's why they worry.

The Vimalakirti Sutra is a very interesting book, especially if you like Star Trek, Dr. Who, any sort of lively thing that tries to show another vision of life in the universe, anything other than the gloomy, mono-linear, Judeo-Christian, big doomsday vision of life. If you don't like that too much, you should read the Mahayana Sutras. Because they completely change the context of life. In the Mahayana Sutras, the Buddha always begins by emanating a certain kind of ray from his forehead or his teeth, or his navel, sometimes even his toenails. Suddenly everybody sees on the ray billions of different planets in all directions, everywhere. In one great Sutra he sticks out his tongue, and the tongue covers an entire galaxy, and in the surface of the tongue, everybody sees billions of different universes, billions of different planets, so they're all stretched on some vast carpet of light, and the spaces in between suddenly don't seem to be very important. And somehow, by the focus of that ray, they see Bodhisattvas everywhere. They see beings doing nice things everywhere, they don't see beings doing nasty things, having holocausts and shoving each other in fires and doing all kinds of stupid things. Instead they see beings giving away things, they see beings being generous to each other, they see beings doing beautiful things for each other. They see beings reshaping different universes, galaxies, they see the universe as a vast carpet of generosity, morality, tolerance, energy, meditation on wisdom. If you see the universe that way, you have less of an excuse: you can't so easily feel, "Oh everybody's a turkey, I'll be a turkey," and you can't feel so proud of yourself if you go meditate for a few minutes, "Oh, I went and meditated, and everybody else watched TV and slept." Because you see whole universes full of people meditating, totally. So you should read this Sutra—you will enjoy it.

The *Vimalakirti Sutra,* the *Arya Vimalakirti nirdesa Mahayana Sutra,* as it is called, is a Sutra mainly taught not by the Buddha, but by Vimalakirti, a lay person who lives in the city of Vaishali. I contend Vimalakirti is a prototype of the Zen master as well as of the Tantric Siddha or Adept. He is one who has no definite position, he was not a member of the monastic order. He was a lay person, wealthy, with a big household. He was a disciple of and supporter of the Buddha, but he didn't have formal spiritual status. He had no special robes and so forth. But he was a very difficult character, he had a big mouth; Vimalakirti was known as unstoppable in his eloquence. He had this really annoying habit of being critical. For example, he would meet a monk or a great elder like Shariputra, or even the Buddha, and he would first bow three times and make offerings, deal with them ritually in the proper way for a religious person. And then he would scold them solidly, usually about the dualism in something they were doing or thinking or saying. Because of his clarity, they would not mind in some way-they would appreciate it, they would learn from it-but it made them rather eager to avoid his presence. So much so that in the fourth chapter, when the Buddha tries to get someone to visit Vimalakirti, because Vimalakirti is sick, no one will go!

It begins with Vimalakirti as an old man, moaning and groaning, and in the Buddhist community there is a custom that you have to go to see someone that is sick. You say, "Hey, what's the matter. Buddha says, 'Hello, are you okay, will you survive, are you remembering to use your sickness as occasion for your samadhi, does it remind you of impermanence, are you not relying upon this fleshly body any more, are you going to die soon, we all need to know, are you being very cheery?'" That's how you cheer up someone in the Buddhist community when they're sick, you go in and say, "Hey, not bad, you're not dead!" That does cheer you up. If you're a nihilist, like some of us perhaps, being dead doesn't mean that much, death is just anesthesia. But if you have the view of former and future lives, which is the day to day ground of Buddhist cultures, then "not dead" means "I don't have to venture my way into a new womb! I'm not having to worry about how I'm reborn, what realm of life, what form of life." So "not dead," remaining human, is a wonderful thing, even if you're very sick, even if you're in pain. Anyway, Vimalakirti is moaning and groaning, "I'm so sick, Buddha doesn't send anybody to see me." Then Buddha reads his mind, and Buddha says, "Oh, Shariputra, elder, go see Vimalakirti," and he says, "Excuse me,

I'd rather not today." "Well, why not?" "Well, last time I met Vimalakirti I was in deep samadhi, and Vimalakirti came up to me and said, 'Shariputra, this is not the way to sit in deep samadhi! Reverend Shariputra, this is not the way to absorb yourself in contemplation. You should absorb yourself in contemplation so that neither body nor mind appear anywhere in the triple world.'"

PUBLICATION OF ZEN CENTER
VOLUME XXII, NUMBER TWO, FALL 1987

Fall 1987

Thanks a lot! You know, Shariputra, he's not an incompetent meditator; he can go into trance and you can hit him on the head with a hammer and he won't even know it, he's so into his samadhi. He's withdrawn his attention, his consciousness, from his tactile sensations totally. Shariputra is a good yogi, and yet, something's wrong. He's not thinking anything, he's not having discursive thoughts, his mind is not wandering, he's completely concentrated in the mental consciousness, in the sixth sense, as they say in Buddhist psychology, and he's totally one-pointed on that. But Vimalakirti isn't satisfied. Why? He said, "This is not the way." I love this line particularly for Zen people; Dogen says this line, of course. You can only sit, you can only practice, you can only meditate, you should only do zazen when you have "cast off body and mind" right away, remember? Vimalakirti says neither body nor mind should appear anywhere in the triple world, that's the way to absorb yourself in concentration.

"You should absorb yourself in contemplation in such a way that you can manifest all ordinary behaviors without forsaking cessation." You should be able to go and walk and talk and do anything without departing from Nirvana—cessation means Nirvana. You are all what you are doing, all being in Nirvana. Not "Today I have to cook and wash dishes and work in the garden, and later I'll attain Nirvana." "No, you should do it in a way where you can do all that without forsaking Nirvana."

"You should absorb yourself in contemplation in such a way that you manifest the nature of an ordinary person, without abandoning your cultivated spiritual nature." Shariputra was a holy monk, a real Arhat, a saint, he had achieved Nirvana already and therefore had a tendency to think of himself as a little bit better than an ordinary person. In India people would bow and touch his feet, and they would bring him offerings, even vie with each other to be the one to give him one on that day. So he was believing his own press releases a little bit, as we've noticed spiritual teachers tend to do. Unfortunately this is a very dangerous thing, so Vimalakirti is not saying something light. He says you should manifest the behaviors of all ordinary people, you should cultivate the yoga of ordinariness, normalness, without forsaking your cultivated spiritual nature. That's challenging, actually. Vimalakirti's main teaching is a teaching of non-duality. Non-duality is a very tricky teaching. It is not the same as oneness. It means the integration of oneness and duality, non-duality between oneness and duality. It means being in the oneness of Nirvana without forsaking the duality of the world. It's a very difficult kind of thing, it's the central philosophical teaching of Vimalakirti.

When the Buddha asks all these people to go see the Vimalakirti, none of them wants to go really. If they go and say, "How are you?" Vimalakirti's going to say, "Who are you talking to, who is me, who are you? Do you think I'm here? I'm not. You're *sunyata.*" You can't say the simplest thing to Vimalakirti. You can't say, "Oh, God." He says, "God? Who's God?" He's right on top of it. He's like a critique machine, constantly operating to remove all sorts of delusions.

Manjushri finally says he'll go see Vimalakirti. You have Manjushri here in this zendo. In the Zen tradition Manjushri is your patron Bodhisattva. He's actually a Buddha who attained Buddhahood aeons ago. Manjushri said "As a Buddha, I want to be innumerable Bodhisattvas, I want to be as many Bodhisattvas as are necessary for the multiverse. Everywhere, anywhere people are seeking the true nature of reality, I will appear." He's the Bodhisattva of science, of wisdom, and he carries a sword of analytical critical wisdom which cuts through the superficial appearances of all things to probe, to find the true nature. And that is why you have him in all of your Zen centers, sitting facing the direction of the meditators. Not to be worshipped as an icon, but to represent your own wisdom, cutting through your own delusions and your own habitual thoughts. He is always young, by the way, always sixteen years old; he's not an old grey-beard. Wisdom in Buddhism is not necessarily arrived at by an old grey-beard. Old grey-beards can remain confused unless they have made special efforts. Experience alone will not necessarily bring wisdom. As the self-delusion habit-pattern is so intense, sometimes old grey-beards can think, "I'm a great old grey-beard!" and be even worse. So the wisdom is a youthful wisdom.

So only Manjushri will go to see Vimalakirti. He says "I'll go, it's okay, he'll bug me, but I'll manage." Because he is the wisdom of all Buddhas, he figures he can handle it. As soon as he goes, everybody says, "Oh, let's go hear what Vimalakirti and Manjushri have to say to each other. That's gonna be some Dharma party, ultimate Dharma combat will take place." When Manjushri comes, he and Vimalakirti start right on Zen. They go totally koan, long before Chinese Ch'an. Manjushri says, "Householder, why is your house empty? Have you no servants?" Because Vimalakirti has a huge establishment. Vimalakirti says, "Manjushri, all Buddha-fields are also empty, my house is just like reality, it's empty." He doesn't just say, "Well, it's their day off," he says Buddha-fields are empty. Manjushri then thinks, "I'll catch him." He says, "What makes them empty?" Is he going to get Vimalakirti into a reification of emptiness? A real reality? The real danger of reifying the absolute into an absolute Absolute? Vimalakirti says, "Well, they're empty because of emptiness." Manjushri gets more excited and says, "What's empty about emptiness?" Vimalakirti still doesn't do the non-dual thing yet, he says, "Constructions are empty because of emptiness, mental constructions are empty because of emptiness." Manjushri says, "Aha, can emptiness be conceptually constructed?" Then Vimalakirti says, "Even that construct is itself empty, and emptiness cannot construct emptiness." He empties emptiness, and returns to non-duality. Emptiness is this relativity. Manjushri was probing lest he be reifying emptiness.

Did you ever reify emptiness? When you heard about emptiness, e.g. when you said the *Heart Sutra,* and you thought you'd sit there and if you really concentrated hard enough, everything might disappear, and you might disappear, and that might be Nirvana, and you'd be in a place. Or when you didn't disappear, did you feel disappointed that you hadn't understood emptiness? I think you might recognize that kind of distinction, because that is the false reification of emptiness. Who would there be to "go into" emptiness? There would only be an empty person; would that person recognize being in an empty emptiness? No. You're just as empty before you ever sit down as you are when you sit down and try to concentrate on emptiness. Emptiness is empty of itself. Emptiness means precisely that it is not outside of this relativity. The absolute is this relativity, and therefore the wisdom of that emptiness means no longer seeking to escape from this relativity. Seeking, realizing that this relativity is the absolute, and thereby being totally committed to this. And that means that this wisdom is great compassion, which is the intercommitment of beings to each other.

Now I want to read to you a great quote about the further implications of this non-duality. Manjushri has just asked Vimalakirti, "How does a Bodhisattva conceive of living beings if he thinks of the world as empty?" And Vimalakirti responds with this wonderful set of metaphors of non-existent things. He says, "A Bodhisattva should regard all living beings as a wise man regards the reflection of the moon in water, or as a magician regards men created by magic. He should regard them as being like a face in a mirror, like the water of a mirage, like the sound of an echo, like a mass of clouds in the sky, like the previous moment of a ball of foam, like the appearance and disappearance of a bubble of water, like the core of a banana tree, like the flash of lightning, like the fifth great element, like the seventh sense medium, like the third rebirth of a one-time returner, like the existence of desire, hatred and folly in a saint, like thoughts of avarice, wickedness, hostility

Robert Thurman.

in a Bodhisattva who has attained tolerance, like the instincts of passion in a Buddha, like the perception of color in one blind from birth, like the inhalation and exhalation of an ascetic absorbed in a meditation of cessation, like a track of a bird in the sky, like the erection of a eunuch, like the pregnancy of a barren woman, like the unproduced passions of an emanated incarnation of the Tathagata, like a tortoise hare fur coat." They have a little humor.

So, in other words, the way to be compassionate for a Bodhisattva who has the great wisdom of emptiness, is to not perceive any living beings. True great compassion does not perceive any beings. It's a very strange thing. It's a great compassion that's completely combined with the wisdom of emptiness. And that doesn't mean that the Bodhisattva does not see beings at all. It means that they do not see beings as they simultaneously see the beings. A Bodhisattva sees simultaneously how a being gets free from suffering as well as seeing it with its suffering, and that means that gives the Bodhisattva a true great compassion that is truly effective.

But everyone always gets puzzled, "Well, how can you feel compassion for beings when you do not perceive them?" And then Vimalakirti replied, "Manjushri, when a Bodhisattva considers all living beings in this way, just as I have realized the Dharma, so should I teach it to living beings. . . . Thereby, he generates the love that is truly a refuge for all living beings, the love that is peaceful because it is free of grasping, the love that is not feverish because it is free of passion, the love that accords with reality because it is equanimous in all three times. The love that is without conflict because free of the violence of the passions, the love that is non-dual because it is involved neither with the external nor with the internal. The love that is imperturbable because it is totally ultimate. Thereby he generates the love that is firm; its high resolve that is unbreakable, like a diamond. The love that is pure, purified even in its intrinsic nature, the love that is even, its aspirations being equal, the safe love that has eliminated its enemy. The Bodhisattva love that continuously develops living beings, the Tathagata's love that understands reality, the Buddha's love that causes beings to awaken from their sleep, love that is spontaneous because it is fully enlightened spontaneously, the love that is enlightenment because it is unity of experience. The love that has no presumption because it has eliminated attachment and aversion; the love that is great compassion because it infuses the universal vehicle with radiance; the love that is never exhausted because it acknowledges voidness and selfishness. The love that is giving because it bestows the gift of Dharma free of the tight fist of a bad teacher, the love that is morality because it improves immoral living beings. The love that is tolerant because it protects both self and others. The love that is wisdom because it causes attainment at the proper time. The love that is liberative technique because it shows the way everywhere. The love that is without formality because it is pure in motivation; the love that is without deviation because it acts from decisive motivation; the love that is high resolve because it is without passion; the love that is without deceit because it is not artificial, the love that is happiness because it introduces living beings to the happiness of the Buddha. That, Manjushri, is the love of the Bodhisattva."

It's very difficult to stop, but Vimalakirti did stop the Sutra. Let me just close with one of the very famous moments in the Sutra where, in the ninth chapter, there are twenty-five Bodhisattvas, plus Manjushri, and they are each giving a description of non-duality, of ultimate reality, calling it the entrance into the Dharma door of non-duality. They all give a brilliant insight into the non-dual, such as "form is emptiness, emptiness is form," as you've all heard in the *Heart Sutra,* very intense things, and then Manjushri says, "You guys did great, I love it!" You go deeper and deeper if you read it with your heart, and Manjushri says about non-duality, "But there was one big mistake that you all made, which is that you all spoke!... Non-duality, absolute reality, cannot be captured in words, it is inexpressible, it cannot be described. So just by talking about it with syllables and words, you blew it!" And of course, *he* blew it.

And I should say, too, there was an earlier time when Shariputra maintained a pious and portentous silence. There was a goddess who was badgering him, a goddess of perfect wisdom, and she came out to celebrate the teaching of selflessness and compassion, etc. She scattered flower petals everywhere. The place was strewn with beautiful smelling flowers; these flower petals were stuck on his robe, and all the other monks' robes. Shariputra tried to get rid of these flowers. She says, "What's the problem, Shariputra, it's just flowers." She's the goddess of *Prajna Paramita,* transcendent wisdom. He didn't know that, he thought she was just a fairy, and he says, "We're monks, we can't wear flowers, we don't wear ornaments, it's against the Vinaya, we don't do this." She says, "Flowers are not unseemly, Shariputra, mental constructions are unseemly! You have some prejudice about flowers. The prejudice you have is unseemly, Shariputra!" Then they really get into it. "Now, what makes you say so," he says, and they go on and on, and she again stops Shariputra every time, cold. Poor Shariputra! Every time he gets wasted, he changes the subject. He says, "Oh, I got it, these are nice flowers," he says, trying to change the subject, but she gets him every time, she gets after him. Finally, he's so stuck, that he finally begins to respect her. And he's a saint, he's not a bad guy, it's just part of his culture; he's a little bit of a male chauvinist. This goddess appears and tells him all these weird things, and completely blows him out.

Finally, he says, "Goddess, you really have great wisdom! How come you are incarnated in the body of a woman?" She says, "What body of a woman? For all these years, innumerable aeons, I've been looking for my body of a woman, and my female escape (she uses this expression) and I haven't found it yet! My womanhood is empty of intrinsic womanhood," (meaning, she's staying on this ultimate level). She says, "Shariputra, would you ask someone who was a holographic projection, who was a magician's image, the emanation of a Buddha, how come you're incarnated in the body of a woman?" He said, "No, I wouldn't. Such a person would be an illusion, they wouldn't be real, I wouldn't ask them how come they incarnated as a woman; it would just be an illusory woman!" She said, "How come the Buddha said all beings are like illusory creations, that in the ultimate there is no male and female?" Shariputra again is struck dumb, silent.

Earlier he had tried to maintain a silence when she asked him how long he had been enlightened. It's like asking your teacher how long have you been enlightened? A week, a month, ten years?

So Shariputra himself was a little bit uptight on that, and he didn't say anything. The sage refrains from speech, very profound. But what did the goddess say? She said, "What's the matter, Shariputra, the cat got your tongue? I asked a simple question, you don't give me an answer? You're the foremost of the wise disciples; how come you can't answer my question?" "Oh, since enlightenment is beyond expression, I thought I'd better be silent," implying that he was enlightened, of course, because spiritual people like to imply that, they're fond of it. And she says, "Excuse me, Shariputra, do not point to enlightenment by maintaining silence; enlightenment is not to be found within or without, or between, and even so, words are neither within, without or in between. They have the very nature of enlightenment, words do. Do not try to point to enlightenment by maintaining silence."

That's why I told that story, I'm still trying to end here. But in between, I have to finish the other one. Then she says this to Shariputra, "There's no male or female," and he says, "Yes, I heard Buddha say it." Then you know what she did? Don't you wish you could do this, with some of your male interlocutors, all you dakinis? She then used her compassion power to transform Shariputra into her body. She transformed herself into Shariputra's body. Shariputra suddenly was a woman. She said, "Shariputra, how come you have incarnated yourself in the body of a woman?" He said, "I'm a woman, I didn't make myself like this; I did, but it's not real!" She said, "Just so, Shariputra, all women are like that, do not put presumptions on them that they are such and such." Then, before he got totally hysterical, she changed him back. Then the Buddha calmed him down, and said, "Never mind, Shariputra, this goddess has been in the retinue of ninety-two billion Buddhas, in different universes. She has unlimited abilities, unlimited insights. Don't exercise yourself." You can have a pretentious, fake, inaccurate silence. Someone can be in a certain context, or with a certain attitude. You can maintain a silence which is pure pretension, very sanctimonious and silent.

But in this setting, when Manjushri said, "Don't say anything, all of you made a big mistake," then he turned and said, "Vimalakirti, it's your turn to tell us of the Dharma door of non-duality. What is the nature of ultimate reality? Please, it's your turn now." And Vimalakirti was then silent. When he was so silent, eighty thousand living beings achieved the tolerance of the inconceivability of all things. All that were present were completely confirmed in their own entrance, never to be exited from, into the Dharma door of non-duality. Their relative existence was ultimate reality, without any dualism. Somehow, his silence accomplished that, and it is called, in the tradition, the lion's roar of the silence of Vimalakirti. That's a marvelous high point, and it gives me sort of a logical excuse to shut up. Thank you.

Thich Nhat Hahn is one of the most influential living Buddhist teachers today. A Vietnamese Zen teacher, he has endured much in his life and is a leading advocate of engaged Buddhism. He was nominated for the Nobel Peace Prize by Martin Luther King, Jr. This lecture, given in 1989, was a progress report on Buddhism taking root in the West. –M.W.

Watering the Seeds of Buddhism

Thich Nhat Hanh

FALL 1989

If we pick a flower, like a rose, and we leave it a little too long on the table, it will die. Even if it does not die yet, if we put it into a pot of water, it will not continue to bloom, it will feel tired, wilted. Because of what? Because the cells at the stem become dry, and when we put them into water, even when there is water in the pot, communication is no longer possible between the water and the flower. That is why the flower continues to be very weak, very sad.

The flower is still young, but it does not seem to be very alive. Therefore, when we see a flower like that, we have to rescue her. The way I rescue a rose is to take it out of the flower pot; I dip the flower under water; I take a pair of scissors or a knife, and I cut it in the water, because the water will come right away to the new cells where it will not be dry. After that, I put it in a flower pot with water. I'm sure that one hour later the flower will be young and fresh again.

Communication between the flower and the water is very crucial for the life of the flower. We know that. We human beings, we are exactly like flowers. Sometimes we bloom happily, very fresh; sometimes we are not so fresh. Even if we are still very young, we are still like that. So we must need someone to come and rescue us—but not exactly in the same way—we don't have to cut anything. But they should do their best so that communication with the water of life is possible for us again.

A flower would not be able to live happily without air and water. We, also, would not be able to live without love and understanding. Where do we get that love and understanding? From our family and from our society. If there is no love in our family and in our society, we will be exactly like the flower without a pot of water, without air—exactly the same. So, in order to rescue us, people in the family have to generate love and understanding— that is the only way.

People in the society have to generate love and understanding— otherwise, we will feel we are alone—we cannot go on. The practice of meditation is to find out ways to be in touch again, in order for communication to be possible again, and life to be possible again.

When the Buddha held a flower in his hands, he invited his friends and students to be in touch with the flower. The only way to be in touch with the flower is to be awake in the present moment, and to really see the flower.

This is not something very difficult to realize, but strangely enough, not many people think so. Look at the flower and breathe, and you can see the flower, you can be in touch with flower. But why are so many people unable to be in touch with the flower? Because they have so many things in their heads—their worries, their anger, their thoughts, and so many things that block them from being in touch with life. It is like the dry cells of a stem of a wilted flower here. They prevent the flower from being in touch with the water. Therefore, there must be a way to save them.

We have to remember that each of us is a flower, and we have to keep our flower blooming freshly and happily. Every time we feel there is something blocking, then we have to stop and breathe, to smile, to look and see what prevents us from being in touch with the wonderful life. We may do that with the help of grown-up people or with the help of younger people like us.

A rose can only be happy being a rose. If happiness is not there, it is all because communication is not there, and real contact is not there. In us, we find the seeds of everything—the seeds of awareness, of understanding, of love. Watering the seeds of Buddhahood, you water yourselves. You water the seeds in your self, and you water them in your environment. Where do I water the seeds of American Buddhism? I water them in my heart, I water them in my body, I water them in my family. Because all these seeds are there. I go back to Christianity and I water the seeds of Buddhism there, because you find the seeds of Buddhism in Christianity, and you find the seeds of Buddhism in Judaism, you find the seeds of Buddhism in the Native American culture. You don't have to go to another country to bring the seeds of Buddhism over. They are there. That is what we have tried to see yesterday.

Fall 1989

If you want to build American Buddhism, you have all the elements within your own culture, within your self, within your family structure, within your religious institutions. If you go back to Christianity and water the seeds of Buddhism there, you renew Christianity. If you go back to Judaism and water the seeds of Buddhism there, you renew Judaism. It becomes something new, fresh, young again, and that is for our sake. It is for the sake of the Buddhist, and it is for the sake of the non-Buddhist. But you know, between Buddhism and non-Buddhism, it is very hard to draw a line.

Sometimes we have to be careful of how we talk about Buddhism. Because Buddhism does not recognize branches. I remember that a Zen teacher in China, he did not like the way people dealt with Buddhism and the word "Buddhism." The way they talk about Buddha makes people hate the Buddha. And therefore one day he said, "Well, every time I pronounce the word 'Buddha,' I have to go to the bathroom and rinse out my mouth three times." This is the way to warn me, to warn you, to warn us that using the word "Buddha" and "Buddhism" will do harm to Buddha and Buddhism.

Another person, quite a friend of the former one, said, "Well, every time I hear you pronounce the word 'Buddha,' I have to go to the river and wash my ears three times." So be careful. The less you look like a Buddha the more you are truly a Buddhist.

We should be able to recognize Buddhist elements within Christianity, within Judaism, within the Native American culture, within our daily life. Without that, how can you water the seeds of American Buddhism? We have to recognize that first, in order to water. Everything that has the capacity to bring us to awareness; everything that can generate understanding, mutual acceptance and love, could be termed as seeds of Buddhism, even though Buddhist terms are not there. This is quite important. If you feel that you are a stranger to your family, a stranger to your culture, that is not because you are not born from that culture, that family, but because there are some cells that are dry and communication is no longer possible.

Sometimes you feel you want to reject your society, your family, and you want to have nothing to do with that institution, because you don't see the beauty in that institution, and you suffer very much from that feeling of being apart from your family and from your culture. But you also know that staying out of it, you never have the opportunity to regenerate it, to change it. Therefore, the only way is to go back and to be rooted again in that atmosphere, in that environment. Acceptance is to be within: this is the only way to change.

The practice of Buddhism is the practice of healing. The Buddha has been described many times as a physician, the King of Physicians. Therefore, the practice of awareness brings about more love and understanding which is healing.

But as I see it, in America, you should have at least two centers for healing. The first center is the family. The second center is the community practice place. Buddhism in America, as I see it, will be mostly lay Buddhism. Children, like the ones we have seen, can only grow in the context of a happy family. The practice of Buddhism should bring about harmony, understanding, happiness within the family. That is for the growth of our flowers, our children. Therefore, you have to go back to your family as an institution, to reorganize it so that you have a practicing center. That is the basic practice center for your society, because society is composed of individuals and families. If you do not practice in your family, you do not use family as a unit of your practice, you cannot reach out to society and change it. That is why, to me, go back to the family, build it in a Buddhist way into a practice center. Practice Buddhism with joy; that is possible.

In Plum Village, all the children go and sit with adults in the early morning, and they are happy to do so. Because they are not forced to do so. They join us. They are children like any other children. I asked one person in Rochester if their two children could sit with us. She said, "I'm afraid not." "How long can they sit?" Their mother said, "Maybe four seconds!"

I said I would try. I invited the children to come and sit with us and I told them, "Sit here with us and enjoy your sitting. You can sit as long as you want. One minute. Two minutes. Three minutes! And every time it becomes boring, you just bow, stand up, and slowly walk out of the meditation hall." And that day, the children sat for eleven minutes! Their mother never believed it. So we have to organize our practice in a way that is joyful and pleasant for our children.

There are two kinds of practice. First is the practice to prevent. To prevent suffering, to prevent disease, to prevent unhappiness, to prevent destruction. That is the best practice. You do not need to have to have malaise in order to begin practice. In a family, we practice that. We practice happiness. We practice nourishing happiness.

I would like to share with you some of the things Vietnamese Buddhist families practice in order to maintain happiness. Because we believe that without happiness between the members of the family, nothing is possible, including a peaceful society, including peace for the future. And therefore, the family is the basic community of practice. We call it family Sangha. Sangha is a community. Family is a community. There should be harmony, there must be principles of living in harmony. In America, I believe that you will go back and build up that center of practice everywhere, with or without a teacher.

I suggest you create a practice center which is not a temple, which is not a church, but which is a center where you come to

Arnold Kotler, Richard Baker, Thich Nhat Hanh, and children at Tassajara.

celebrate life, to be happy, and to practice healing in case we need it. We do not wait until we are very sick in order to come to the center. That would make the center a kind of mental hospital. Nobody prevents us from setting up a hospital like that in order to help people who are heavily afflicted. But we should have a center where people have joy and happiness. When they come, they practice in order to prevent the kind of destruction that can happen to their lives.

Without monks and nuns, such a center could also be operated. These are two dharma doors that I would like to propose today. Those who help us in running such a center should be happy people. We need skill, but we need happiness much more than skill! A person that is not happy cannot help us. That is very plain and simple. People are either monks, or nuns, or lay persons. If they are happy, if they live a happy life, they are qualified to help us.

This is the only qualification for us. Who transmitted that qualification? Good practice can convey to a person the capacity of sharing that happiness with other people. That kind of transmission I think is obvious. We do not need a ceremony. We do not need a certificate. We only need the awareness that such a person can be a brother to me, can be a sister to me, and can help me in the practice. Whether you call that a friend or a teacher would not make a lot of difference.

I think that the teaching of love in Buddhism is important to learn. Because love, in the context of the Buddhist teaching, has another sense from love that we understand in other contexts. We know that love in the context of Buddhism is impossible without understanding. If you do not understand a person, you cannot love him or her. Where understanding is, love is. Love is another name for understanding. Understanding is the fruit of meditation. Stop, look, and you understand. When you understand, you cannot help but love. This is the way.

For the guidance of the establishment of these two kinds of centers of practice—family center and community center—we should learn and teach the art of loving and understanding. In Buddhism, of course, both are linked to meditation in the easy, simple definition. Meditation is to stop and look, in order to see. Out of that comes understanding, acceptance and love.

I would like to tell you the story of what happened to the Buddha when he was thirty-nine years old.

One day there was a young person who lived with his son of six or seven years old. His son had died because of disease, so he suffered very much; he had almost lost his mind. He wandered around the capital, and he called for his son, "My son, where are you? Come back to me!" He spent many days like that, calling the name of his son. Someone saw that, so he brought the unhappy father to the Jeta Monastery, in order to see the Buddha.

The Buddha was staying in a thatched hut and he went out to meet the unhappy man. He asked, "Why? Why are you so unhappy? Please tell me."

The man said, "I just lost my son, and I suffer so much."

The Buddha commented, "I know love involves worries and despair..." He made that statement. But upon that statement, the man got very angry. He stood up and he shouted at the monk Gautama, "No, you are wrong! Love never creates worry and despair! Love can only bring us happiness!" So he left the Buddha in anger. He did not allow the monk Gautama to explain further.

After the king heard about this, he went to see the Buddha. The king said, "It seems that Your Reverence said that love involves suffering and despair and worries." The Buddha said, "Yes, I did say so, but I had not finished my explanation when the man left me in anger. So if Your Majesty would like to hear more about it, I would be glad to tell you."

The king said, "To me, love is very important. Life without love is not worth living. The world would be very sterile without love. Why do you advocate that we not love?"

The Buddha said, "I don't advocate not loving. I only advocate the true kind of love. Because the true kind of love can make people happy. I agree with Your Majesty that love can make life beautiful and happy. But I would like to insist it must be true love. The kind of love that has as its nature the desire to possess, the desire to forbid, the desire to monopolize, the desire to satisfy one's own ambition, that kind of love I would not call love, because it will bring a lot of worries, despair and suffering." Then the Buddha told the king about the way to love. He talked about *maitri* and *karuna*.

"Maitri is loving kindness. Maitri is the willingness to make one person happy without any condition whatsoever. Without asking anything in return. I love him. Not because he is my countryman; I love him because he is a human being. I love him not because he is of the same religious belief. If I love him because he is of the same religious belief, I don't really love him. I love my religious belief. So maitri is the kind of love that has no condition whatsoever. You do not need to get something in return. You just want that person to be happy.

"In order for the person to be happy, you have to understand him or her, because a person has pains, has sufferings, has hope, has aspirations. If you do not understand the pain, anxiety, aspiration, hope of that person, it will be impossible for you to love that person. Therefore, understanding is the basis of any kind of love that can make the person happy.

"Karuna may be translated by compassion. Maybe there is a better word. Karuna is the willingness to remove a person's pain. In a person, there is a source of pain. You see that and you would like to take it out of that person, again, without any condition. Without asking for return. If you do not know exactly the nature of that pain, you cannot help to remove it. Again, understanding is the base for that kind of love.

"Compassion means to suffer with. When you see someone suffer, you sit beside him or her and you suffer together. That relieves a little bit of his or her pain. But karuna is more than that. Karuna is the kind of practice that removes the suffering from the person. And you don't necessarily have to suffer. Because you have wisdom, you have understanding, you have energy, and you are capable of helping the person remove her suffering. And if you yourself suffer so much, how can you help? What energy is left for you to do the work? Therefore, maitri and karuna should come from a very strong source of understanding and love and energy.

"So, King, you have a princess and a prince. You said you have to love your prince and princess first. I agree. As a parent, you should love your children. But do you understand the anxiety, the aspiration, the suffering of Prince Jeta? If you don't, how can you say that you can love him properly? The same thing is true of Princess Varjari. If you are not able to understand what is in her heart, what her true aspiration is, what her own problem is, then you cannot love her.

"If you are capable of loving the Prince and Princess, you will be capable of loving all the young men and young women in your country. Because the young men and young women of your country, they do have their problems, their sufferings, their aspirations, and their needs. If you can love them the way that you love your Prince and your Princess, then suddenly you have countless daughters and sons. Love now does not know any limit. Love does not know any frontier. This is possible.

"As the king, you have the duty of loving all the young men in your country as your son. If you do not practice maitri and karuna, how can you do that? You would be hesitating to send your son into the battlefield, you would feel the same with all the young men in your country." The conversation went on, but I would not like to continue because it is a little too long. I would like to say here, that after that conversation, King Prasanjit became a very close friend of the Buddha.

So it is not easy to make the statement, "I love you." That statement is difficult to make. Maybe "I have the willingness to love you" is truer. I want to love you. But am I really capable of loving you? That is quite another problem. So, as a wife, I would practice like that. I would select a moment when I could be alone with my husband in a quiet place. I would practice breathing for some time. Then I would hold his hand in mind and ask, "Dear one, do you think I love you properly? Does my love suffocate you? Do I make you unhappy because of my love? Please tell me so that I can learn the art of loving. I know that I am not perfect. Because of loving you, I might deprive you of your liberty. I might kill the deepest of your aspirations. That is not what I want to do, but because I want to know with all my heart, please tell me. Do I love you properly? What can I do in order for my love to be only nourishing and not destroying?" If I am aware and I am capable of asking such a question, then the door of happiness will be open. If I ask with all my heart.

And if I am a husband, I would do the same. "My dear one, maybe my love is only a prison for you. I want to monopolize you. I want you to be the way I want, and I don't let you bloom freely like a flower. So please tell me so that my love will not feel like a prison any longer, so my love will be something nourishing." That is very important.

If you love a breeze, a gentle breeze in the summer (and who does not love a gentle breeze in the summer?) and if, at the same time, you want to possess, to monopolize, then you would like to imprison the gentle breeze all for yourself. You put the gentle breeze into a steel can, hermetically sealed, just for yourself. A cloud is beautiful floating in the blue sky. Who doesn't love such a cloud? But if you want to possess, to monopolize, you put the cloud in your steel can, hermetically sealed, and then the cloud will die, like the gentle breeze.

A person is like that. If we imprison him or her, in our prison of love, we kill him or her. That is not the way of loving. That does not come from understanding. So most of the suffering comes from the fact that we want to monopolize, we want to dictate the behavior to the ones we love. Maybe we have done exactly what

Trees reflected in Tassajara swimming pool.

other people have done, put our love into a steel can, hermetically sealed.

How can happiness exist in the family for the children to grow? Loving a child is the same. We should be able to ask a child whether our love is suffocating to him or to her. Because the child is the object of our love, we want the child to be happy. We want to remove the suffering, the pain, of the child. Therefore, understanding is indispensable. So we should also be capable of holding the hand of our child and asking the questions. Do not think that since we are a grown-up person, we can decide the best way to love. Look to see whether the child is happy within his skin. To see whether the child is blooming like a flower. There we need understanding.

If we can practice loving like that in the context of our family, the family becomes the basic center of practice. With families like that, we can change the society. The community center is where we come, several families, to contact a day of mindfulness, a day of happy family living together. To get in contact with other friends who are practicing this same kind of love, of understanding. For the children to meet each other to play and to learn the way of happiness. I think both kinds of centers are crucial for our practice. The family Sangha and the greater community center.

Of course, you can visualize such a center. It is not exactly a place for worship. It is a place to celebrate life. It should be possible for you to practice walking meditation, to enjoy each step. It should be a place where you can sit and enjoy sitting and breathing. There should be a park where children can practice jumping and playing. The forms of practice you will see as you go on, as the path of your understanding and love. I think these things are not difficult. Why don't we write a song for the children: "Flowers need water and air, I need love. I need understanding." The children can sing it, the adults can sing it. Because all of us need love, not just children. But the true kind of love: maitri and karuna.

Robert Buswell practiced Theravada Buddhism in Thailand, Zen in Korea, and Hua Yen Buddhism in Taiwan—three different Buddhist traditions in three different cultures and languages. He then studied at UC Berkeley in order to understand their relationship to each other. This lecture on Buddhist path systems shows a way to see the connections between all the different schools of Buddhism. –M.W.

The 100-Foot Pole and Buddhist Path Systems

Robert Buswell

SPRING 1990

I want to explore the *Marga* or path systems of Buddhism and how I think its different versions work together. But I thought what I might do first is give you a sense of why these issues are important to me personally, and why I became interested in studying these sorts of problems in Buddhism. Though I consider myself primarily a scholar of Zen Buddhism, I am especially interested in how Zen resonates with the rest of the Buddhist tradition. I first began studying Buddhism when I was a teenager. I remember I had from my own interest in philosophy at the time this very strong question: how you can live without exploiting other people? At the time when I was growing up, this was a very real problem that I really had no way of knowing how to resolve. As I began to read more and more Western philosophy, there seemed to be lots of answers, but there really wasn't any method or system by which one could come to realize those answers. I became progressively frustrated with philosophy, scholarship, and that kind of thing.

One day, by chance, I happened to come across a book by a teacher named Nyanaponika, a German Theravada monk, who wrote a book called the *Heart of Buddhist Meditation*, which was a real revelation to me. I remember I sat in my room and ravenously devoured this book. It really seemed to provide an answer; not only an answer, but a means to realize the answer of what to do in order to learn to live without exploiting other people. At that point, I began to read everything I could about Buddhism, all of which finally led me to believe that the Theravada system offered a method, an approach, or a regimen one could follow in order to realize enlightenment. After studying everything that I could about Theravada Buddhism when I was in college, and there really wasn't much at that time, I finally decided that I needed to go to Asia and see what Theravada monks actually did.

I arrived as a nineteen-year-old kid in Thailand, with one contact, ready to become a monk. Of course I was very quickly disillusioned. The first question I was asked by a Thai monk, when I was ordained in Thailand, was when I planned to disrobe. This is really a common question in Thailand, because monks are very rarely ordained for more than a few months at a time, so this is the first thing they always ask, but to me it was almost sacrilege to think that you would become a monk with the intention of immediately disrobing. Finally, I ended up with a teacher named Maha Boowa, who was a Theravada teacher who lived up in the forest around the Laotian border. He is one of the teachers featured in Jack Kornfield's book, *Living Buddhist Masters.*

It seemed to me that this teacher was almost diametrically opposed to all of my presuppositions about what Theravada practice actually involved. I had arrived after reading Nyanaponika's *Heart of Buddhist Meditation,* which has a very strong slant towards the Burmese Vipassana style of practice. There's a very methodical regimen that one follows in doing Vipassana practice: you watch your steps, you watch the lifting, touching, placing of your foot; you watch your postures, you feel the sensations, the pillow against your seat, your knees against the floor as you're sitting. In the system, if you follow the directions, you should be able to come out at the other end enlightened. I thought this shouldn't be too hard: all I have to do is just follow the directions, and a year, a year and half, two years later, I should be pretty well done with this. I arrived up in the forest to meet this teacher and expected him to give me his method. I was going to come in, and he was going to tell me you do this this day, next day this and next day you do this, and pretty soon we'll have you out of here. So, I arrived there and the first week he wouldn't even talk to me. After a week there he sort of noticed there was a new guy around, and he finally consented to talk with me.

The first question of course I asked him was: "Please tell me your method and what I should do in order to achieve enlightenment." His response to me was very telling, and it proved to be very influential in my own development as I began to look at other traditions of Buddhism later on. His answer was, "I cannot tell you how you can become enlightened. I know what I did for myself, but I can't tell you what is going to work for you. Each of us is different. Each of us is unique, each of us has his or her own predilections, backgrounds, interests and propensities, and all these things can only be understood by you personally. So all I can tell you to do is to watch yourself, to watch your own life, try different things out and see what works for you. What works, keep doing, what doesn't work, discard and go on to something else." So here I was, expecting to get some method and I was told basically the only method is no method, which was not terribly helpful at the time when I was still quite young and immature.

Eventually, after a few months there, I had to go to Bangkok for visa reasons and I spent several months there. One day I was trying to figure out how you simply watch your mind, having no method as to the approach you're taking, and still gain something from it. I was sitting there thinking about all of this and suddenly outside my window there was this snarling pack of dogs. In Bangkok and in Thailand the people have this belief that you should not kill animals, and being the good Buddhists that they are, what they do is take all their stray dogs and bring them to the monasteries. So you end up with these dog packs all going after the leftover food from the monks. If you ever want to have a vivid example of what hell must be like, I would recommend going to one of these large Bangkok monasteries because, however idyllic it may be for the monks inside their rooms in these monasteries, it is very definitely not idyllic outside. You have packs of dogs, twenty, thirty in a group, constantly battling with one another, all torn up, skin ripped off, legs broken, and hopping around on three legs. I remember wondering, "What am I doing here in Thailand?" And this is not at all to denigrate the Thai people—I have a very strong respect for Thai Buddhism as a tradition—but one has to realize that tradition always goes hand in hand with culture and society.

I decided, at that point, that it behooved me to get out of Thailand and go somewhere else. So I tried a contact in Hong Kong and ended up going to a very small hermitage place called Landau Island, a small island out of Hong Kong sound, where I spent a year with a Chinese monk and a French monk who also spoke some Chinese. This was almost the exact opposite of the large Thai monasteries with a lot of monks and lots of activity, both good and bad, occurring in the temples. It was a very quiet, calm, secluded place, much more in tune with what I thought Buddhist monastic life should be like.

Wind Bell

PUBLICATION OF ZEN CENTER
VOLUME XXXIV, NUMBER ONE, SPRING 1990

Spring 1990

The Chinese monk I was with had his own schedule. He usually sat in meditation for about ten to twelve hours a day for several days, and sometimes weeks at a time, and when he got bored with that he put out his woodblock edition of the Flower Garland Sutra, the *Avatamsaka Sutra,* which is the biggest text in Buddhism, and stacked the folios up on his meditation seat, and started chanting through the whole text from page one to page four thousand. He would spend a week doing that, then he would go back to his meditation, going back and forth between his reading and his practicing. I spent most of my time there reading. Actually I was studying Chinese on my own. I would prepare a Chinese Buddhist text and the teacher would sit with me every morning for two to three hours and we would read through the Chinese text. This was really good for my scholarship, but, after a year of this, I felt I really had to have a Sangha again. A Korean monk whom I had met in Thailand said, "Why don't you come to Korea?" There were, at that time, no books at all on the Korean tradition of Buddhism, and there were no travel books about Korea. So I had no sense at all of what I was getting into. But, what the hell, I would try it out see what happens! So I arrived in Korea unable to speak one word of Korean and not knowing at all what their Korean tradition of Buddhism was.

I ended up at the temple called Songgwang-Sa, with a teacher named Kusan. I was lucky to spend five years at Songgwang-Sa. For the first several weeks there I communicated in classical Chinese, I could write Chinese and the Korean could write Chinese, and we could communicate back and forth by writing. Very slowly I managed to acquire some of the language. I began to be able to listen to the master's instructions, and I learned that the temple was predominantly of the Zen tradition. At that point I had read nothing at all about Zen. I had managed to avoid reading Alan Watts and D.T. Suzuki; somehow I never came across them when I was doing my initial explorations of what Buddhism was all about. I still had this sense that Buddhism was somehow a methodical system of practice: do this, and this is what happens. It is very much the way Theravada can be portrayed. I don't think that's what it is, but that is certainly the way I was still attached to.

At any rate, after three months in Korea, I began my first Zen retreat. In Korea the retreats are usually for three-month periods at a time: three months in the winter, three months in the summer, and a three-month off-season in the fall and spring. I entered my first three-month retreat barely able to speak Korean, with no knowledge at all about Zen, knowing nothing at all about what my teacher was saying to me, or what I was supposed to be doing while I was in this three-month retreat. So I struggled for the whole period trying to figure out exactly what I was supposed to be doing. We were studying a koan, "Chao-chou's 'Mu,'" the "No" Koan, one of the most famous ones in the collections, and he asked me what Chao-chou meant and what his mind was like the moment just before he said this answer: "no" ("mu"). I ended up going back to the meditation hall many times and trying to figure out why I should care what Chao-chou's mind was like. So that become my koan. After three months, I was very much impressed with the sincerity and the practice of the Korean monks. They're very diligent, very energetic and very enthusiastic practitioners in Korea. The Korean monks practice twelve hours a day for three months. But I really didn't have any sense at all about what I was doing or why I was doing it. In order to survive in Korea, it was very clear to me that I had to figure out what the koan technique was about, and, in more general terms, what Zen was about, and how Zen could possibly portray itself as a Buddhist tradition.

This is finally how we get down to the question of the continuity of Zen with the rest of Buddhism. I began to read as much as I could in Korean Buddhist works out of the Zen tradition, I began to discover what I thought were some rather compelling things. Here I would like to return to a scholarly perspective after bringing your attention to the point of how this question appeared to me. In order to do this, I will give you a metaphor that is commonly used in Zen materials, and very often in Dogen's work: "to step off the 100-foot pole."

The final transition from the conditioned world of birth and death to the unconditioned realm of Nirvana takes place when you finally have the courage to let go of all your old attachments to your body, your mind, your society and your tradition. You let go of all of that in that final leap off the 100-foot pole. The first thing you have to do, of course, is to find out where the pole is. If you want to find where this 100-foot pole is, it might be very helpful to have some sort of a road map, telling you where this pole is located. You figure out which way the map should be oriented, and you finally start following along the road. If you follow the map accurately, you get to a point in the road where, off in the distance, you can see this 100-foot pole, and you realize for the first time that this pole really does exist and that it wasn't just a myth. At that point, the map is no longer necessary. You know where the pole is, you can see it directly in front of you, and you reach the pole. Well, a 100-foot pole is pretty high-I don't know if I could get up a 100-foot pole or not-but supposing you can climb it, and after you finally get to the top, and the view is so great, you just hold on and look around and, my God, it's just marvelous!

Unfortunately, as you are holding on to this pole, your grip starts weakening and you start sliding back down the pole until you're down at the bottom again and you realize, well, maybe that's not the way to go either. So, finally, after reaching the pole, climbing it, and getting to the very top, rather than holding on, and looking around, and enjoying the view, and revelling in your achievement, at that point, finally, you are able, just for the Marga, to let go and take that final leap off. Then you're enlightened. This would be the model for the Marga that we would set up here: looking for the pole, finding the pole, climbing the pole, and jumping off the pole.

Going back to the Marga, or path schemes: looking for the pole would be like the initial stage of cultivation *(laukika bhavana marga)* when you're following various road maps that Buddhism offers, such as through Morality, Concentration and Wisdom. By following these different techniques, you may finally find out where the pole is located. By following the map carefully, you can see the pole off in the distance, and seeing the pole out there is your *darsana marga* (path of vision). Through this vision you realize that that pole really does exist, you see where it is, you finally realize that I know I can make it now, I see it myself, I don't have to rely on this road map any longer. After reaching the pole you start climbing up, and this would be like your transcendental cultivation stage, *lokottarabhavana-marga,* that comes after your vision. You not only get to the pole, but you have to climb it now. But, if the person is not able to take that one final step, to generate that final total detachment to the whole experience of Buddhism itself, the person is eventually going to backslide and slide back down the pole again.

Finally, what Buddhism is saying to you is, well, we've given you these directions, we've helped you to get to the pole, we've assisted you to climb the pole, but, in order to take this last leap and realize Nirvana, what you're going to have to do is to let go of all these past directions. In other words, you have to let go even of Buddhism itself, in order to make this transition into the unconditioned. So this leaping off and letting go of the pole would be like final realization, the last stage of awakening, called *nistha marga.*

There's a very famous Sutra in the *Majjhima Nikaya,* called the "Simile of the Snake." It is a very interesting Theravada text in which Buddha talks about the Dharma, the teachings of his religion, as being very dangerous, like a poisonous snake. You may go out looking for a snake, you find the snake, and go to grab it, but rather than grabbing the snake by the head where you have control of this snake's power and his poison, you make the mistake of grabbing it by the tail. Instead of serving you, the snake rears around and bites you on the hand. This is the analogy that Buddha uses for the Dharma. The Dharma has a certain utility as long as it is used correctly, as long as its purpose is one's own personal development, not as a way of lambasting rival sects, or getting into debates, or proving that Buddhism is better than Christianity or Judaism, or showing that Zen is better than Theravada, or any of the other sectarian battles that go on. As long as Dharma is used simply for the purpose of achieving enlightenment, you're using it correctly and you have control over its power.

Robert Buswell.

What Buddhism is saying is that, to truly realize this perfect detachment from both one's body and one's mind, one has to let go of all sense of identity, including the identity that one has as being a Buddhist. One has to follow the path leading to this state of realization. As long as you have any grasping, you might have a very advanced spiritual achievement, yet it still won't be enough to realize Nirvana, to take that last step off the pole. This is the final challenge that Buddhism is making to us: do we have enough courage to let go of this pole?

In another simile that appears in this Sutra, the Buddha talks about this massive stream you have to get across. There's no possible way you can swim across, but as you walk along the bank you find twigs, branches, a little bit of twine here and there, and you manage to lash them together into a makeshift raft. By paddling furiously on top of this raft you're able to get across this creek. He says that of course after you've gone across the stream you wouldn't pick up this raft and put it on your head and carry it off. You would leave it there and go on with your journey at that point. The raft has served its purpose, just leave it behind and go on. Well the Dharma, the Buddha says then, is very much like this makeshift raft which he's fashioned to get you across this stream of birth and death. It is a technique which even though very makeshift, does work, if you paddle furiously. But in order to make use of this accomplishment, or to be able to go on from there, you have to let go of the teachings of Buddhism at that point, to truly realize the ultimate. Buddhism is the only religion that I know of that you have to abandon to truly understand it.

Now we have this metaphor of looking for the pole, seeing the pole, climbing the pole, and jumping off the pole as our four stages of the path. If you were to look at Theravada, for example, I think what Theravada is doing is taking a very expansive vision of what this path encompasses. Theravada tells us it's fine to say you have to take that final leap off that 100-foot pole, but if people don't even know the pole exists, what good does it do them to tell them to take this final leap off? What is more important is to give them some sort of a guideline, a map, so they can find out where that pole is.

What Theravada does is kind of step back and appeal, in a sense, to the lowest common denominator of people, most of us probably, people who really don't have a clue as to where they're going or what they're doing with their lives. So they give you all kinds of techniques and guidelines that you can follow, and, hopefully, by following them correctly and diligently, you will be able to see off in the distance the 100-foot pole that you're going to have to climb. It is the most expansive path in the Buddhist scriptures. People have to get started somewhere, and if that means you have to hit them with morality, hit them with concentration, well, we'll do that, to get them started. Hopefully they will be able to follow the directions precisely and eventually be able to find the pole and climb it themselves and let go of the whole thing.

Other traditions, for example the Chinese Flower Garland tradition, tend to have a different view. They say, well it's fine to give people these maps of the path, but these maps have nothing whatsoever to do with seeing that pole off in the distance. In other words you can give somebody a map, but if they turn it upside down, or have it crooked, they will not be able to follow the guidelines on that map at all, so the map really is useless. What is important is not the map of the pole, but seeing that pole in the distance. The Flower Garland (Hua-yen) school starts off by saying that Buddhism begins with an initial sudden awakening. It's like seeing the pole off in the distance: you know it's there and, after seeing it, you then go on to cultivate that initial insight until finally it's integrated into your life and you achieve realization/awakening.

In Hua-yen, you have moved from the beginning of Buddhism one step farther up the path. They've jettisoned the initial path of cultivation and said Buddhism really starts at the path of the insight, the *darsana marga* stage of seeing the pole. So in a sense what they're saying is that Buddhism is following an approach of an initial sudden awakening, or seeing the pole, followed by gradual cultivation, or walking to the pole, climbing and letting go of the pole. Whereas, Theravada is really following a regimen of gradual cultivation followed by awakening. They're getting this map, gradually following the guidelines of the map, and eventually seeing the pole out there.

Now other traditions of Buddhism may be a little different. Let's take, for example, the Rinzai school of Zen. They say that maps don't do any good, seeing the pole doesn't do any good, in fact even climbing the pole doesn't do you any good because who knows if you will finally have the courage to let go of it. The only thing that counts is letting go, letting go of that 100-foot pole, because until then you don't really know what Buddhism is all about. What they're doing is jettisoning not only the initial path of the cultivation, but also the path of the insight, and the subsequent path of the cultivation that follows the insight. They're saying that all that counts is that last stage of realization/awakening. What is Rinzai? Well, this would be a sudden awakening, sudden cultivation system. Cultivation and awakening are simultaneous as soon as you let go of the pole. So cultivation and awakening go hand in hand; there is no division between them.

I think that this vision of Zen practice is what has led Zen to claim that they are somehow special, that they are separate from the rest of Buddhism, because they're not concerned with all these initial guidelines and maps. All they care about is the final moment of realization, letting go and truly realizing for oneself the truth of the reality of Nirvana. But I think if we keep this metaphor of the pole in mind, maybe we can begin to see that Zen is really not so much different from the rest of Buddhism, but, rather, is simply targeting a different stage that is more conclusive instead of talking about the guidelines that help you get to this moment of final insight. It is focusing just on the very last moment of the Marga.

But if one has not already gone through these preliminary stages to reach that moment of insight, how much chance is there going to be that the person is going to have the courage to let go of the pole? In other words, unless you've already been guided to find the pole, to climb the pole, and do all the preliminaries to that, how are you going to have the ability to actually let go of this pole and make that final jump? I think that if you look at much Zen writing, especially in the Rinzai tradition, you'll find that they are targeting what they believe to be a very small number of people who no longer require these guidelines to practice provided by the rest of the Buddhist schools. Rather what they're saying is that what they do is to help those who are already at the top of this pole to find some way to gain the courage to let go and jump off. So they are, in a sense, jettisoning all the rest of Buddhism, because they are focusing on that last moment of insight. Theravada, on the other hand, is focusing on the masses of people who are more disturbed by how they are leading their everyday life, rather than concerned with taking this final leap off the pole.

As I read more on Zen, I have the sense that Zen is not so much a separate tradition of Buddhism as it is a tradition of Buddhism that is targeting the very final moment of the path, while other traditions of Buddhism have focused on earlier stages along that path. In my view, there is a strong continuity between Zen and the rest of Buddhism. In fact I believe there is really one comprehensive Buddhist Marga into which all the different systems of Buddhism can be incorporated. When we have this wider vision of what this Marga is, I think that many of the controversies that crop up in Buddhism become irrelevant. I think this is especially important because we in the West are faced with very serious challenges, because, in the process of learning about Buddhism, we have received not just one system of Buddhism but a multitude of systems. We have the challenge that the Chinese had very early on of how to reconcile all these different traditions, all of which claim to be Buddhist, but which in fact may present diametrically opposed visions of what Buddhism involves, not only in its thought, but also in its practice. Our challenge is, from my point of view, to develop a more comprehensive way of looking at Buddhist issues, a way that will allow us to see the value in all the different traditions, a way in which all the different traditions can be seen to be harmoniously working toward their final goal: realization of enlightenment. Thank you very much for your attention.

Rita Gross, author of Buddhism After Patriarchy, *is a Tibetan Buddhist, feminist, and sociologist. Meditators often ask about strong emotions such as anger. This article is an exploration on how to relate to this difficult emotion.* –M.W.

Meditating with Anger

Rita Gross

CITY CENTER, 22 JULY 1998

SPRING 1999

I thought that this would be a good occasion to talk about what I have experienced and learned about anger through practice.

I want to begin by telling a story of an event that took place a year-and-a-half ago with one of my teachers, Khandro Rinpoche. She is one of the few women rinpoches in the world of Tibetan Buddhism, and I have been very much magnetized by her presence and her teachings. She was giving a set of teachings, and a woman asked her: "What should we do with anger? How should we deal with anger?" And her reply was very sharp and very cutting: "Anger is always a waste of time." And the woman was sitting not too far from me. I could feel her energy, her kind of frustration and puzzlement and disappointment at that answer. She said, "But"—you know there's always a "but" with anger—"what about things that are wrong? What about things that deserve anger?" And Khandro Rinpoche replied, again very sharply, "I didn't tell you to lose your critical intelligence." And that's the frame in which I want to discuss anger, because that actually has been my experience through practice with anger. "It's always a waste of time. I didn't tell you to lose your critical intelligence, to get rid of your critical intelligence."

As many of you know, I've done a lot of work, a lot of contemplation, about women and the dharma. I was a feminist before I became involved in practice. I was pretty angry when I began to sit. And I did not begin to sit because I wanted to find a way to work with my anger. In fact, I think if someone had told me that it might not be so easy to keep my head of steam going I might not have been quite so interested in sitting. I had a really good head of steam going, and I felt quite okay about it. I think that's often the case with people who are involved in some justice issue. We feel that anger is a motivator to keep us going. If we didn't have anger to keep ourselves involved in a particular issue, what would we have? What would keep us going? A lot of us, in the early '70s, felt that anger was a much better alternative than what we had lived with before. I still agree with that. As someone who was socialized in the '50s, I actually went through a long period of self-hatred before I came to anger and anger is probably better than self-hatred. The kinds of things I wanted to do with my life didn't fit into the female gender role. My first solution to this problem was just to turn it in on myself. And I spent years basically cursing the fact that I had been born female. One day, I had an insight that it really wasn't me that was the problem, it was the system I was living in. That was a tremendous relief to feel that: "It's not me, there's nothing wrong with being female." But that didn't solve the anger problem. It turned outward. So I became very good at cutting rhetoric and white-hot outbursts of rhetorical fury. Of course I was always trying to control that too, because it's not politic and it's not polite. Needless to say, I wasn't doing too well even though I felt pretty okay with being angry and felt it was quite justifiable under the circumstances. I think that's probably about the position of the woman who said, "But, what about things that we should be angry about?" With that kind of head of steam I somehow became involved in sitting practice. That's pretty unusual for academics to do, especially academics who are in the study of religion and the study of Buddhism, but it happened. I found myself, for quite a while, in a kind of wasteland, a kind of no-man's-land situation. When I first got involved with Buddhism, I already had a pretty good reputation as a feminist theologian or a feminist scholar of religion. And all of my friends in academia, especially my feminist friends, thought I had lost my mind. It was like, "What has happened to Rita? Rita's sold out." It was understandable to them that you could inherit a male-dominated religion and try to work with it. Some of them were making that choice, but that you would convert to a male-dominated religion? I had to be out of my mind, according to them. I think you're aware that Buddhism still looks pretty male-dominated to much of the outside world, and I don't think that reputation is totally undeserved.

My Buddhist friends, meanwhile, were saying to me, "Oh Rita, that's okay. When you grow up, when you get to be a real Buddhist, then you won't care about this feminism shtick anymore. You won't have any attachments." They said that when I got to be a real Buddhist I would be detached and not care about justice issues.

I think that for some reason feminism among justice issues gets trivialized and becomes the object of hostility a lot more easily than many other justice issues. And I don't want to try to explore that tonight, but I think that's the case. So they had a particu-

Rita Gross.

larly live one on their hands—a Buddhist feminist, an oxymoron.

I was pretty much alone. I live in Eau Claire, Wisconsin, which is not exactly a hotbed of Buddhism. I have very strong ties with Vajradhatu, and I do a lot of programs in Boulder, Colorado, and in other places, but that still means that, day by day, my practice is by myself. And in some ways I'm very glad for that because I haven't had too many people always trying to yank me and jerk me; you know, do this and do that, develop this way. So in some ways it was good.

What happened to me was actually very scary. After a while of practicing really intently, I realized that I just couldn't work up that head of steam. It just wasn't there. It wasn't very satisfying. I started to get really scared: "What's happening to me? Maybe my Buddhist friends were right. Maybe I'm not going to have this thing in my life anymore." Clearly what was happening was that I had made a pretty good ego out of anger. As that started to dissolve, I got scared.

Simultaneously, I noticed that people were listening to me better. When I talked to people, instead of putting up a wall and going the other way, people were listening to me. And that's where it's at—that as the emotionalism, as the cloudy murky rage starts to subside, the intelligence can come through, and people can actually hear what we're saying. That's what Khandro Rinpoche was talking about when she said, "Anger is a waste of time. Don't lose your critical intelligence." Very powerful, very provocative.

As I was experiencing that, I was starting to be able to distinguish between pain, which is the pain of the human existence, which isn't anyone's fault, and the kinds of things that we do to each other through passion, hatred, and delusion. I was starting to see something that I think is really important for those of us who are trying to do our Bodhisattva work in an engaged way in social justice issues: that there's always going to be basic human suffering. That's not the fault of any particular thing wrong with the way the world is put together, period.

I think it's very helpful to know that and to be able to find one's way into accommodating the basic pain and having some distinction between basic pain and the things that are the result of passion, aggression, and ignorance.

So what was happening with practice—and I didn't realize this until much later—was like a test tube that has a number of ingredients in it and it's all shook up. You shake the tube, and nothing is clear, nothing is settled. And then with practice, that situation settles and stills, and the emotionalism subsides, and it leaves some intelligence, some clarity. In the Tibetan Vajrayana tradition, anger is connected with the Vajra family. The Vajra family is in the eastern gate of the mandala and is connected with the element water. This is very telling because water, when it is turbulent, is murky, and you can't see anything. But when water settles, it becomes an absolutely clear, perfectly reflecting mirror surface. When anger transmutes, it transmutes into clarity. The energy of anger becomes mirror-like wisdom. Same energy, different application. So this means, among many other things, that it's not so much that we need to throw away our anger as that we need to distill it: to settle the emotionalism, that cloudy, heavy, painful feeling. You feel this energy in your body that hurts, and you know you can't say anything sensible while you feel that way. And yet, that's when people really are tempted to sound off. To go back to Khandro Rinpoche's statement, she said, "Anger is always a waste of time." And that's absolutely true in my experience. I think what began to happen to me, when I could no longer get up a head of steam, was that I was beginning to see: "Who is this helping?" Who it was helping was me, myself, and I. The pain was so great, an outburst of anger would give momentary relief. But it didn't do anything. It did not pacify the situation. It did not make people more understanding of the predicament I felt. It did not make people more willing to take a feminist critique of society or Buddhism or whatever very seriously. It's hard to take angry people seriously, partly because of what they bring up in us, partly because of the defensiveness we feel when somebody is lashing out.

So I think that's very important: to somehow begin to see the absolute total counter-productivity of these tumultuous *klesha*—driven outbursts of anger—that they're not helping anything. They're not good skillful means. Is there an alternative?

I think one of the problems we face in our culture is that everything is always couched in either/or terms—either we stand up for ourselves or we're going to get rolled over. Certainly I think that's the logic that fuels a lot of our reactions. I certainly felt that way: that if I didn't put up this good front, I was just going to be pushed aside. But I think that there is a middle path between acting out aggressively and caving in. One holds one's ground gently and non-aggressively, in body, speech, and mind; one doesn't go away; one doesn't stop talking unless that would be the most skillful thing to do at that moment. I think that to reach that place between acting out aggressively and just caving in, we need to develop a kind of self-confidence without arrogance, to develop *maitri,* more self-acceptance, more ability to be with who we are. There's a phrase in *Shambhala, the Sacred Path of the Warrior* that I really like, which describes this situation as "victory over warfare." That's a wonderful phrase, victory over warfare. I think that's what it's about; that we have unconditional self-confidence so that we can stand our ground without being defensive, which is of course not

View of mountains and clouds from Tassajara.

always so easy to do. What I now do is try very hard to refrain from speech until I feel that I've reached that point. If something really riles me up and I'm tempted to flash off a letter or a speech, I check my body energy and often decide I'd better wait awhile.

So, I think that's some background to Khandro Rinpoche's statement: "Anger is always a waste of time." I think we have to unpack the word "anger." It's not so much avoiding feelings of irritation and frustration-it's acting out on them. Maybe we should use the word "aggression." But then, you know, then there's the "but." That's what this woman had in mind when she said, "But what about things that are really terrible?"—like battery, or murder, or all kinds of very aggressive things that are done to people that we need to take issue with. And that's when Khandro Rinpoche said, "I didn't tell you to leave behind your critical intelligence."

In this particular perspective on anger, as one of the five basic energies of the five Buddha families, as I've already said, anger masks or veils clarity. The clarity is there, but as long as we're totally caught up in that body energy I talked about, it's very hard to get to the intelligence. That's why it's so important to let the anger settle. But anger or aggression, in this particular set of teachings, always contains some kind of intelligence. There's something going on that is worth paying attention to. The problem is we can't pay attention to it until we let the aggression settle. If we start investigating this a little bit, what we usually find is that very close to the surface of anger is pain. Very, very close. If we look at ourselves, in some ways it seems like pain is an even bigger problem to deal with, to admit, than anger. I think it's very helpful, when we're dealing with people who are angry with us, to stop, and instead of getting defensive and starting to give it back, try to see where and what the pain is. What is really behind this?

When I was an ideological angry feminist, it wasn't that there wasn't anything worth attending to in what I was saying. There was a tremendous amount of insight in my critique. It was just not being expressed very well. So finding a way to get down to the genuine insights and letting them out—that's a very important part of dealing with anger. It's not so much that we need to get rid of our anger as that we need to distill it: to boil out the stuff that isn't so productive and get down to the stuff that has some intelligence in it, and begin to develop skillful means for working with that situation.

One of the most important things to distill out for me has been ideology or fixed mind-cherished beliefs and opinions. If you think about it, heavy opinions are pretty much the opposite of the mirror-like wisdom that reflects everything absolutely without distortion. Opinionatedness is actually very aggressive, if you think about it. If you ask a teacher, "What do you most want your students to give up?" often the answer is fixed opinions and beliefs.

Well, you know, this is going to bring up another one of those "buts," but if we're going to be concerned about the world, about justice issues, about poverty, sexism, homelessness, racism, homophobia-if we're going to be concerned about those things, don't we need strong convictions to be socially engaged? And I would say, no, what we really need is flexible wisdom, a kind of very flexible mind, not a know-it-all opinionatedness, because that's just going to turn people off. I think this is the middle path. People often think that if we don't have strong opinions about something, then we don't give a damn, right? No, there's a middle path between cherishing opinions and just not caring, period. We need to find that flexible mind, that curious, open, very malleable, very workable mind that is a mind of *bodhichitta,* is a mind of caring, but caring in a very open and flexible way.

So what is it about practice that allows this to develop—what is it? In this particular context, I want to bring in a couple of slogans that get used with meditation practice a lot in my tradition. One of them is touch and go: that when we practice, we don't censor or judge the thoughts that come through, which is one of the great reliefs of practice. It's not about censoring, it's not about judging all the stuff that comes up. But it's also about: don't lead, don't follow. In other words, the thoughts come but they also go. We don't entertain them. We don't dwell on them. And my favorite statement for that is that we don't believe in our thoughts, which to me is a tremendous relief—that I don't have to believe in all my crazy thoughts. Now, there is usually a lot more space around the thought. And I can recognize, "I don't have to believe in this thought."

I want to conclude by suggesting that for engaged Buddhists, for people who have something that really is of concern, some real care about the world and things that are going on in the world, finding this kind of practice and this kind of way of working with anger is absolutely essential for staying the course. You know, the story of a lot of people who are very involved in social issues is that they have a lot of fire fueling their social concern, they're very zealous, and then they burn out. It gets to be too much. I think the missing ingredient there is practice, where we can learn to touch and go with our thoughts, not leading, not following them, developing a mind in which we don't have to believe in our thoughts, so that we have the energy to actually work with the situation intelligently and in a caring fashion.

Kazuaki Tanahashi is an artist, translator and social activist who has been loosely associated with Zen Center for almost twenty-five years. This article traces his study of Eihei Dogen, the thirteenth century founder of Soto Zen Buddhism in Japan, and of Dogen's importance today. –M.W.

Why Dogen?

Kazuaki Tanahashi
FALL/WINTER 1999

Dogen said, "Miracles are practiced three thousand times in the morning and eight hundred times in the evening."[1] You must already have experienced two thousand seven hundred miracles this morning; so there are three hundred more to go. [laughter] During Dogen's time in the thirteenth century, and in fact through most of the history of Buddhism, the midday meal was the main meal and often the last meal of the day. People were sleepy in the afternoon, when it was miracle-free time. [laughter]

An attraction of Dogen to many of us in a time of advanced science and technology is that he didn't regard miracles as magical or supernormal phenomena which might be brought on by prayers or rituals. According to Dogen, miracles are such daily activities as fetching water and carrying firewood. Every encounter we have is a miracle. Every breath we take is a miracle. But, as we often focus on imperfection, lack, and failure, we become cranky and unhappy. So Dogen's words can be a good reminder of the miracles of each moment.

People say, "How many years did it take you to put the Dogen book together?" I sometimes say, "It took us seven hundred fifty years." It's true in a way if we consider that Buddhism practically didn't exist in the West until recently. In the sixteenth century a Portuguese missionary reported a strange kind of demon worship in Japan. When this was the typical European perception of

---

[1] "Miracles," translated with Katherine Thanas.

Buddhism, there was no need for Dogen in the West. Zen was formally introduced to the United States in 1894, when Soen Shaku gave a lecture at the Parliament of World's Religions in Chicago. D.T. Suzuki, one of his students, wrote a lot about Zen but seldom mentioned Dogen.

In my twenties when I was a beginning artist and looking for a spiritual guide, I read Dogen's poems and essays, which blew my mind. Let me read some of the lines that inspired me most:

> Birth is just like riding in a boat. You raise the sails and row with the pole. Although you row, the boat gives you a ride and without the boat you couldn't ride. But you ride in the boat and your riding makes the boat what it is. Investigate a moment such as this. At just such a moment there is nothing but the world of the boat. The sky, the water, and the shore are all the boat's world.[2]

I had been studying European literature and philosophy, in particular the writings of the existentialists. Camus, for example, points to the impermanence of life, realizing that we are all on death row. In my view, existentialists couldn't find any way out and expressed helplessness, despair, and boredom. Then I saw Dogen, who was so positive, as if he were presenting a next step to the existentialist understanding.

I didn't have a firm grip on what Dogen was talking about, and perhaps because of that, I was drawn to him. In 1960 I had my first art show in Nagoya; it took place in a rented gallery for six days, as was common in Japan. There was an old man, Soichi Nakamura, who came to my show every day. We became friends. I realized that he was an accomplished scholar and Zen teacher. I said to Nakamura Roshi, "Dogen is amazing but few people understand his writings. It would be a great help to many people if you would translate Dogen into modern Japanese." He said, "I would, if you do that with me." So I said, "I would be happy to help you."

---

[2] "Undivided Activity," translated with Edward Brown.

I thought I would work with him for a few years, get that done, and then do something more interesting. [laughter]

Prior to that, when I was thirteen years old, soon after World War II, I practiced Aikido and its spiritual foundation, Shintoism, with Morihei Ueshiba, founder of Aikido. My family and I were living in the master's dojo complex. So in a way I had to study Aikido. Later my father started a Shinto church. I was the only person around, so I ended up practicing Shintoism with him for some years until his church grew larger. I started going to a Christian church and then to Nakamura Roshi's temple. My father was wondering why his first-born son was interested in other religions. My explanation was: "We should understand what other people are doing. Some day we may have to convert them." [laughter]

Kazuaki Tanahashi.

Translating Dogen's paradoxical words from medieval Japanese and Chinese into modern Japanese was extremely painstaking. Sometimes we worked for a whole day on just one line. I started studying Sanskrit with a tutor and Chinese and Buddhist teachings. At one point I was invited to have a show in Washington, D.C. It was January 1964, and I was twenty-nine years old. I first landed in Honolulu, where I met Robert Aitken, who was not a roshi yet. He gave me a list of Zen places to visit on the mainland and suggested that I meet Rev. Shunryu Suzuki.

I visited Soko-ji and had a friendly conversation with him for about one hour. I guess he was wondering what I was. Finally Suzuki Roshi said, "Are you a salesman of Buddhist goods?" [laughter]

I said, "No, I am not. I am a student of Dogen."

Then I said to Suzuki Roshi, "I understand you teach zazen here. What kind of text do you use?"

He said, *"The Blue Cliff Record."*

I said, "Why not Dogen?"

"Dogen is too difficult for American students."

"Don't you think you should present your best when you teach foreign students? It doesn't matter if they don't understand it. [laughter] Don't you think Dogen is your best?"

After a few moments of silence, he said, "I am scheduled to give a talk to my students on Sunday. Would you please talk about Dogen for me?" [laughter] I had never given a public talk in English. I borrowed a copy of his Dogen book and wrote a lecture. My topic was "time" based on "Time Being," a fascicle of Dogen's major work, *Shobogenzo*.

After showing my artwork in North America for one year, I went back to Honolulu and translated "Genjokoan," another fascicle of *Shobogenzo*, with Aitken Roshi. Returning to Japan, I suddenly found the work of translating Dogen into modern Japanese much easier. Translating into English had changed the dynamics. When you translate something into another language, you have to deconstruct the structure of the original sentence and try to find the best possible syntax to make it sensible in that language. Some kind of breakdown process had taken place, which opened up my mind. I said to Nakamura Roshi, "It might be a good idea if you would let me do the translation by myself and comment on my draft afterward." I dictated my modern Japanese translation into a tape recorder and asked a team of volunteers to transcribe it. We completed the entire ninety-five fascicles of *Shobogenzo*, which were published in four volumes with an extra volume of dictionary, in 1972.

At one point I thought of translating more of Dogen's writings into English. As Suzuki Roshi had passed away, I wrote to Baker Roshi. When I met him in Kyoto in 1975, I expressed my wish to collaborate with those who were practicing Zen. Baker Roshi asked me directly: "Are you a Buddhist?" I said, "Well, I am not. But I am a Buddhist scholar." Then he said, "Why don't you come to Zen Center and work with us?" Since 1977 I have had the pleasure of being part of the Sangha and working with friends who are deeply engaged in Zen practice.

Dogen was extremely serious and formal, a high spiritual leader and excellent community organizer. I'm the opposite. I like to be informal. I like free thinking and identify myself as a drop-out. In no way am I a good student of Dogen's. But I am attracted to his world view and teaching, and wish to support, in a modest way, those who are following Dogen's path.

Dogen said:

> By the continuous practice of all Buddhas and ancestors, your practice is actualized and your great road opens up. By your continuous practice, the continuous practice of all Buddhas is actualized and the great road of all Buddhas opens up. Your continuous practice creates the circle of the way.[3]

We receive a great teaching, and we actualize it. We receive a great heritage, whether it is a common human heritage or a Buddhist heritage, and it is we who make it vital. Teachers make students, and vice versa. Teachers are students and students are teachers.

Enlightenment Unfolds has been a three-year project of Zen Center. An obvious part of this collaboration is that some of the teachers in this community have worked with me and Zen Center has provided financial support. A less obvious part is that all of you who practice together have helped. Let me give you an example. There is an East Asian expression that is usually translated as "sitting in a crossed-legged position." Norman Fischer suggested "sitting in a meditation posture" as an alternative translation. This translation radically widens the concept of meditation posture. Some of you say, "I can't sit in the cross-legged way. I need to sit on the chair," or "Can we meditate in a wheelchair?" When you raise these issues, you are our teachers in redefining the concept.

Once my wife, Linda, said, "Why do you say 'Patriarch,' as in 'the Sixth Patriarch'?" In Chinese this word has no gender, so I realized that "patriarch" was not a good translation. Some of us translators came up with the word "ancestor," which is commonly used now. In this way we could correct our understanding of dharma and make it more accessible. My partners and I examine each word and try to find the most appropriate translation that is justified in light of the original thought. When we had meetings to review the draft translation of *Enlightenment Unfolds* at Zen Center, I said, "We are the humblest people in the world." Of course real humble people don't say such things. [laughter] What I wanted to say was that we are open to everyone's comments and hope to make the book, and the practice, accessible to as many people as possible.

In this book we have included Dogen's fundraising letter. People like the idea that even Dogen had to do fundraising. [laughter] Fundraising is a way to offer people an opportunity to give, which is an important practice. Fundraising is also a way to clarify the meaning of your practice and explain it in a way that others can understand. Dogen was trying to build a small monks' hall soon after he had come back from China. In his letter he said, "We will thoroughly engage in each activity in order to cultivate proper conditions to transform the ten directions."[4] This is an outrageous statement. By taking care of every small detail of life-sitting, walking, cleaning, and cooking-he wanted to change the world. One of his tasks was to establish a practicing community by encouraging its members to be sensitive to other people's feelings, be fair and open, and not to overstep others' responsibility. What Dogen was doing was small, but the effect of his thinking and practice has proven to be enormous, and his influence is still growing. It is ironic and inspiring: being thoroughly engaged in each activity, while working with others harmoniously, may be the most immediate way to bring forth large-scale transformation.

Traditional
Practice:
warm hand
to warm hand

This 1973 First Memorial Service Lecture for Suzuki Roshi is full of stories of teachers and their successors. It was given by Suzuki Roshi's successor, Zentatsu Baker Roshi. –M.W.

Memorial Service Lecture

Richard Baker

23 DECEMBER 1972

Suzuki Roshi died just over a year ago and today we will have the one-year Memorial Service for him. It is an old, old Buddhist custom to treat your teacher as if he were still alive and to offer food to him on the anniversary of his death. Do you know the story of Tozan and Nansen at Baso's Memorial Service? Tozan Ryokai (807-869) is the founder of the Soto line in China, our lineage. During Tozan's time the five lineages stemming from Hui Neng, the Sixth Patriarch, were all interconnected, everyone visiting and learning from each other. Nansen Fugan (748-838) is the great teacher who is famous for the koan about "killing a cat." He was one of the five main disciples of Baso Doitsu (709-799). For Suzuki Roshi, Baso was one of the greatest Zen masters of all time.

Tozan was quite young when he asked his first teacher, probably a local village priest, why the sutra said "no eyes, no ears, no nose, no tongue, no body, no mind, " when he had eyes ears, nose tongue, body, and mind. Amazed by Tozan's ingenuous clarity and matter-of-factness, the village teacher said, "I am not good enough for you, please go to Master Reimoku." Tozan did so and had his head shaved under Reimoku (747-818) who was one of the many heirs of Baso Doitsu. When he was about twenty-one he began journeying about visiting various teachers. The first teacher he visited was Nansen. When Tozan arrived the monastery was preparing for the annual Memorial Service for Nansen's teacher, Baso. Nansen said to everyone, to all his disciples, "Tomorrow we will serve food to Master Baso. Do you think he will come?"

I may ask you the same question. This afternoon we will perform the first annual Memorial Service for our teacher, Master Suzuki Roshi. We will offer him food and drink. Will Suzuki Roshi come and eat the food we serve him today?

When Nansen asked this question there was the "silence of no one answering." and then from the back of the assembly young Tozan stepped forward and said, "Master Baso will wait for a companion." Nansen then said, "Oh here is a fellow, although he is quite young, he is worthy to study Buddhism." Tozan answered, "Please do not slight me in that way!" Let's run through this again. Nansen asked, in effect, "Is there a student in the house? Will one of you come forward? Is there anyone here who knows that Baso is always present, that he neither comes nor goes?' All these questions are held in Nansen's question. After none of Nansen's disciples replied, Tozan felt someone should come forward — or more likely he was gripped by the question and by the presence of Nansen, and even by Baso. And Tozan said, "He will wait for a companion. He will wait for someone who knows the immediate presence of the true relationship—that is outside of history and time—between disciple and teacher." Then Nansen, both recognizing and cautioning him, said, "Are you pointing yourself out as a student, as a companion?' Tozan replied, "Please do not insult me. I am pointing out Master Baso."

How does a teacher really exist? You must make an effort to be a disciple. You must come forward to be a teacher's companion in a common realization. You must make an effort, a great effort to realize Suzuki Roshi's teaching, to realize your own True Nature, to be Suzuki Roshi's companion forever. It means actually eating with Master Baso and Suzuki Roshi, walking with them, knowing how they exist and existed. It means to think with them, hear with them, see with them. This is a story about how each one of us actually exists with each other—and ultimately with our teacher and the lineage embodied in this life.

There is also a story about Tozan when he was in his fifties preparing for a Memorial Service for his own teacher Ungan Donjo. You know about Ungan from our morning chanting of the lin-

Suzuki Roshi's funeral at 300 Page Street.

eage. Beginning from the Sixth Patriarch, Hui Neng or in Japanese, Daikan Eno: Daikan Eno Daiosho (great teacher), Seigen Gyoshi Daiosho, Sekito Kisen Daiosho (the author of the Sandokai), Yakusan Igen Daiosho, Ungan Donjo Daiosho, Tozan Ryokai Daiosho . . . and up to Dogen and Keizan, and now us. For twenty years Ungan was also a disciple of Hyakujo who was also an heir of Baso Doitsu.

During the preparation of the vegetarian food for the offering to Ungan, a monk asked Tozan, "What teaching did you receive from Master Ungan?" Tozan answered, "Although I was in his community for many years, he gave me no instruction." [Tozan is also saying, "Pay attention to the instruction which is not presented as instruction. Pay attention to the ever-present instruction even of the insentient."] But sincerely seeking instruction, this monk persisted, "If he did not instruct you, why are you preparing food and offering a Memorial Service to him now?" Tozan said, "How dare I contradict him?" ["How dare I not acknowledge his not instructing me?"] The monk then said, "You visited Nansen first and became known at that time, why do you offer food now in Ungan's memory?" Tozan said, "I am not making this offering because of Master Ungan's virtue or Buddha-Dharma, but because he refused to reveal the teaching to me. In this way, I revere him."

Another monk asked at the same time, "Master Tozan, you are about to conduct a Memorial Service in honor of your teacher, Master Ungan, do you still agree with his teaching?" Tozan replied, "I half agree and half disagree." [Remember Tozan also said, "How dare I contradict him!"] The monk, who wants something to be in agreement with, asks, "Why do you not agree with him completely?" "To do so [in the present moment] would be to do him an injustice," replied Tozan.

1973

There is still another story about Tozan I would like to tell you again. After Tozan left Nansen he went to see Isan Reiyu and asked him about a famous statement of Nan-yo Echu. Isan (771-853) was an heir of Hyakujo and co-founder of the Igyo lineage. Nan-yo (d.776) was an heir of the Sixth Patriarch and he is often known by his title of Chu Kokushi, or State Master, and by his request for an untiered or seamless burial mound. Tozan told Isan that he did not understand the deep meaning of Nan-yo's statement that inanimate objects expound the Dharma. Isan said, "Please repeat the story." And Tozan did so: A monk asked Nan-yo, "What is the mind of an ancient Buddha?" Nan-yo replied, "A wall and broken tiles." "But are they not inanimate objects?" the monk said. "They are," replied Nan-yo. The monk asked, "Do they know how to expound the Dharma?" Nan-yo said, "They are always expounding the Dharma vigorously and unceasingly." The monk asked, "Why do I not hear it?" Nan-yo replied, "Although you do not hear it, do not hinder that which hears it!" The story goes on, but this is the statement I want you to hear: "Although you do not hear it, do not hinder that which hears it."

At the end of the whole story, Isan says, "I have something to say about this too, but I have not yet found a man to whom I can speak." Tozan said, "Will you please teach me, I do not understand." Isan raised his whisk and said, "Do you understand?" Tozan said, "No! Will you explain it to me?" Isan said, " This mouth from my parents will never explain it to you."

After that Isan told Tozan to follow the bending grasses to the mountain cave where Ungan lived. When Tozan arrived at Ungan's cave, he immediately asked, "When the inanimate expounds the Dharma, who can hear it?" Ungan said, "The inanimate hear it!" Tozan said, "Venerable Ungan, do you hear it?" Ungan said, "If I heard it, you could not hear my expounding of the Dharma." Then Tozan asked, "Why do I not hear it?" Ungan raised his whisk and said, "Do you hear it?" Tozan again said, "No!" And Ungan replied, "If you cannot hear my teaching, how can you ever hear the teaching of the inanimate?" Tozan said, "What sutra says, 'Inanimate objects expound the Dharma?'" Ungan said, "Do you not know that the *Amitabha Buddha Sutra* says, 'Streams, birds, trees, groves, all chant the Buddha-Dharma?'" Finally, Tozan realized. He said:

Wonderful, wonderful!
The Dharma of the inanimate cannot be conceived.
Listening with the ears, nothing is heard,
Hearing with eyes, everything is known.

Suzuki Roshi was like this, he would not say much about the teaching. He just lived here with us. In the first years he was here in America, it was very hard to recognize in him more than that he was a very nice and remarkable man. To most people, he was just one of the local Japanese priests for the Japanese community. It was not until he had relationships with several disciples that we began to see him through these relationships as a teacher and then find our own relationship to him as a teacher. By coming forward in ourselves and treating him as a teacher, we found he came forward in himself and treated our new relationship as the teacher. It felt like and often was a discovery of ultimate friendship. By the end of his life many people could see him directly through his reflections in his many disciples—and through his reflections in them. In the first years, many of the people who came to sit zazen for a while, went away not knowing who Suzuki Roshi was. But by the end of his life everyone wanted to stay with him and there was much space around him in which to stay.

Our relationships with him continue and many people can see Suzuki Roshi through us. Our relationships with him are not gone, if we continue to come forward, continue to hear with the eyes, and see with the ears—if our knowing is not limited to the five categories of the senses the seemingly seamless world they help provide. We should treat Suzuki Roshi as if he were alive. One of the ways we remind ourselves is we offer food to him and call it a Memorial Service. This has wisdom in it. "I was with him many years, but I did not receive any teaching." Although, we do not know what we have learned, when necessary it will come out spontaneously according to circumstances, something we did not even know we knew. Do you know how to come forward to make the body of Suzuki Roshi and of Buddha visible in the Memorial Service, to join Suzuki Roshi today in this Memorial Service?

Which came first, Buddha or you? Buddha or Suzuki Roshi? There is no first Buddha. The potentiality of Buddha is always the mountain grasses! It was the same in Buddha's time. This possibility to come forward, this actuality exists right now. The teaching is always waiting. Suzuki Roshi is still waiting. Don't worry! Everything exists, just as you exist now! It is something incomprehensible, something unthinkable. "Although we do not hear it, do not hinder that which hears it!" This line we can practice with!!! Engo said, "Ten thousand Holy Ones have not handed down a single phrase of the pre-voice." I say the pre-voice of the ten thousand things is heard everywhere. Do you hear it? Can you practice in this realm of the incomprehensible? This actual being, this actual practice is beyond being and non-being, so we offer food to Suzuki Roshi. Please come forward and make the body of Buddha visible, animate and inanimate. Please continue this practice and teaching.

During the afternoon everyone gathered in the Buddha Hall to begin the Memorial Service. Baker Roshi standing, before the special altar set up for Suzuki Roshi, called out:

> At Baso's Memorial Service,
> Tozan said, "He will wait for a companion."
> At Ungan Donjo's Memorial Service,
> Tozan said, "I spent many years with him,
> But he refused to reveal the truth to me!"
> O Suzuki Roshi, What do you say?
> Will you refuse to reveal the teaching to us?
> We come forward as one person,
> Hearing the ten thousand things bless you.

Beginners Mind Temple, at 300 Page Street.

This ceremony is the first formal initiation into Buddhism.
The version that we used in 1986, with commentary here by
Abbot Tenshin Anderson, remains the one that we use today
with just a few minor changes . –M.W.

Lay Bodhisattva
Initiation Ceremony
with Commentary by Reb Anderson
FALL 1986

The Lay Bodhisattva initiation is a ceremony of sudden Awakening, like going through the door. Just as a fish swimming in water may take it for granted, we moving through life may take it for granted. But if we put a door down into our life and walk through it we may suddenly realize, "Oh, I am alive." In this way we awaken to our life, to the simple truth that we are alive and that we are life. It is an initiation into a fresh new life and at the same time a coming home.

In this ceremony we are initiated into our home and family: the great assembly of enlightening beings (Bodhisattvas). We are formally introduced to our close family members. It is a way to remember something very familiar. It is a re-initiation. Like a friend of mine says everytime he falls in love, "It's never been like this before, again."

Sometimes the ceremony is called *Jukai,* which means "receiving the precepts." It may also be called *Zaike tokudo,* which literally means "staying home and accomplishing the way." The priest Bodhisattva initiation is called *Shukke tokudo*—that is, "leaving home and accomplishing the way." Both of these ceremonies offer a means for being one with Buddha's way.

Our Lay Initiation Ceremony is composed of eight basic elements:

I. Invocation
II. Confession and Resolution of Action
III. Ritual Water Purification
IV. Taking Refuge
V. Receiving the Three Pure Precepts
VI. Receiving the Ten Grave Precepts
VII. Receiving a Buddhist Name and Robe
VIII. Receiving the Bodhisattva Precept Lineage

I. Invocation

ABBOT:

Invoking the presence and compassion of our ancestors
In faith that we are Buddha
We enter Buddha's Way

Homage to all Buddhas in the ten directions
Homage to the complete Dharma in ten directions
Homage to every Sangha in ten directions
Homage to our first teacher Shakyamuni Buddha
Homage to our succession of Bodhisattvas and Ancestors
Homage to Eihei Dogen Zenji
Homage to Shogaku Shunryu Daiosho
Now may their presence and compassion sustain us.

Let us chant the names of Buddha

INITIATES AND AUDIENCE:

Homage to the Dharmakaya Vairochana Buddha
Homage to the Sambhogakaya Lochana Buddha
Homage to the Nirmanakaya Shakyamuni Buddha
Homage to the future Maitreya Buddha
Homage to all Buddhas in the ten directions, past, present, and
    future
Homage to Manjusri, the Perfect Wisdom Bodhisattva
Homage to Samantabhadra, the Shining Practice Bodhisattva
Homage to Avalokitesvara, the Infinite Compassion Bodhisattva
Homage to the many Bodhisattva Mahasattvas
Homage to the Maha Prajna Paramita

COMMENTARY: We call within. We call up the wisdom and compassion of the Buddhas and ancestors. In this way the beginning of this ceremony is Buddhahood.

II. Confession and Resolution of Past Action (Karma)

ABBOT:

In order to be fully awakened in the practice of Buddha's precepts we start with the pure practice of confession.

ABBOT AND INITIATES CHANT TOGETHER THREE TIMES:

All my ancient twisted karma
From beginningless greed, hate, and delusion.
Born of body, speech and mind,
I now fully avow.

ABBOT:

You have gone beyond the karma of body, speech, and mind; and have been freed from greed, hate, and delusion. O good disciples of Buddha, now you may live in the Way of the Three Treasures. Even after acquiring Buddhahood, will you continue this truthful practice?

INITIATES:

Yes, I will.

COMMENTARY: This is a group confession for the avowal and confession of our past actions. Then, to clear away any reservations, any resistance, any hesitation to accepting the truth, to accepting the way, we confess. We avow all the things we have done, from beginningless time, with our body, our voice, and our thought, through all kinds of confusion, aversion, and attachments. We avow *all* these actions and we burn them up by this complete avowal, setting ourselves free and ready to receive the precepts of the Buddha way. And we really feel free from our past karma. As though we can actually change and start fresh, on the path.

III. *Ritual Purification (Abhiseka)*

THE ABBOT, USING A LEAF, SPRINKLES WATER ON THE INITIATES
AND THE ASSEMBLY.

COMMENTARY: The basis of this wisdom water purification is the
Buddha Nature which we all share. We have this water that has
been passed down to us for thousands of years. And we take some
of this water, and sprinkle it on all the people, to purify each person—just to make sure they are not holding on to any dust of past
action. Then everybody is clear and pure.

IV. *Taking Refuge*

ABBOT:
> We have purified our mind and body. Now you may receive
> the path of the precepts of the Three Treasures. You are seated
> with Buddha and are really Buddha's child. Will you receive
> these precepts?

INITIATES:
> Yes, I will.

ABBOT CHANTS EACH LINE AND INITIATES REPEAT:
> I take refuge in the Buddha
> I take refuge in the Dharma
> I take refuge in the Sangha
>
> I take refuge in the Buddha as the perfect teacher
> I take refuge in the Dharma as the perfect teaching
> I take refuge in the Sangha as the perfect life
>
> I have completely taken refuge in the Buddha
> I have completely taken refuge in the Dharma
> I have completely taken refuge in the Sangha

ABBOT:

You have returned to your original nature free from attachments and limited ways. From now awakening is your teacher, all beings are your teacher. Do not be fooled by other ways. This is the path of mercy for all existence and things. Do you agree to follow this compassionate path of the Three Treasures that I am now passing to you?

INITIATES:

Yes, I will.

COMMENTARY: In this ceremony we give the sixteen great Bodhisattva precepts, which are the Three Refuges, the Three Pure Precepts and the Ten Grave Precepts. Taking refuge in the Threefold Gem is the beginning and end of the Buddha Way. It is the heart.

For Dogen Zenji the first step in practice was to take refuge in the Triple Treasure. Before we practice ethical conduct, concentration, and insight, we take refuge, and after we have accomplished these practices we take refuge again.

This pattern is demonstrated in Dogen Zenji's life. Towards the end of his life he wrote the *Shobogenzo* fascicle, "Taking Refuge in the Triple Treasure." He hoped to revise it but due to ill health he was unable to do so. And as he was preparing to die, the practice of this great and learned Zen master, this ancient Buddha, was to write "Buddha, Dharma, Sangha" on a pillar in his death-room, and then walk around the pillar taking refuge. He said, "I take refuge in awakening. I take refuge in the teaching. I take refuge in the community." This is what the old Buddha did, as he was dying.

A Buddha is constantly taking refuge in Buddha. So a Buddha is constantly taking refuge in him or herself. Doesn't that make sense?

At the beginning of our practice, we also take refuge in Buddha's mind, in Buddha as our own mind, and in our mind as Buddha. When you feel like you're beginning practice, or entering the way through initiation ceremonies, you rely on and return to "this

Lay Bodhisattva Initiation at Page Street zendo.

mind as Buddha." When you have become accomplished in the
way, you take refuge in "no-Buddha, no-mind."

The Japanese expression for taking refuge is *ki-e*. According to
Dogen Zenji, *ki* means to unhesitatingly throw yourself into something and it also means to return, to come again.

Therefore, to take refuge in the Three-fold Gem is to throw
your awakened mind into the awakened mind, into the perfect
teaching, and into the oneness of all being. It is to jump, unhesitatingly, into awakening; into the true teaching; into the interconnectedness of all being. That is *ki*. And *e* means to "rely" or
"depend" on, to find true safety and asylum in Buddha, Dharma
and Sangha. Ultimately there is only one Treasure: Awakening.
But for the sake of helping people, Buddha is seen through three
aspects. One is awakening as a teacher for us. Another is awakening as doctrine or teaching. And then there is awakening as
revealed through discipline and thus through those who practice it.

The feeling and spirit I have when taking refuge is to unhesitatingly plunge into the Buddha mind. To rely on, to find safety
in, and return to the Buddha mind. With no hesitation I jump into
the true teaching, rely on, return to and depend on the true teach-

ing. With no hesitation, with no reservations, I dive into the community of fellow practitioners, of good friends, into the interconnectedness of all living beings.

This is what we do and this is zazen.

In the *Sixth Ancestor's Platform Sutra* there is a Bodhisattva Initiation Ceremony. Therein Hui-neng, the Sixth Zen Ancestor asks people to take refuge in the Body of Buddha as their own physical body. The Body of Buddha is the law body, the bliss body, and the transformation body. These are the Three Bodies of Buddha. He asks the people to take refuge in their own body as the Three Refuges and the Precepts. So basically it comes back to deeply trusting in yourself. It all comes to that. Deeply trusting in your own goodness. Deeply trusting in your own imperturbable Buddha mind.

"Deeply trusting" means to stand, or sit steadfastly in your imperturbable awakened mind. To do all the activities of daily life with imperturbable Buddha mind is to take refuge in Buddha.

v. *The Three Pure Precepts*

ABBOT:
Now will you receive the Three Pure Precepts?

INITIATES:
Yes, I will.

ABBOT RECITES EACH PRECEPT AND INITIATES REPEAT:
I vow to refrain from all action that creates attachments
I vow to make every effort to live in enlightenment
I vow to live to benefit all beings

ABBOT:
Abiding in the Three Pure Precepts even after acquiring Buddhahood, will you continuously observe them?

INITIATES:
Yes, I will.

COMMENTARY: All Buddhas have taught these precepts. In their most simple form they are:

1. Avoid all bad actions
2. Do all good actions
3. Live for the benefit of all living beings

The practice of these precepts is the body and mind of Buddha. To avoid all wrong actions is Buddha's law body (Dharmakaya). To do all right actions is Buddha's bliss body (Sambhogakaya), and living for the benefit of all beings is Buddha's illusion body (Nirmanakaya).

Once there was a Zen master who meditated in a tree. He was known as "Bird's Nest." A great governor-poet came to see him and said, "What a dangerous seat you have up there in the tree."

"Yours is more dangerous than mine," the teacher replied.

"I am the governor of this province, and I don't see what danger there is in this."

"Then sir, you don't know yourself very well. When passions burn and mind is unsteady, this is the greatest danger." "What is the teaching of Buddhism?" the poet asked.

The teacher recited a stanza from the *Dhammapada*:

"Not to commit wrong actions
But to do all good ones
And keep the heart pure.
This is the teaching of all the Buddhas"

"But any child of three years knows that," said the poet.

"Any three-year-old child may know it, but even a person of eighty years finds it difficult to practice," said the teacher in the tree.

VI. *Receiving the Ten Grave Precepts*

ABBOT:
Now you will receive the Ten Grave Precepts?

INITIATES:
   Yes, I will.

ABBOT:
   A Disciple of the Buddha does not kill
   A Disciple of the Buddha does not take what is not given
   A Disciple of the Buddha does not misuse sexuality
   A Disciple of the Buddha does not lie
   A Disciple of the Buddha does not intoxicate mind or body of
      self or others
   A Disciple of the Buddha does not slander
   A Disciple of the Buddha does not praise self at the expense of
      others
   A Disciple of the Buddha is not possessive of anything
   A Disciple of the Buddha does not harbor ill will
   A Disciple of the Buddha does not abuse the Three Treasures.

ABBOT:
   Abiding according to the Ten Grave Precepts even after acquiring Buddhahood, will you continuously observe them?

INITIATES:
   Yes, I will.

ABBOT:
   You have received Buddha's precepts and are a child of Buddha. To sustain and confirm the practice of these vows, for reality is in living them, I will now give you Buddha's name and
   lineage and robe to clothe you throughout this life and times
   to come. This will be your name, true family and dress. Now
   you can really work for all beings and realize your own Buddha Nature. You yourself and all beings are the Tathagata.

COMMENTARY: Taking refuge in the Triple Treasure is the heart of
Buddhism. The precepts are the blood. This precept vein is a vital
link between all the Buddhas and Ancestors and us. To truly receive
these precepts is to be awakened. While receiving these precepts

one should be mindful that they are our own true body and mind. They are the way of complete freedom.

1. A Disciple of Buddha does not kill. If I remember that all living beings tremble when their life is threatened and fear the end of it, I will not kill or allow others to kill. If I remember that life is dear to all living creatures I will not kill or let others kill.

2. A Disciple of Buddha does not take what is not given. Material accomplishment may occur, we all possess something. But we must be sure that it comes by right livelihood.

3. A Disciple of Buddha does not misuse sexuality. This is using our life energy only for the benefit of all beings and not to produce attachments.

4. A Disciple of Buddha does not lie. Since this precept is concerned with refraining from false speech, one way to practice it would be to simply not say a word. But lying may also be done with silence. There are lies of omission. Sometimes we must speak and speak honestly. But this, of course, is not so easy. Many of us do not know how to tell the truth, and need to enter a difficult process of learning. What is the truth? An Ancestor says, "Turning away and touching are both wrong, for it is like a mass of fire." It is vast, inconceivable, and we cannot be known as an object. It remains elusive. So we may be tempted to simplify it in order to grasp it. However, this is slandering the truth and is a kind of lying. Developing a tolerance for complexity and being willing to admit confusion may help us in our practice of telling the truth.

5. A Disciple of Buddha does not intoxicate mind or body of self or others. If we look for the advantage of one thing over another, anything may be an opportunity for intoxication. If taken in the right way, alcohol may be helpful. It all depends on our basic attitude. Suzuki Roshi emphasized that this precept warns against intoxicating people with spiritual teachings. It encourages us to go beyond all dependencies, even on Buddha's teachings.

6. A Disciple of Buddha does not slander. The first thing that comes to mind here is to be strict with ourselves, but gentle and forgiving of others. Being strict with ourselves in this case means

to be sure that our speech is motivated by compassion. If we practice this way, we might not have much to say about others.

7. A Disciple of Buddha does not praise self. If we can remember how limited our awareness is, we may be able to observe this precept. As Dogen Zenji says, "When dharma does not fill your whole body and mind, you think it is already sufficient. When dharma fills your body and mind, you realize that something is missing."

8. A Disciple of Buddha is not possessive of anything. First of all, this precept points to the disharmony and injustice of amassing material possessions while others are lacking them. People who possess lots of precious things are often feared and hated. On another level, this is an encouragement to Buddhist teachers not to be possessive of the teaching. The challenge of their lives is to share the teaching with everyone.

9. A Disciple of Buddha does not harbor ill will. Deep in our hearts we all know how destructive it is for our own health and happiness to hold on to anger. It may be even more harmful for those towards whom we express angry words or gestures. Therefore, we must sincerely practice patience to protect ourselves from producing anger.

10. A Disciple of Buddha does not abuse the Three Treasures. Although this precept comes last in the list, it is also in a sense first and most important because it refers back to the first three precepts, the refuges, which are the foundation of the precept practice.

In the *Shobogenzo,* Dogen Zenji tells a story about precepts.

Two billion, six hundred million hungry dragons came to see Buddha. They had been having quite a hard time for hundreds of thousands of lifetimes, suffering. The most troubled of all the dragons was a blind female dragon, who is described as being in terrible shape. She was putrifying, rotting, in all the possible dimensions of rot and putrescence. She cried out to the Buddha for help. Buddha said, "How did you get into this situation?" She explained that in a previous life she had been a nun and she had done a series of really terrible things—after having taken refuge as part of becoming a nun. She had really done some bad things. She said she conned people in the monastery out of possessions; she used the temple as a place to set up her sexual activities. She really violated the precepts royally. So this was the terrible result. Buddha said, "If what you said is true, if you did take refuge in the Triple Treasure, in a past life, then I can help you." He reached out and scooped up some water, and said, "In a past life I gave my life for a dove." He poured the water into his mouth and sprayed it on her, purifying her rotting body. Then he said, "Now if you wish to receive the Three Refuges, you can do that." And she did.

Dogen says, "This is all that could be done for her. And it is because she took the refuges in the past that Buddha could do this for her."

Now, by these acts of invocation, confession, purification, taking the refuges and receiving the precepts, we become the working basis of the Buddha way. We have become, by those actions, the ground for the arising of the Buddha mind—of the *bodhicitta*. And therefore we are ready to receive a new name, new clothes, and a new family lineage paper.

VII. *Receiving New Buddhist Name and Robe*

Abbot calls each person by old name, and new name, and each initiate receives name and robe and returns to seat.

I (new-name), Buddha's Disciple, receive this robe of five strips, each strip made from one long and one short piece. I will wear this robe of Buddha with the mind and body of its sacred meaning.

Each initiate removes robe from its envelope and places robe on head, and chants:

Great robe of liberation
Field far beyond form and emptiness
Wearing the Tathagata's Teaching
Saving all beings

COMMENTARY:

NAME: Now that we have the new life of the sixteen Zen precepts, we may also receive a new name. I say "new," but it is also a traditional name. Our Buddhist names are usually composed of some elements taken from the names of our ancestors. It may be that no one has ever had your name before, and yet it is just like all the others.

ROBE: We are fortunate to be living at a time when the correct method of sewing and transmitting Buddha's robe is known and practiced. I am deeply grateful to Zen teachers like Eko Hashimoto and Kodo Sawaki for revitalizing the tradition of the correct way of sewing, wearing and caring for Buddha's robe, and to Eshun Yoshida and Joshin Kasai for coming to Zen Center and teaching us how to sew Buddha's robe. If we wear the properly transmitted robe even once for only a short time, it will serve to protect our practice of awakening.

Being willing to respect and care for small and apparently unimportant things brings the great mind of awakening into our daily life. Even though we may not understand what difference it makes, to care for our robes in accord with Buddha's instruction helps all beings to realize the essence of the way.

VIII. *Receiving Lineage Papers—*
The Blood Line of Bodhisattva Precepts

COMMENTARY: The blood lineage chart describes how we are connected with all Buddhas and Ancestors through the precepts. It also shows that we are the latest edition of the lineage and its source.

By studying this diagram of the blood line we realize that we are Buddha's disciples, we are the Ancestors' children and at the same time we are Buddhas, and the life of the lineage comes from our practice of the precepts. The lineage chart has Shakyamuni Buddha at the top. From him a red line goes down through ninety ancestors—2,500 years—to the people in this ceremony. This red blood line goes from Shakyamuni, going down, down, down, through India, through China, through both Rinzai Zen and Soto

Zen, up to Dogen Zenji and down through Soto Zen in Japan, to America, and to us. After the red line goes through the person ordained, it goes back up to Shakyamuni Buddha.

We are actually taking refuge in the nature of our own mind. We're disciples, and at the same time we are Buddha. This is the blood line—it gets pumped all the way around, back through all the Ancestors, into you, and back to the Ancestors, through them, and into you—round and round the Buddha blood goes.

ABBOT:
> We offer this ceremony to the enlightenment of all beings
> We live like a cloud in an endless sky
> A lotus in muddy water
> One with the pure mind of Buddha.
> Let us bow to the Tathagata.

EVERYONE:
> All Buddhas, Ten Directions, Three Times
> All Beings, Bodhisattvas, Mahasattvas
> Wisdom Beyond Wisdom, Maha Prajna Paramita.

The primary practice at San Francisco Zen Center is seated meditation or zazen. Pat Phelan, who spent many years here, is currently Abbess of the Chapel Hill Zen Center. She expanded the original 1987 zazen instruction for this book. —M.W.

Zazen Posture

Pat Phelan

SPRING 1987

The fundamental practice in Zen is engaging in the actuality of our being as it arises moment by moment. We develop this through the practice of Zen meditation called zazen or *shikan taza*. Zazen is basically the practice of awareness, of bringing our attention to the present moment, this whole and complete moment, by bringing our awareness to our physical presence, including our posture, sensations and the breath. The wonderful thing about practicing awareness of our body is that it is always in the present.

Zazen can be done sitting cross-legged on a cushion, sitting in a chair, or lying down while paying attention to most of the same points of posture. If you are sitting cross-legged on a cushion, please experiment with where you place yourself on the cushion. Many people sit close to the edge of the cushion. Only your spine needs to be supported by the cushion, not your legs. Although it is fairly common for the feet or legs to fall asleep when sitting cross-legged for thirty or forty minutes, I distinguish between the leg falling asleep and then waking up several seconds after being uncrossed, and between the foot or leg becoming completely numb or deadened. This usually happens due to pressure against a nerve in the leg. If this happens, you don't want to do this day in and day out. Try sitting closer to the edge of the cushion and see if that relieves the pressure against the nerve in the leg.

I also recommend trying out different heights of cushions—sit on a thin cushion, sit on a thick cushion, try sitting on two cushions. Experiment and see how different heights effect the alignment of the lower back with the upper back. Cross-legged sitting is considered a stable way to sit because there are three points of support, your two knees and your sitting bones. If you are sitting on a cushion your knees should be supported. If they don't touch the floor or a support cushion, it will be hard to have the strength you need in your lower back to support your upper back. Try placing a cushion under your knee or knees if they are not touching the floor so they won't be dangling. I also recommend alternating which leg is on top or in front. Even if your less flexible side feels pretty awkward, try alternating your legs so your body won't become asymmetric over time.

Many people who find that sitting cross-legged doesn't work for them, sit Japanese style or *seiza* by kneeling and sitting on their feet, usually with the assistance of a cushion or a small wooden bench which takes the weight off the feet and knees. If this is difficult for your feet, try letting your toes hang over the back edge of the zabuton or place a rolled up wash cloth under your foot just in front of your toes so the foot isn't stretched out so much.

If you are sitting on a chair, your feet should be flat on the floor with your knees about a hips width apart. Ideally the back of the seat of the chair will be slightly higher than the front of the seat so you can gently arch your back. Sitting on the very edge of the chair will also take care of this. If you need back support, try to place a cushion against the back of the chair so your back is supported in a well-aligned position. If you have a physical difficulty that won't allow you to sit, you can practice zazen lying down. When you do, bend your knees and place your feet flat on the surface. This allows your lower back to come into line with the upper back.

This is all preliminary to taking zazen posture. Find a position that you can be in for a while relatively still.

Two characteristics of zazen are being alert yet relaxed. There should be some energy or effort in your zazen practice. This is an intentional activity and it requires some effort, but not too much effort. If there is too much effort, you will become tense and your zazen practice will be a strain. While sitting, you should be relaxed but awake. On the other hand, if you become too relaxed, your

Suzuki Roshi adjusting posture at Sokoji temple in San Francisco, circa 1961.

mind will become dull and it will wander in its usual way or you may fall asleep. We each need to find a balance between effort and ease in our zazen practice.

In *Zen Mind, Beginner's Mind,* Suzuki Roshi said, "The most important thing in taking the zazen posture is to keep your spine straight." So whether you are lying down, sitting in a chair, or sitting on a cushion, try to keep a straight back. Push in a little at the back of your waist, or arch your back a little, but just a little. You do not want to be sway-backed, and when you push in at the waist if your back gets sore, that's too much pushing. Your spine should be straight all the way up your back and neck through the top of your head, and your head should be parallel to the ceiling or, if you like, parallel to the sky. Although we say to keep your back straight, we don't mean to force your back into an upright position as much as we mean to allow your back to find its own uprightness.

Two ways we can practice mindfulness of posture both in zazen and in our everyday activity are: Bring your attention to the position of your back throughout a period of zazen or throughout the

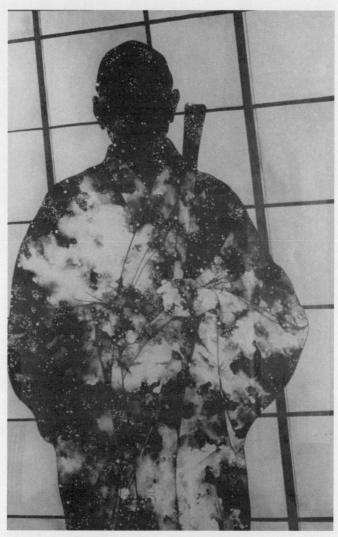

Robert Quagliata's watercolor of Suzuki Roshi.

day, and if it isn't well-aligned, readjust it. So you are noticing your back over throughout the period of zazen and readjusting it if it is not straight. I think of this as growing a new posture, and it is a good way to practice for a beginner. Another way to practice mindfulness of posture is to bring your attention to the position of your spine and note its position. Is your back lengthened and extended, or is it crooked or curved or leaning? Notice your mental or emotional state and how you are breathing. Without changing your position, just notice it and get to know the relationship between your spine, breath and mind and how the position of your back affects your experience of this moment.

Relax your shoulders and bring your ears over your shoulders. We sit with our eyes open and usually sit facing a wall. To do zazen with your eyes open means that they shouldn't be wide open and they shouldn't be closed, but somewhere in between. You shouldn't be staring at anything and your eyes don't need to be focused. They may be out of focus, softly focused or somewhere in between. The eyes should be opened enough to allow some light in. The gaze of the eyes is looking downward so it comes to rest about three feet in front of you. When gazing downward, keep your face straight ahead so that if your eyes were wide open you would be looking straight ahead. Only your gaze is cast downward, not your head. Having the eyes open, whether we actually "see" anything or not, helps keep us grounded in the present and helps us keep from falling asleep.

Place your tongue on the roof of your mouth and hold your teeth so they rest together without grinding them or holding your jaw tightly. You might notice both in zazen and in your daily activity the connection between having your teeth apart and your inner dialogue or chattering mind. This is an example of how we use the stability of the body, holding the teeth together, to support the stability of our mind. Even if the lips are shut, if the lower jaw is dropped, our mouth, that place of talking, can easily begin to move and generate mind chatter.

Pull your chin straight in slightly so that you are facing straight ahead with the top of your head parallel to the ceiling. This is almost more an attitude than a physical action and it is an aspect of the posture you will need to experiment with. When done sufficiently, it will bring alertness to your zazen; if done too much, it will create tension.

Usually at this point if we are sitting on a cushion, we rock from side to side, staring with wide arcs that slowly become smaller until we come to rest in the center of our posture. This is to help us keep from leaning to the left or right or forward or backward.

The next point is the position of our hands, called the *mudra*. We place our hands, one on top of the other, with palms facing upward. Fingers should overlap and thumb tips come together just barely touching to form a circular shape with the hands. The edge of the hands should be held against the abdomen with the thumbs about the height of the navel. The thumb tips should remain in contact, touching with enough pressure to support a single sheet of paper. I find that my thumbs don't just barely touch automatically or unconsciously. It takes an ongoing presence in this area. I find that when my attention wanders, my thumbs tend to drift away from each other; and when I have a sense of the contact between my thumbs, I am present in my immediate experience. Suzuki Roshi said that we should hold this universal *mudra* with great care as if we were holding something precious. In a sense what we are holding is our consciousness.

This is a description of an ideal zazen posture. But we have to start with the body we have, the body we are. Actually, we have no choice. Instead of trying to force yourself into some statue-like ideal, Zen practice emphasizes being present with our actual experience. By placing our attention with the minute details of our physical posture, we get to know our selves, where we have tension, where we are crooked, where we are holding, where we let go, where we are at ease. Our body reveals who we are. Through this awareness, we enter the path of practice.

This collection of statements by lineage holders at Zen Center gives a taste of the breadth and depth of how people understand and embody Buddha in our community. It is excerpted from several issues. —M.W.

Dharma Transmission
Zen Center Transmitted Teachers
Spring 1988, Summer 1994, Winter 1996, Winter 1997, Summer 1997, and Spring 2000.

"Studying Buddhism is not like studying something else. It takes time to accept the teaching completely. And the most important point is you yourself, rather than your teacher. You yourself study hard, and what you receive from your teacher is the spirit of study, the spirit to study. That spirit will be transmitted from warm hand to warm hand. You should do it. That's all. There is nothing to transmit to you."

—SUZUKI ROSHI

Transmitted teachers, from left: Mel Weitsman, Ananda Dalenberg, Blanche Hartman, Paul Discoe, Reb Anderson, Hoitsu Suzuki, Kobun Chino, Katharine Thanas, Jerome Peterson.

Steve Weintraub

I want to make a distinction—a tentative distinction—between the outer meaning of Dharma Transmission and its inner meaning. The metaphor that is used in Dharma Transmission is lineage, birth, "your Dharma son" or "your Dharma daughter." It's a lineage. So there's blood involved. There's blood that runs through the transmission. The meaning of that blood is not something just for Dharma Transmission. The meaning of that blood is for anyone who takes up practice. For anyone who takes up practice, this blood is transmitted. So I ask you: What is this blood?

We can say the outer meaning of Dharma Transmission is like graduation. The outer meaning is that you have accomplished something. It looks like you know something or have something. But Avalokitesvara is "coursing deeply in the prajna paramita"—she hears all suffering. She is coursing deeply in the *Prajna Paramita,* coursing *deeply* in practice. This coursing deeply is the feeling of Dharma Transmission. This blood courses deeply in us. We recognize it and allow it to course deeply in us, and we course deeply in it. It is not some knowledge or ability; it doesn't have anything to do with that. That's just the way it looks. Inside, in fact, it may be "pretty terrible." This is what's given from generation to generation, and what's given to each of us—not just this fancy ceremony. What's given is this opportunity to course deeply.

Steve Stucky

I am primarily moved by gratitude for the extraordinary treasures that we have, the Three Treasures: Buddha, Dharma and Sangha. During the Dharma Transmission process, I felt some clearer sense about how Buddha, Dharma and Sangha work together and how important these treasures are for me.

There is true heart, the Buddha, our own lively mind. And true teaching, the Dharma, this wonderful wisdom culture which we are developing. It's a tremendous gift for ourselves and it's a tremendous gift for the world. And we have each other, the Sangha, true friends. It's very important for us to appreciate and recognize each other's whole being, each person's whole capacity.

Please be kind to each other and to children in particular. Clarify your own motivations and really appreciate this indescribable gift that we are all in the middle of together. My promise is that I will do my best to continue being a student of the Dharma, and I ask you all to help me.

Paul Haller

The Dharma Transmission ceremony has been built up, layer after layer, for about 800 years. Sojun said, "It's just grown into this form." So layer after layer of particularity, steeped in Soto tradition, has created this lacquered container called Dharma Transmission that absorbs the person placed in it and gives them the experience of just being who they are. Out of it's womb,

through it's umbilical blood line, the gene of Soto Zen is transmitted. To me, it felt very simple, just being human. We have our particular way just as the crickets have their particular way. If you listen to their chirping, it's beauty, it's art, it's music, it's just crickets being completely crickets, and it's beyond our comprehension. Even the transmission of one human heritage requires endless study of the obvious.

One thing that has surprised and amazed me is the amount of support and help I have received while preparing for this ceremony.

So many people have helped sewing robes and obtaining materials and objects. It's helped me realize that I don't own the robe, that it belongs to all the people who helped in so many different ways. This reminded me of an expression of Suzuki Roshi's; once he held up his glasses and said "These are your glasses. I'm just borrowing them." Somehow it got through my dumb brain how much help and support I have received in all the time I have been at Zen Center, and that the people who helped me are my Dharma parents. This is their robe; I'm just borrowing it.

Pat Phelan

For eight days or so, Gil and I traveled to many different altars, offering incense and bowing; and each day we come to the zendo and chant the names of the Buddhas and Ancestors, and with each name we offer incense and do a floor bow. And also we

Gil Fronsdal and Pat Phelan.

have been writing all the names of the Buddhas and Ancestors on white silk with a paint brush. We've done that three times now. This may sound like some form of ancestor worship that has been imported from a different time and place, but in Zen we use the body as an entrance to our whole being. So in a sense, by chanting the names it enters our tongue, our ears; by doing the bowing it enters our muscles and legs. By writing it enters our hands and fingers. Part of Dharma Transmission is realizing the connectedness with the causes and conditions that have made this way of life possible. So we embody the Ancestors.

Gil Fronsdale

It seems like the day before yesterday that I came to Zen Center for the first time, knocking on the door to receive zazen instruction and to check out Zen. And only yesterday that I returned a few months later to be a guest student. I have memories, almost smells, of being in the men's dorm downstairs. Even now there are times I feel that my place at Zen Center is in the basement in that guest student dorm.

So I find it strange to be sitting here in a brown robe. The ceremony was quite moving for me, and I am very grateful for the people who were there helping, especially Blanche Shunbo Hartmen and Vicki Shosan Austin. Also I feel very grateful for Mel—Sojun Mel Weitsman Roshi—not only for the teachings I received over the years, but also for his trust in me. The transmission ceremony is a meeting of two people in trust.

In going through the transmission ceremony I feel I have stepped through a gate, there is no turning back, and I don't know what is on the other side. I certainly feel a greater sense of responsibility both for the lineage which I have now joined and for Zen Center. I have great appreciation, gratitude, and love for our Zen practice and I hope we can continue to share in it together.

Fran Tribe

Fran was given Dharma Transmission by Sojun Weitsman while at Kaiser Hospital in Walnut Creek. It was a very happy occasion for her as well as a closure of her practice. A few days later, a number of folks came together and in a few days' time made a one-piece okesa (robe) which we took to her in the hospital. On that occasion, she was witty, smiling and composed. Upon hearing that she was an inspiration to all of us, she said, "Please don't be too quick to canonize me." During her illness of six months, as her health gradually declined, she became more and more radiant and calm. Her smile had a wonderful sweetness. Accepting her condition and her impending death, she seemed more concerned for those around her with an openness and equanimity worthy of a true Bodhisattva. With her passing we feel a great loss, but her wonderful spirit is present to all of us who knew her.

Ed Brown

I have a new robe. Since it is dark brown, we decided when we found the fabric that I could be known as Dark Chocolate Sensei, and that eventually I might become Espresso Roshi. Then I

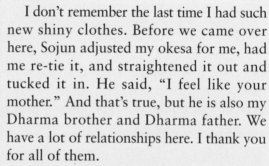

have a second robe which is a lighter brown, so when I wear that one, I will be Latte Sensei.

I don't remember the last time I had such new shiny clothes. Before we came over here, Sojun adjusted my okesa for me, had me re-tie it, and straightened it out and tucked it in. He said, "I feel like your mother." And that's true, but he is also my Dharma brother and Dharma father. We have a lot of relationships here. I thank you for all of them.

Yet many people make an event like Dharma Transmission possible. Many people make any of us who we are, and we are all here making each other who we are. Thich Nhat Hanh mentions that it takes thirty leaves on the apple tree to make an apple. So we are making each other into apples, but fortunately we get to use the same leaf more than once. We get more apples that way.

Jiko Linda Cutts

Dharma Transmission is about two people using the form of the ceremony as a vehicle, bringing forth their effort. And equal to the effort that is made, the meaning comes forth. That's always true, that whatever you bring to your activity, equal to your effort and sincerity the meaning will be revealed. This is everyone's practice, not just Dharma Transmission ceremony. It's the ceremony of life.

Transmission, not as something from A to B, but as identification, points directly to the teaching that each of us is already Buddha. And to be identified with your teacher means to walk together with all the Buddhas and Ancestors, and yet to express the teaching in your own unique way. This is not copying, but individually expressing the Dharma.

I feel extremely grateful to have experienced this wonderful ceremony and all the years preparing for it. I want to thank all the people who helped me. Among them are Abbot Norman Fischer who offered me a sabbatical to prepare for the ceremony, Gary McNabb and Katharine Thanas who served as preceptor. Finally I offer my gratitude and love to my root teacher Tenshin Reb Anderson. Words cannot reach it.

Layla Smith

I received Dharma Translation from Zoketsu Norman Fischer March 3, 1998, during the Spring Practice Period at Tassajara. It was wonderful to be doing a practice period at Tassajara again—my first in many, many years. The same remarkable strong current of practice continues in that deep valley. Lying on my bed in the yurt with the door open one warm spring morning, the fragrant air coming in and the sound of the creek in my ears, I experienced a strong sense of past and present uniting. The early 1970s—Tatsugami Roshi sitting implacably in the stone zendo, the kitchen under construction, struggling to learn to hit the bells and chant in Japanese—and the late 90s—new baths at the flats, study hall out in the yurt, now me leading the services—the same moment of eternally present "timeless spring."

I was very grateful to Norman, and to Mel who helped him, for the warmth, presence, and care they brought to the Dharma Transmission ceremony, and moved by the energy and support of Zen Center and its resources to do this ceremony in its full, traditional, powerful form. I was grateful for the friendship and support of my fellow Tassajara practitioners, and grateful to Suzuki Roshi for bringing this simple profound lineage of non-attainment to us. Now I'm continuing to wander onward in my life, but with a greater sense of permission to teach the Buddha Dharma and a greater sense of responsibility to do so.

Lee de Barros

I received Dharma Transmission from Zoketsu Norman Fischer, Abbot of San Francisco Zen Center in a red room at Tassajara Zen Center. The instructor during the proceedings was Sojun Mel Weitsman, my original priest ordination teacher. Dharma sister Layla Smith received transmission just before me. Layla and I spent many days together doing ceremonies and copying lineage materials in preparation for the final event. I will always feel a close bond with her. I have deep gratitude for Zoketsu Fischer for transmitting to me his most precious non-possession and I thank him, Sojun

Weitsman and Tenshin Anderson for looking after me all these years. Because of the efforts of every single Zen student and every single supporter of Zen Center all these years, the Dharma of Buddha unfolds right here. Central to Dharma Transmission is the Vow to make every effort to continue and extend the Dharma of Soto Zen. I so vow and will do my best. May all beings be liberated.

Layla Smith and Lee de Barros.

Gary McNabb

The Ceremony of Zazen

At first
It seems like
Something
We do.

Then
Gradually
Deepening
Truths

Perhaps
It has waited
For us
Through so many realizations.

Until
All
Rituals
Practices Ceremonies

Kindly
Re Mind
Us
Together.

One practice precept
Radiance
No one
Anything out

Much Love
Nine Bows

Maylie Scott, Sojun Mel Weitsman, and Alan Senauke.

Maylie Scott

I received Dharma Transmission from Mel along with Alan Senauke. Driving to Tassajara for the ceremony, it became clear to me that the time had come to move to Arcata to be a full time teacher for the community I'd helped develop there. I'd been thinking about the move for some time, but the impending ceremony clarified the decision. Mel readily agreed. Consequently, transmission marked a great change in my life, both in terms of circumstance and in being principally committed to being a teacher. The co-mingling of live and deceased Ancestors that happened in those five days on the Tassajara grounds continues to take care of me, even though I will never live up to it. Fundamentally it is a life of gratitude.

Alan Senauke

A year and a half later, the experience of Dharma Transmission from Sojun Weitsman feels like a dream. Daily life of family, practice, and work continues to unfold, and I am still very much at Berkeley Zen Center, practicing and studying with my teacher. And yet something is changed. It is like my experience of marriage. We are doing the same things as before, yet something is different.

September of 1998 was warm and sunny at Tassajara. Across from our "scriptorium," where my sister Maylie Scott and I copied documents onto silk each day, roofers were hammering away steadily (and loudly!). During the days we sweated in our robes. In the dark and chill of early morning we offered incense and deep gratitude to Buddhas and temple guardians. Later in the morning we did our daily bows to Buddhas, Ancestors, and the first woman practitioners.

In these activities and the ceremonies themselves I felt wonderfully supported by Shosan Victoria Austin, Kokai Roberts, Paul Haller, and the Tassajara community. But the extraordinary generosity and effort of Sojun is impossible to convey. Even as it happened there was a dreamlike quality of intimacy to the various ceremonies and rituals. Sojun moved through this dream with his customary air of nothing special, even though our activities were rare and special indeed.

Myo Lahey

Amid rain and snow, I spent March of '99 at Tassajara, performing the Dharma Transmission ceremony with my teacher, Reb Anderson. It was physically challenging for me, and deeply affecting on many levels. The students who were at Tassajara at the time, and particularly those who were able to volunteer to provide various kinds of "practical support" for the ceremony, will always have my profound gratitude, as will Preceptor Linda Ruth Cutts, Tanto Vicki Austin, Chief Jisha Fu Schroeder, and Abbot's Assistant Kokai Roberts; my gratitude to my teacher is beyond comment. Near midnight on the final night, a dazzling moon flooded the space in front of the kaisando as I stood  there alone, preparing to enter. The sliding door to the chamber was ajar, and the draperies, lit from behind, leaked red light, red as our own blood. That's really all I have to say.

Fu Schroeder

Watering the plants,
putting the toys away,
making the beds and washing
the dishes.
With these things accomplished,
opening the door and leaving home.
The Path, as always,
directly beneath the feet.
In a moment of repose and bliss,
the Great Okesa finds
its way around the body of all things.

Victoria Austin

The twenty-one days of Dharma Transmission sealed a gift that my teachers have been trying to confer all along—that everyone mutually supports and actualizes the Way. The conditions of this ceremony were so unusual that the only constant was this support, expressed through the rituals acknowledging it. Every day I bowed to the Buddhas, Bodhisattvas, protectors and Ancestors, my teachers, including teachers Zentatsu, Tenshin and women teachers of the past and present, and the welfare of the Sangha. The first day, a red-tailed hawk stood guard over Tassajara. Guests and summer students left, and work period volunteers came, all with helpful arms and open hearts. The fifth morning, as my helper and I offered incense, a giant thunderclap shook the zendo and rain poured from a clear sky. The next day the other participants in the ceremony arrived—and the Ventana Wilderness forest fire began.

Sojun Mel Weitsman and Vicki Austin.

One day, in the midst of some delicate calligraphy, we all went to lunch. The Director called us outside, saying, "I don't want to alarm anyone, but you have a half hour to leave Tassajara. The forest fire is very close." Mel, Blanche, Kokai and Alan, gently and firmly packed everything back into the cars and set it all up again—in San Francisco—by suppertime. City Center staff and residents made big adjustments to accommodate a major shift. Everyone was so helpful.

In Dharma Transmission, verifying and entrusting arrives through all time from the Buddha to oneself, and oneself to Buddha. Body and mind joins in the great astonishing dance to the beat of the warm red heart. May I require the kindness of my teacher, Sojun Mel Weitsman, and of everyone else who so clearly and fully express the meaning of Dharma Transmission to me.

Michael Wenger

My experience of Dharma Transmission was of recognizing the deep connection to my teacher Sojun Mel Weitsman, to all those who came before him, to all those who will practice in the future and even a sense of connection to all living beings, period. It's funny in a way to have a special ceremony celebrating the unity of beings and yet, what could be better?

Barbara Kohn

This fall I began, at City Center, a three-week process that culminated at Tassajara in the dark of a beautiful November night. During those weeks I had bowed to the Ancestors and to the Sangha members who assisted as I went from altar to altar offering my appreciation for this practice which has so altered my life. Myo has called it a meditation on the Ancestors and so it is. It also became a meditation on appreciation. I was stunned by the myriad ways that people offered themselves during those days. My intimacy with my teacher, Blanche, grew as my intimacy with

all the sangha developed. Time, things, encouraging words, skills, friendliness—all were given freely, usually before I even knew what was needed. My own ability to care increased in this barrage of lovingkindness. I knew it wasn't just for ME, but for myself as another of so many who have been offered the opportunity to vow to continue this practice by giving it to others. On the day of the ceremonies, compressed into one night to accommodate a variety of schedules, Zenkai came down with the flu. She rose to the occasion with a voice that was especially deep and she and I became the first two hens at SFZC to delve in these realms together. We laughed and were amazed, touched by each other and our relatedness to all things. My overwhelming feeling the next day and since has been one of gratitude for the generosity, intimacy, compassion, humor, honesty, and wisdom embodied in these rituals of bloodline which when all is said and done, has opened wide the connection to all beings.

Daigan Lueck

On November 15, 1999, I received Dharma Transmission from then Abbot Zoketsu Norman Fischer, at Zen Mountain Temple. What can I say? Words can hardly reach it. That it was a traditional ceremony, a rite of passage, a family affair, intimate and irreplaceable. That it happened to take place in the autumn of the year which, fitting enough, matched the late autumn of my life. That the russet shades of autumn were like the color of my robe. That the robe itself, stitched together by my clumsy fingers, felt impregnated with the thoughts and feelings of a lifetime. That when the ceremonies took place on two consecutive

nights in the red-draped room, all my past and present relations with the world were there with me, shining in my teacher's eyes. That gratitude overflowed my heart and tears caught in my throat. That when it was over, I came away feeling something precious beyond precepts, lineage, verification, empowerment, yet at the same time nothing special at all, but simple, a commonality with the earth itself, natural and unhindered; and that a warmth enclosed me not unlike the warmth riding from a compost heap, rich and steamy, spreading in all directions. And that having said this much I've really not touched its true character. All I can say finally is thanks to all my teachers, bow again and again. And may I be a worthy recipient of this robe.

Taigen Leighton

Dharma Transmission is an amazingly wonderful and totally challenging process, possible only with the assistance of innumerable beings. I am deeply grateful for more than two decades of extraordinary patience and subtle guidance from my teacher, Tenshin Anderson. Abbess Linda Cutts was also extremely helpful as instructor for my ceremony, as she has been for many years. The Tassajara students were  especially kind and encouraging, helpful in specific instances, but also just in the strength of their practice keeping the jewel of Tassajara beautifully functioning. The real transmission of Buddha's Way is in the ongoing generations of students who engage the practice of facing and opening the deep self that is not separate from the whole interconnected universe. I am honored and humbled to now be taking on this new responsibility for upholding and maintaining this wonderful Dharma.

Everyday Zen

Harry Roberts was part Yurok Indian, trained from childhood to be a Yurok Shaman and deeply immersed in Indian knowledge of the natural elements, plants, soil, sunlight, and air. He was also a Western university-trained agronomist with a lifetime of experience on the California Coast, including developing seed stock, nurseries, and even working Green Gulch as a cowboy forty years ago.

He came to Green Gulch for extended visits, teaching us and helping us to know the land. The following story is one of a collection, about the way of the Yurok people. –M.W.

A Yurok Story

Harry Roberts

SUMMER 1976

My uncle was sitting in the morning sun in front of his house fixing the feathers on the long headdress wands for the brush dance. He had made a pot of sturgeon glue and was very carefully smoothing the feathers down and gluing new feathers in where the old ones were damaged or torn loose. He was working very carefully and slowly for this was very fine, difficult work to do.

I looked over one of the wands that he was repairing and I could barely see where the feathers were damaged. I told him that I didn't think that he had to repair that one as I could barely find the damage. My uncle just looked at me for a while, and then he asked me what it was that the wand I held in my hand was. And I said that it was a brush dance headdress wand. My uncle waited a while and then asked me what it was for, and I told him that it was for wearing in your headdress when you danced the brush dance. And that since one danced at night no one could see that it was very slightly damaged. He looked at me some more, and finally he said, "But I know."

We sat in the sun and I helped him fix the headdress. After a while he said that it was about time that I should begin to study to be a man. He would start asking me the questions that a man must be able to answer so that I could understand the law.

I asked my uncle what was so hard to understand about the law. It seemed very simple to me because there was but one law and that was merely "Be true to thyself."

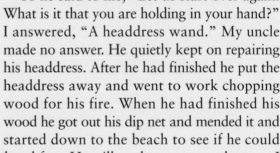

My uncle asked me, "If you understand the law, why do you not understand why I am fixing my headdress wands?" This I could not answer.

So he said to me, "Let us start over again. What is it that you are holding in your hand?" I answered, "A headdress wand." My uncle made no answer. He quietly kept on repairing his headdress. After he had finished he put the headdress away and went to work chopping wood for his fire. When he had finished his wood he got out his dip net and mended it and started down to the beach to see if he could catch some fish for breakfast. He still spoke not a word to me. I asked him if I could go fishing with him. He merely looked at me and said nothing. I could not understand why he wouldn't speak to me. Finally I asked him what was the matter. Had I offended him? He smiled and said no, that it was he who had not wished to offend me by interrupting my thoughts before I had finished answering the question.

Summer 1976

I said, "But I answered the question. I told you what it was." He just looked at me some more and said nothing.

So I thought and thought and thought. Finally I told him, "It is a headdress wand for the last night of the brush dance." He looked at me and slightly smiled and said "Unh," by which I knew that he meant yes, that's a little better, it will do as a start; now let's get after the answer. So I said, "It is to show how rich you are because it is the best and most expensive of all of the headdress wands on the river." Whereupon my uncle looked upon me with disgust and said, "I thought that you wished to be a man. Why don't you start to think like one?" After having so expressed himself, he left and went fishing, and not one more word was addressed to me that day.

The next morning my uncle was again sitting in the sun in front of his house. This time he was making some bone arrow points. He had been soaking the bone for several weeks in the creek and it was nice and soft and just right for cutting into shape. I sat beside him to watch how he carved the bone and to see how he cut with the grain so as to cut more easily.

Finally he looked at me and said "Well?"

This was very bad for me. For elder uncle only spoke this way when he was very, very angry. I had seen big grownup persons cast their eyes aside and blush when he so addressed them in council meeting. I had even seen important men leave the council and start out on long pilgrimages to the high places when so addressed.

I was only a small boy, and so I just cried and ran and cuddled up to my dog and told my dog how hard it was for a little boy to have such a great man for an uncle. And my dog understood and licked my face all over, and especially my ears.

Presently my uncle came to me and inquired if my ears were now clean enough to listen with, and did I still wish to be a man?

I said, Oh yes, I did.

My uncle said that since I was such a little boy he would help me a little more. So I should tell him again what it was that the brush dance wand was. This time I told him that it was the wand which one wore in his headdress on the last night of the brush dance for the final curing of a sickness in the person for whom the dance was being held.

My uncle smiled and said that that was a little better, but what was the brush dance really all about anyway? I said that it was to drive out the evil spirits which were making the person sick. Uncle looked at me and shook his head. He said, "You sound like a superstitious old woman. I shall be kind to you this time and tell you all about it."

So he spoke: "When a person is sick of a sickness which people cannot see, it is then that for that person we hold a brush dance. In the brush dance we sing fun songs and make jokes to let that

person know that there is fun
in the world. While everyone
dances around the sick person,
the doctor talks to the patient
about what it is that troubles
him. When that person sees
that he is surrounded by friends
who are singing happy songs to
make him feel better, then he
feels that it is that people care
for him. He feels safe and tells
the doctor what it is that both-
ers him, and the doctor tells the
patient what he can do about
his troubles.

Harry Roberts.

"On the last night of the
dance everyone brings out their
very best costumes. These costumes represent hundreds of
hours of very careful work. They are made of the rarest and most
difficult to obtain materials. They have been kept in absolutely
perfect condition. Never does a costume ever show any wear or
that it has been used before. Everything is perfect. These costumes
are the most beautiful things that an Indian can make. Thus when
one dances before the sick person in this costume it means that
the dancer has cared enough for the patient to go to all of that
trouble in the hope that he can help the patient.

"Now. How could I respect myself if I only went halfway, or
three quarters of the way to help someone? If I'm not going to
help all of the way, it is better that I don't go to that dance at all.
So when I make a brush dance the patient knows that I am all of
the way for him. Then he feels reassured and will quite likely get
well.

"This is what the brush dance wands represent. This is the way
to be true to yourself. Now let us see if you can think like a man
the next time we have a question."

Then it was that I saw that the law was not quite as simple as it appeared. Thus it was that I realized that to be a man meant to be proud to yourself in everything; you could never be less than all of yourself without breaking the law.

When I finally understood what a person who entered a brush dance was doing, I then wanted to know just what the dance meant. Why it was danced the way it was danced. I asked why the dancers did not all dance up and down in unison.

This is what my uncle said: "The dancers do not all go up and down together because the world is like a canoe. If everyone leans to one side of the boat together, and to the other side together, they rock the boat and pretty soon it turns over."

I asked what the solo dancers were doing when they jumped in the middle and acted so strangely. He said, "Don't you remember the story of how, when the world was reborn, creation appointed the giant woodpecker to go around the world and report to him how things were going? So in this dance men who have pure spirit jump in the middle and jerk their heads back and forth like a woodpecker and spread their arms and fly around and sing the woodpecker song and everyone wears woodpecker scalps and heads. This is to remind the great woodpecker spirit that there is someone who is sick and he should go and report it to Creation so that Creation will lend his strength to the doctor so that the sick person or child can get well."

Stone steps at Tassajara.

The relationship between Buddhism and Psychotherapy is addressed by long time Zen practitioner and psychotherapist Steven Weintraub. This is a popular subject in America, where psychology studies behavior and consciousness. Where are they the same? Where are they different? Where will you go for an answer? –M.W.

Facing the Darkness in Buddhism and Psychotherapy

Steven Weintraub

FALL 1988

Robert Gethner, a practicing psychotherapist and a student of Zen Buddhism, in an article he wrote on the parallels he sees between these two disciplines, states: "For the most part, the reason that people begin to practice Zen and the reason they come for psychotherapy is the same. People come because their lives are not working, and they have faith that by practicing Zen or by entering psychotherapy, things will change and that they will get some relief from their suffering... In psychotherapy and Zen practice, the way is the same: through, not out." But, we may ask, through what? That is, what territory is it that needs to be gone through, needs to be explored and examined? Generally speaking, I feel, it is those areas of our mental/emotional life that we would prefer to turn away from, to not look at. They are often dark, and they are often secret, and they are often fearful. J.D. Frank comments: "... psychotherapy, by persuading patients to face what they fear, enables corrective learning to take place." To go "through," then, is to face the darkness.

This movement in psychotherapy, and in Buddhist practice, is one which is, in the mainstream culture at least, discouraged in modern American times. We go to great lengths to avert our view from the face of death, we shut away the old and infirm in institutions, hoping someone else will tend to them, we idolize youth. The media are full of Barbie Doll and GI Joe ideals, or the latest, hippest version of their descendants. And if there is a problem, when difficulties or suffering arise, which they inevitably do, we say: "fix it"; as though people are machines, and the only question is: who's the best mechanic? In the field of psychotherapy, this tendency to go "out, not through," the attempt to avoid, escape, minimize, or otherwise obliterate one's problems, difficulties, suffering, is unfortunately reflected in any number of popular, "fix it" therapies; and as well, in a good deal of modern mental health care, in what Jonathon Adams aptly identifies as the "Brave New World . . . of cost-conscious health care providers." This is a corporate mentality misapplied. Such an ethos violates my own sense of what psychotherapy is all about, what it attempts, most fundamentally, to address.

The mechanistic, and darkness-avoiding mentality is sharply in contrast to the traditional Buddhist Path of self development, and to certain major currents in Western, psychotherapeutic tradition. In the latter, I think primarily of the Jungian orientation, but a similar viewpoint is echoed in other schools of psychology as well. Roy Shafer, for example, speaking about brief psychoanalytic psychotherapy, advocates that " . . . the therapist tries to establish as much of an exploratory or investigative atmosphere and discipline as possible." His formulation of the goals of brief therapy makes the same point, even more strikingly: " . . . [the client] develops a more definite and more comprehensive idea of the scope, multiplicity, and complexity of his problems." When I first came upon this, I thought: "Yikes, these are goals!?!" From the point of view of "fix it," from the point of view of "get that machine running and get it back on the road" (though no one knows quite where the machine is going, or what the point of getting there would be, anyway)—these are indeed modest accomplishments. But from the point of view of the traditional religious or spiritual understanding of human life (the "perennial philosophy"), these insights are the first major steps on the right path.

Two illustrations come to mind from the traditional mythic biography of Buddhism's founder, one from the beginning, the other from the turning point of his career. It was prophesied to Shakyamuni Buddha's father that his son would become either a

Moon over Tassajara.

great king or a great religious leader. Wanting to promote the former of these paths, the father kept Siddhartha (Buddha's name as a young man), shielded from the harshness of the world, never allowing him to leave the palace grounds, always surrounding him with gaiety and diversions. Nevertheless, Siddhartha did, at some point, visit a nearby city. The story goes that on each of three successive days, he saw, respectively, a sick person, a dying person, and a dead person. His shock, (never having been exposed to this darkness before), was overwhelming—and it was this experience that propelled him onto the path of self-knowing that he explored so thoroughly. Later in his career, after numerous false starts and tribulations, he came to sit and meditate under the tree where, seven days hence, he would achieve enlightenment. Mara, "the evil one," (more on who Mara is later), seeing that his game would be up if Siddhartha accomplished his goal, immediately sent hordes of wrathful beings to attack the future Buddha. Siddhartha saw them coming and remained sitting calmly. As they furiously shot their arrows and flung their spears at him, the weapons turned to lotuses and fell at Siddhartha's feet. Mara then sent beautiful women and enticements of all sorts to distract and allure Siddhartha from his intent. Siddhartha continued to just sit. Not to be easily outdone, Mara himself then went to where the future Buddha was, and began to upbraid him, attempting to instill an insidious doubt in Siddhartha's heart about his readiness and ability to achieve awakening. Buddha continued to sit quietly, and called the earth as his witness, to witness and confirm the intensity and direction of his intention. When the earth did attest and confirm Siddhartha, (she shook), Mara had to withdraw, finally defeated.

In both these instances important aspects of the archetypal path of "through, not out" are demonstrated. In the first instance, it is not at all incidental that the motivating forces that move Siddhartha to begin his search, his visions of old age, sickness and death, are expressions of basic human archetypal forms of suffering. And it was going toward this suffering, going through it (rather than the contrary alternative of attempting to avoid it) that eventuated in the final resolution which he came to. This first instance points to the paradoxical usefulness of suffering. In the second instance, Buddha demonstrates the prototypic activity which, to this day, is the mainstay of actual Buddhist meditation practice: he sits calmly and unmoving. Face to face with wrath and seduction: he doesn't run in fear, he doesn't succumb to temptation. (Yay for Buddha!) In Freudian terms, we could say that the spears and dancing girls represent his own aggressive and sexual impulses. And he succeeds, first, by owning these impulses, (not running from them), and, second, by sufficiently disidentifying with them, so that he can face them without being thrown totally off course. The happy result is that the spears turn to lotuses.

Allen Wheelis, a psychoanalyst practicing in San Francisco, addresses our sense of owning (or not owning) our difficulties and suffering: "We feel our suffering as alien, desperately unwanted, yet nothing imposes it." And later in the same piece: "Modern psychiatry found its image in the course of dealing with symptoms experienced as alien." But, of course, symptoms are not alien—they are the current, somewhat distorted, expressions of something very much our own. If we own what is our own, and this is the import of psychotherapeutic treatment and of Buddhist meditation, there is some possibility of undistorting the situation. This possibility arises out of the willingness to face the darkness. Shafer, again in his addressing brief psychoanalytic psychotherapy, points out that the second goal of such therapy is that "most of all ... [the client] realizes something of the extent of his active participation in bringing about the difficulties that to begin with he experienced passively..." I take issue with Shafer only in that he implies that a person's difficulties are somehow mostly their own "fault." For an adult who was the victimized child of a sexually abusive parent, there may be little "active participation in bringing about the difficulties." Yet, I do agree with Shafer, continuing the same example, in that such a person is, in some sense, actively participating in the current configuration of their difficulties. There are many cases where such a person is, for example, symptomatically extremely depressed and self deprecating, as a result of such abuse. This would be the distorted, "alien," expression of a deep inner pain and tangle. The example of abuse also allows me to make a related point about the nature of averting the darkness in one's life. Namely, such an aversion may be a necessary adaptive mechanism, a mechanism of psychological survival in very difficult circumstances. What is needed, in any case, is encouragement to face what may be the extremely painful darkness of an undiscussed, unresolved, past.

Looking at the same material from a different standpoint, many of these points resonate with the Jungian idea of individuation. Marie-Louise von Franz describes the first approach to the unconscious in these terms: "The actual process of individuation—the conscious coming-to-terms with one's own inner center (psychic nucleus) or Self, generally begins with a wounding of the personality and the suffering that accompanies it. This initial shock amounts to a sort of "call," although it is not often recognized as such." Here we have that paradoxically "helpful" suffering explicated. In Wheelis' terms, this is the "symptoms experienced as alien"; in Buddhist terms, this is the old age, sickness and death which Buddha saw. Jungian theory also clarifies what happens if such forces within our consciousness are not integrated, if the call is not heeded: what we turn away from, what we refuse to confront and grapple with, makes its existence known nevertheless. It comes up as shadow. This is not all that the Jungian shadow is, but avoided psychic material constitutes one of its major manifestations, probably the most problematical one: "The shadow becomes hostile when he is ignored or misunderstood." Mara personifies this unintegrated and therefore hostile shadow, in the Buddhist story. And in the case of the adult who was victimized as a child, the depression and self deprecation are hostile shadow elements which need to be brought into the light. Von Franz's "solution," or, more accurately, the first step on the path of individuation "is to turn directly toward the approaching darkness without prejudice and totally naively, and to try to find out what its secret aim is and what it wants from you."

Wind Bell

PUBLICATION OF ZEN CENTER
VOLUME XXII, NUMBER TWO, FALL 1988

Fall 1988

Adolf Guggenbuhl-Craig, a Swiss Jungian, makes the connection between individuation and what has traditionally been the motive force in spiritual development more explicit. He distinguishes between the path of well-being, which has to do with "the avoidance of unpleasant tensions ... possession of a physical sense of comfort ... the possibility of satisfying some of the so-called material wishes without inordinate effort ... " etc.; and the path of salvation: "Certainly not belonging to the state of well-being are tensions ... painful emotions ... difficult and insoluble internal and external conflicts ... the felt need to come to terms with evil and death." He clarifies that he is using the word "salvation" in a broad sense: "In the context of religious language, salvation means seeking and finding contact with God. In philosophy one speaks of the search for meaning, for an experience of the meaning of life." Still, by subsuming individuation in the category of salvation, he associates it irrevocably with religious pursuits. And though the paths to salvation are numerous, they, nevertheless, share "certain features in common. I know of none in which a confrontation with suffering and death is not necessary." Here we have the facing of the darkness again. In his concept of psychotherapy, Craig allows for both well-being and salvation: "To promote well-being involves helping the patient to adapt to his environment and to learn to make his way successfully through the world. But we speak further of individuation... this does not necessarily concern mental health, well-being, or a sense of happiness. As a healer, the psychotherapist seeks to help the patient toward a feeling of well being... He seeks also to support the patient in his search for salvation, for individuation."

Because the client's facing the darkness is the crucial work s/he must do in psychotherapy, it is requisite, most simply, that the client have the courage and willingness to do it. This may be something the client brings with her/him to the first psychotherapeutic hour. If not, if there is some version of wanting to just "fix it," nevertheless, sooner or later, s/he will have to confront the fact that it is not as simple as that; that, as Wheelis points out, "the symptom does not afflict the patient, it is the patient"; that it is or will be required of her/him that s/he own or see some things s/he might rather not. Using Buddhist practice metaphorically, the client has to mobilize the motivation to sit still long enough to look at some things that may not be pleasant. And as courage is required of the client, encouragement is required of the therapist. This attitude of encouragement may encompass a number of aspects. It will mean that the therapist understands and expresses to the client her/his empathic understanding of just how difficult a task it may be to face the darkness. Even better, and perhaps necessarily, this empathy would naturally arise out of the therapist having confronted, to at least some degree, her/his own darkness. Third, though this may not look like encouragement, I think it is important that the therapist not try to solve the problem. This willingness to resist the temptation to be helpful in the more obvious sense comes from the conviction that solution is in the problem.

And this brings us full circle. Finally, it is not a matter of getting "out" of the problem, it is not a matter of getting out of suffering, but rather one of going "through" it.

Tassajara work circle.

How does Buddhist practice inform our life with kids and family? Lee Klinger-Lesser wholeheartedly examines this question in her own family. —M.W.

Karma, Dharma, and Diapers

Lee Klinger-Lesser

FALL 1989

The vivid image of a two-year-old boy I once took care of, sitting quietly at a table with his shoulders hunched up to his ears, remains with me after more than ten years. This was a posture I had seen frequently on his mother when she was nervous or tense. Her son was simply adopting it through observation. Alice Miller writes in her book, *Thou Shalt Not Be Aware, Society's Betrayal of the Child,* "Whatever we put into a child's soul we naturally will find there, but if we become conscious of what we are doing, we then have the chance to free ourselves from the constrictions of our past." (New American Library, 1986, p. 154). Children learn from everything we do and don't do, from everything we say and don't say.

Each month, when I see the full moon in the sky, I find the words from the Full Moon Ceremony returning to me: "All my ancient twisted karma, from beginningless greed, hate and delusion, borne through body, speech and mind, I now fully avow." Now, instead of being in the zendo I am in the midst of my home, realizing that my own karma is constantly informing the lives of my children, as theirs does mine. The more conscious I can be, the less I will interfere with the unfolding of my children in accordance with their own natures, and we will be able to meet true nature to true nature, as I vowed to do with my husband when we married each other.

It is distressing to me how deeply we ignore and undervalue the quality of family life in general in our society, and that we have continued this neglect in the cultivation of our spiritual practice. I can think of no other areas in which the impact of our own mindfulness is as profound as it is in the raising of children.

After practicing Zen from 1978 to 1983 in the formal, monastic setting of Green Gulch and Tassajara, I find that my family is now my Practice Center. One of the challenges of family as Practice Center is the lack of established forms. I have to be responsible for how I practice in a way that is distinctly different from following strict schedules and shared formal practices.

Elements that I have found important to family practice are: personal practices for myself; shared family practices and rituals; and being with other families who are exploring how to practice together. I meet at least once a month with a Buddhist teacher to help me explore my own personal needs in practice and to help me create a context for practice at home. Being with other families interested in practice has been encouraging and stimulating.

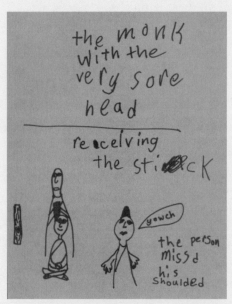

Drawing by Dhyana Cabarga, age ten.

Gradually we are building a "family sangha" through being together during "Family Days of Mindfulness," sponsored by the Marin chapter of the Buddhist Peace Fellowship, during meditation retreats that include children, through shared writing and conversations. This past spring Thich Nhat Hanh offered a retreat specifically for young people. Fifty-two families came from around the country: one hundred and four people in all. The young people who participated ranged in age from four-and-a-half to nineteen years old (there were also three infants). For children to be with other children who are practicing mindfulness and meditation makes the whole process more accessible, fun and real! Using our thoughtfulness and creativity to develop practices that are welcoming and age-appropriate to our children is important, especially when it is done with joy.

In my own home, our most basic practice is breathing together. Becoming quiet and aware of breathing is possible for each of us at any moment. We work with this in different ways. During the recent retreat for young people with Thich Nhat Hanh, we learned a song that is linked to breathing with each line accompanying an inhalation or exhalation: "In, Out, Deep, Slow, Calm, Ease, Smile, Release, Present Moment, Wonderful Moment." We sang this song throughout the retreat, during sitting and walking meditation, and when we gathered together for other events. It has now become a part of our family life. The tune itself is soft and calming. When I am aware of being agitated or irritated, I can sing this song as a form of meditation that brings me back to myself in the midst of any activity.

One evening, as I was preparing dinner, my twenty-month-old daughter was being her familiar inquisitive self. She went from discovering a glass of water, and emptying it onto the floor, to exploring the contents of the compost bucket, to pulling on the dog's tail. At the same time my six-year-old son was pleading with me to help him make some paper airplanes and complaining about being hungry. I began to notice the distinct signs of irritability rising in me, my shoulders tensing, my stomach tight, breathing shallow, movements sharper, a desire to yell. It seemed like an opportune time to stop and sing. After singing "In, Out..." five or six times, I found I was smiling. And I was content and grateful to be where I was. Jason watched with quiet curiosity, as he saw me transform my state of mind. Several weeks later I overheard Jason trying to help Carol quiet down and perhaps go to sleep in her room. He was singing "In, Out..."

I taught this song to two mothers with whom I participate in a mother's group. Neither of them practices Zen or Buddhist meditation. They told me that the song has become a part of their lives. One who has a four-year-old daughter told me that her daughter asks her to sing the song when she is out of control, crying or deeply upset. One night when her mother wouldn't let her have a snack, five minutes before their dinner, she began to cry. Her crying built out of control. Still sobbing at the table, she pleaded, "Mommy, sing the song!" Her mother did and gradually she became calm. This had become a tool which helped them both to seek comfort, even in the midst of conflict with each other so that emotional distress moved to conscious breathing, to calm, and even to connection with each other.

My other friend's family has adopted the song to calm their six-month-old baby. Her four-year-old daughter and her husband both sing the song to the baby and the baby stops crying. Singing this song does not guarantee that the baby will stop crying. It can however provide us with the opportunity to maintain our own calmness no matter what happens.

Another tool we use in our family for connecting us with our breath and returning to the present moment was inspired by our experience two years ago in a meditation retreat with Thich Nhat Hanh. It was our first introduction to a "Bell of Mindfulness." After the retreat we bought a bell for our home. It lives on the altar in Jason's room where anyone can get it at any time and bring it to sound it anywhere in the house. Just as we experienced during the retreat, whenever the bell is sounded, we all stop whatever we are doing and breathe three times. Then we continue mindfully with what we were doing. Our bell has been sounded to greet new guests, on the way to the bathroom, in the midst of bustling dinner preparations, during meals, in the heat of arguments, and directly after angry outbursts.

Once, when I was afraid that Jason and my then infant daughter might have whooping cough (we were waiting for test results), Jason and I were working together in the kitchen when he did something I had asked him not to do. I roared at him with the full force of my preoccupation. A few minutes later I heard the sound of the bell. As I breathed with the tears that instantly arose in me, I heard a clear, little voice say, "Mommy, I rang the bell so you wouldn't be so angry."

I find there is so much for me to learn and practice with in relation to the anger and frustration that arises in me with my children and immediate family members during even the most trivial of interactions. During one of his talks at the young people's retreat,

Zen Center picnics.

Thich Nhat Hanh spoke of anger, saying it needs a friend and the friend is mindfulness. Families provide wonderful opportunities to practice the cultivation of this friendship. It is important to me that Jason knows that sometimes I am mindful and sometimes I'm not, that I can come back to my true self, and that he can help me. I think he understands this about himself, too. Having the bell, a tangible practice we share, I believe is empowering for Jason, especially in the face of what can be overpowering adult emotions and judgments.

I know that as Jason gets older our rituals will change, and this too is part of our practice. Most likely the altars we have all around our home will stay. In each of our bedrooms, in our bathrooms, and in our kitchen, they are invitations to be aware. For the past one-and-a-half years, at night before bed, Jason and I have offered incense on his altar. Jason's altar is a place where he puts things that are special to him. He has two Jizo figures standing side by side on top of a purple silk sandbag that I made for him after I made one for a friend of mine who was dying; a clay face that a friend made as a portrait of Jason; a big conch shell; some favorite rocks; a photograph of a lion that Jason took at the zoo; photographs of Jason with his grandfather in a frame with a special letter from his grandpa; a scarf that belonged to my mother, whom Jason never knew; a piece of shedded snake skin, and a variety of everchanging items.

Jason lights the match and gives it to me to light the candles. He doesn't feel comfortable enough yet with the fire in his hand to do it himself, so he goes instead to turn off the lights. He offers a stick of incense; then he sounds the Bell of Mindfulness, sits down on my lap and we sit and breathe together for three breaths in front of his candlelight altar. Sometimes we sit there for ten or fifteen breaths. When Jason is ready he snuffs out the candles; we turn on the lights, get into bed and read a story.

The other day in the car, as my husband Marc and I were talking about a Day of Mindfulness, Jason blurted out, "I hate meditation!" After a slight pause I said, "But we sit meditation every night in front of your altar and you seem to like that." With tolerance for my ignorance he replied, "No, I don't mean that. I like that. I mean real meditation like they do at Green Gulch for forty minutes."

I trust that someday Jason will know that sitting in front of his altar breathing quietly three times is also real meditation. And I trust that the experience of happily sitting together will remain with him, as will the transforming power of being in touch with breathing moment by moment. It has been a refreshing lesson for me to experience the influence of stopping in the midst of what I am doing and simply following three breaths. I can become more present. My own practice does not have to be sitting forty minutes of meditation. I have to find what is conducive to the realities of our family life. It is an ongoing exploration.

What we are trying to do in our family is give our children practices, rituals and experiences that they can own, incorporating our values into our lives and letting our children grow up tasting them. In my husband's and my experiences practicing at Zen Center, we saw little offered to children that they could own for themselves. We both come from Jewish heritage, but not from Jewish practice. It has been a rich process for us to use our experiences practicing Zen to help us become more open to the wealth of Jewish family ritual and tradition.

Each week, we observe the Sabbath; it is our weekly Family Day of Mindfulness, beginning with a service at sunset on Friday night and ending with a service when the first three stars appear on Saturday night. Adding new rituals to our family life is a slow process. We spent one year just lighting the candles on Friday night and eating a nice meal together before we were ready to give up shopping, television, working or going places on Saturday. Our intention is to do what nourishes us as a family. Celebrating the Sabbath has become a gift for us. It is an opportunity to go beyond the pressures of constant juggling and being squeezed by time, to be together in the spaciousness and simplicity of the structure of the Sabbath. It is like bringing a touch of monastic life into our family life each week, a rich and fertile blend.

It is also a time shared with other generations. Every Friday night we sit down at the table: Carol, twenty months old; Jason, six years old; Marc, thirty-seven years old; myself, thirty-eight years old; and my father, eighty years old. The table is set with my mother's wedding silverware, a lace tablecloth made by her mother, gold-rimmed holiday glasses from my father's mother. As we start to light the candles, Carol knows what is coming and begins to sing with soft bird-like sounds, a blessing of its own to our being together.

I remember a rabbi once describing the lighting of the candles of Friday nights as a marking of the ending of one moment and the beginning of another. In Buddhist practice we speak of impermanence, interdependence and non-attachment. In our family we are borrowing from the wisdom, history and traditions of both Judaism and Buddhism; seeing how they come alive through our daily lives of innumerable beginnings, endings, and present moments. How does the reality of impermanence affect how I live?

As part of my own bedtime ritual I have begun to do three full bows in front of the altars of each of my children. I see them sleeping and quiet. I breathe with them. With the detachment of not needing to interact with them, our connection is refreshed for me. I see them with more quiet eyes. Perhaps I see them more clearly. Sometimes as I watch them sleep I allow the question to arise in me, "If my children were to die, what would I regret the most...?" Continuing to breathe, I open to what arises in me and work to give it room to influence my actions.

Our children are with us so briefly. They change so quickly. What we do now helps to mold them and their future families, and *their* future families. To be conscious and mindful in what we do requires intention and effort. To give our own true mind to the many intricacies and complexities of family relationships is a Buddha field to practice in. If we can be happy and peaceful within our families, it can't help but impact our wider world. If we neglect the opportunities to practice with our families, that too can't help but impact our wider world.

Zen Center has been associated with food. (Bread, Tassajara Guest Season, Greens Restaurant.) Therefore this recipe by former Tassajara guest cook Laura Burgess. It tastes good!
—M.W.

Apple Crisp
Laura Burges
SPRING 1990

I'm teaching third grade at the San Francisco School. On occasional Saturday mornings, I go over to Cal to participate in the Bay Area Writer's Project, a series of classes to help me learn how to help kids learn to write.

Recently, in such a class, we were asked to describe how to make a dessert and this is what came to mind: I learned how to make apple crisp one winter when I was living in a Zen monastery in the Los Padres Wilderness.

We lived in a very simple way up there with simple food that was served Japanese style in the meditation hall. In winter, the cold outside was paralyzing and it was only slightly warmer in the zendo.

But every five days, we'd set the tables in the dining room with red table cloths, light the kerosene lamps, and sit down to what seemed to us, given our usual fare, a feast.

Silent much of the day (to continue our meditation) we were hungry for talk and the clinking of dishes and silverware, the rattle of conversation, filtered out of the dining room like the babble of the rumbling winter creek.

I worked in the kitchen that winter and we worked—mostly—in silence. I learned how to press a special tool through the core of the crisp green apples, which would simultaneously core and slice them. We would toss the apple slices with our hands in a huge stainless steel bowl, with fresh squeezed lemon juice and tumble them into long pans. We'd pile on the topping—a concoction of rolled oats, flour, brown sugar, nutmeg, cinnamon and butter, lightly mixed, press it gently over the bed of gleaming apples, and slide the pans into the oven.

We'd serve it hot with cold whipped cream, carried over to the dining room from the kitchen through the chill night air to the boisterous monks. The crispy sweet topping, the warm, soft, spicy apples, the cold whipped cream—delicious and surprising.

I don't suppose food has ever tasted so good to me—before or since—as it did in that mountain wilderness against a background of bird song, rain, creek chatter. The sharp pleasure of delicious food in that simple, silent way of life.

This is my current version:

Apple Crisp

INGREDIENTS:
6–8 green pippin apples
   juice of one lemon
 1 teaspoon cinnamon
 2 tablespoons flour
 1 cup apple juice

TOPPING:
 1 cup rolled oats
 ¾ cup flour
 ½ teaspoon salt
 2 teaspoons cinnamon
   dash of nutmeg
 1⅓ cup brown sugar (or a bit more if you like)
 ½ cup butter, well chilled
 ½ cup coarsely chopped walnuts

Preheat oven to 350°. Slice the apples thin, leaving the peels on. Mix them in a bowl with lemon juice, flour and 1 teaspoon cinnamon. Place them in a buttered 9 x 13-inch baking dish with the apple juice.

Mix the topping in a bowl. Cut the butter into small chunks and work it in with your fingers. Press the topping mixture onto the apples, but don't mix them together. Cover the pan with aluminum foil and bake for a half hour, then remove the foil and bake another

15 minutes or so. The apples should be soft and the topping should be crunchy.

Serve hot. You can top it off with whipped cream, cold half-and-half, vanilla ice cream—or all by itself. Serves 6–8.

Suzuki Roshi ashes site at Tassajara.

This exploration of Buddhism and self-healing is insightful and witty. You'll feel better just reading it! See Darlene's book, Finding a Joyful Life in the Heart of Pain *–M.W.*

Buddhism and Self-Healing

Darlene Cohen

FALL 1990

I'd like to talk about healing, Buddhism and self-healing, especially what we call self-healing. I have rheumatoid arthritis. I've had it for thirteen years. It is a very crippling disease, and I developed it in my seventh year of Zen practice when I was living at Green Gulch Farm. So that is one reason I would like to talk about healing. Another reason is that I've noticed people in general are interested in healing, especially this thing we in California call self-healing. It seems like many of our friends are being stricken with maladies or getting injured or, as we age, getting more concerned with their bodies. I think this is a topic of general interest to people. Especially people who have some practice of penetration, be it meditation or a mantra, because people who have some sort of practice tend to use their illness and their healing process as a further opportunity to practice a mode of penetration. They use illness and healing as a penetration into the nature of things and into the self.

In *The Blue Cliff Record,* Yun-men said, "Medicine and sickness mutually correspond. The whole universe is our medicine. What is the self?"

When I was first very ill, and other Zen students took care of me, I didn't have much of a place to turn to for healing in general. When I went to the doctor I found that there is no cure for rheumatoid arthritis. It is a chronic disease that you just have. There are many palliatives, drugs to alleviate pain and stiffness, but there aren't any cures.

When you are in a situation like that people give you lots of advice. For instance, my doctor, with all of society's authority behind him, advised me to take toxic drugs; my teachers here at Zen Center instructed me in various things; and my friends—when I think of them now, how kind and concerned they were, I feel like blessing them—advised a great number of treatments. First of all, I was given rice bread to eat instead of wheat. Every week I was wrapped in comfrey-soaked sheets for an hour or so. I had every conceivable massage known to man or woman. I took extract of every benevolent plant that grows in Northern California and China. Unfortunately, my pain got worse, despite all this. My ability to move got less and less. As my body got weaker, and my pain got greater, I had to figure out what is real? What is the important thing to pay attention to in this situation? Where is the place inside of me or outside of me that can help me?

As it turned out, my preoccupation with dharmas, my Zen meditation training up to that point, (I'd had seven years at Tassajara and at Green Gulch) was a very great help. What I mean by my preoccupation with dharmas is studying the objects of consciousness: feelings, perceptions, impulses, and consciousness. Meditation training can help you notice specific areas of your body and all that sort of thing, because paying attention to the objects of consciousness, the minute little things that go on in your mind, attunes you to very fine detail. If you study the Four Foundations of Mindfulness, you learn body awareness, you pay attention to your thoughts, you feel sensations very keenly, and you study your perceptions.

Most importantly, you learn from this study to be less attached to things. This is also very important in the process of self-healing: that you are not attached to something that was before and no longer is, because the function of your body was once something and now it is something else.

So the business of Zen meditation is to observe all these things: sensations, perceptions, your consciousness and your body. In Zen you simply recognize—now I am sitting, this is my posture now, my thoughts are in trying to express these ideas to you, my perceptions are of your breathing, your faces, the presence of all of us in the room. I'm aware of my dry mouth. I'm aware of wanting an ice cream cone. I'm aware of various things that are going on now.

In self-healing, you manipulate the objects of consciousness to increase your health. For instance, let's say you want to walk to the bank to get some money out. As you are walking along, you notice a pain in your back. What object of consciousness do you think would be most beneficial to you now? Worrying about whether you have enough money in the bank to make this withdrawal? Or noticing when the pain in your walk increases or decreases? That letting your pelvis stretch a little from your spine seems to decrease the pain for about five steps. And then it comes back when you come down on your right foot but not your left. It's clear that this kind of attention can help you in the realm of pain.

Fall 1990

In the case of a catastrophic illness, you might want to find the healer itself that resides in you: the state of mind you have when you feel healthy, generous, when all the energy is moving from the middle of your body out to the periphery and you feel your arms and legs actually stimulated by the center of your body; you're aware of your breath filling up your body when you breathe in; when you breathe out all your attachments disappear. That's a great, precious, gorgeous state of mind. If you notice what conditions induce that state of mind for you, then you can regenerate it again and again for your healing.

So it's true that you can use meditation practice to achieve your health goals. You might get rid of your disease or overcome your injury, whatever, but if you practice mainly to get rid of your pain and to function again, rather than to express your life itself and your nature, then it's a very narrow and vulnerable achievement. A clay Buddha can't go through the water, and a wood Buddha can't go through the fire. A goal-oriented healing cannot penetrate deeply enough. You must penetrate your anguish and pain so that illness and health lose their distinction, their meaning, allowing you to just live your life. Your relief from pain and your healing have to be given up again and again to set you free of the desire to get well. Otherwise getting well just becomes another hindrance to you; it is just another robber of the time that you have to live. It's just another idea that enslaves you, like enlightenment. It is just something else to chase after and never quite attain, some ideal you measure yourself by. Fortunately, for our sincere way-seeking mind, recurring illness is like a villain stomping on your finger tips as you cling desperately to your healthy functioning body. We all have to give up our bodies some day. The sick among us get in practice.

The problem with being preoccupied with your health is that you get into this illusion of progress: am I getting better? Am I

getting worse? Who's winning: me or my illness? The problem is that illness and wellness are opposites on a continuum of preoccupation with health and as opposites they have the same nature, like life and death or love and hate: when we pluck wellness out of the void, illness always comes with it. There is no essential difference between sickness and wellness; form is emptiness, emptiness is form. If you are preoccupied with how well you are, you will also notice how ill you are. That's how it works. So, you get on this wheel of despair and discouragement alternating with euphoria and encouragement which condemns you to a life of disappointing setbacks alternating with happy spurts of improvement.

Darlene Cohen.

You become discouraged with your health when you have been idealistic, when you still have some gaining idea, some ideal you are measuring yourself against, like how you used to feel, like how someone as sick as you healed himself or herself. Your health habits are more reliably based in something more stable than your "progress" toward wellness, such as daily practices which do not change with feelings about your body. You can decide how to best take care of your body, and do it dispassionately.

I want to propose that healing yourself is a lot like living your life. It's not a preparation for anything else, a journey to another situation called wellness. It's its own self; it has its own value. There's a spaciousness around events when you decide to just live. It is each thing as it is; form is form, emptiness is emptiness.... You live to express your own sincerity, your own nature. You take care of your body because it yearns to be taken care of and you feel generous toward it. When you have peace of mind, you are disposed kindly toward things, including your body. You are aware when you want to rest, to eat, when you need stimulation, when you want to challenge yourself, and also when you are disappointed with your body, when you don't like the level of function that it has. You can take the restlessness from that disappointment and use it to express your body's yearning to move....

We don't have a lot of role models in our society for this kind of attention to our processes so we are deeply touched when they appear to us. When I was very sick and in bed, I happened to hear a recording of Mississippi Fred MacDowell's Delta Blues music. He strums a guitar and sings in a rough voice. His recordings were made a long time ago, so you can hear the process of recording as well as his voice and the guitar. The way he plucks each string of his guitar it sounds like he's expressing his true nature. When I was lying there and hearing the purity of his effort, I felt that if he could touch a guitar string that way, I could dedicate my life to living as sincerely as I could. Teachers of the heart are so rare for us that finding one can inspire you for years.

When there is no thought of obtaining good health, there is full appreciation for the body as it is. Even if that body is weak or painful, is limited, it's still your home, it's how you're manifesting this life. It's also, from the practice point of view, your penetration into reality. Your body is the only way that you can experience the transparency of all things and their interrelationships.

When I was first sick, my therapist, Meir Schneider, said to me: "I want you to study your despair." I said if I don't try constantly to distract myself, I'll commit suicide. He told me I had to experience where I was before I could go any place else. He said to try to find some open space in my constricted body, some place in my body I could go for a refuge from my pain. I found a place in my chest where I could breathe in and breathe out and just be there without any anguish. Every time my suffering became too much, I would lie down and feel that place in my chest and be comforted, just like a cat lies down in the sun. A place right in the very center of my despair. Ironically, when my body was at its worst, that's the first time I ever appreciated it. Before I was sick I had a very strong, healthy body. It would do anything I wanted. It would sit through sesshins, no matter how much pain. But I used to say, well, why won't it get into full lotus? It would also run along the beach at Green Gulch. But I would say why can't it run faster and longer? Even though it was strong and well-toned, I would say there's too much fat over here. It seems like I never could appreciate it until I was sick and said "Thank God for this one part that still goes up and down."

I have a client in my body therapy practice, Dorothy, who has been in a wheelchair for three years. She has been diagnosed with arthritis of the spine and hip. Her goal in working with me is to get out of the wheelchair. I taught her awareness of her body and many stretching and strengthening exercises so that her weak body could begin to support itself. For a long time Dorothy did her exercises like taking medicine, that is, she believed that these movements were good for her and she did them. But she didn't actually *live* through them. Every session, she would ask me questions about what she should feel and what she should do if the exercise hurt her and how many times she should do each exercise.

Then one day she came to our session with this big grin on her face and she said, "I found out *everything* is information. Hurting or getting tired or not feeling like exercising. I'm noticing everything." And I knew she had gone from mechanical movement and had dropped into that timeless realm of sensation itself. The whole universe was her medicine.

A monk said to Feng-hseuh: "Speech is a matter of subject and object and silence is a matter of subject and object, so how can I get

Green Gulch Farm zendo.

out of subject and object?" Feng-hseuh said: "I like to think of Chieng-nan in March. The partridges chirp among the many fragrant flowers." So how do we develop this appreciation for our bodies just as they are? This broad and generous spirit that allows

Stained glass, at Page Street, of Suzuki Roshi's palms together.

everything to just be just as it is, or as Aitken Roshi puts it, how do we have the realization that our life is a wallet stuffed with hundred dollar bills and we have no thought of picking it up and putting it into our pocket? Especially if we're sick and in pain and think that our wallets are empty?

Our teachers tell us to look into ordinary things. Thich Nhat Hanh says that combing your hair and washing the dishes get you in contact with reality. These activities themselves are an expression of sanity, of reality. So are our sick bodies. If you move a sore leg across your bed and onto the floor, if you lift a spoon to your lips and taste your medicine, if you feel your sore feet accept your weight, you are connected with reality. For some of us, being sick is the first time we slow down enough to actually notice the ordinary things around us, to notice what moves and what stays still. If you're lying in bed, you listen to the sounds that other people consider background noise, like children

playing or cars passing. If you go out of your house after you've been sick for awhile, the first time you go out you actually feel the air as it hits your cheeks. Of course, these kinds of things happen to all of us, sick or well, every day, all the time, but we usually just dismiss them as mundane and don't notice them.

Trungpa Rinpoche writes that human intelligence and dignity are attuned to experiencing the mundane things of life: the colors around us; the freshness of the smells, perceiving the beauty of trees and mountains and sky. I think he's suggesting that our intelligence and dignity themselves are actually developed by our noticing these mundane things. Our awareness of all these things is, to me, a meditation on the synchronization of body and mind, where all of me is synchronized for a particular period of time. This synchronization, in my experience, is a very deep healing. You experience your integrity being all of a piece. It's very unconventional to value these subtle experiences. We're not encouraged to do this in our society. It's much more usual to want to be special. It's actually extraordinary just to be ordinary, to be preoccupied with the mundane things.

Another client, Judy, also has rheumatoid arthritis. For a very long time, I've been trying in our therapy to help her generalize her relaxation exercises to her daily life. She is capable of relaxing—she turns into a noodle on the massage table—but the minute her session is over she jumps up and starts putting on her clothes so frantically to rush to her next appointment she undoes everything she has just done. I tried various strategies to communicate this idea to her of using her daily life as one long exercise in healing, but I never had any success with this; she never "got" it. Then one night she said to me as she was rushing out the door after her session, "Whenever you give me new relaxation exercises, I have to do my work twice as fast and do my exercises as fast as I can so that I can have *some* time for myself." And I realized what the problem was: she divided up her life into tasks she had to do and actual *living*, and she madly rushed through her work so that she could begin to live. No wonder she felt, despite a supportive, loving family and three homes in different beautiful places in California, that she was a deprived person. No wonder she felt so much pressure she was always contracting her muscles and compressing her joints. As soon as I pointed this out to her she said, "Oh!"

Another client of mine was very annoyed and scolded her husband for coming in and telling me a joke while I was massaging her at her house. When I asked her why she minded so much, she said to me, "He was using up my time with you." What she meant of course was that he was distracting my attention from her and my paying attention to her was the only acceptable way she could spend time with me. This indicates a very deprived, starved state of mind—not one that is satisfied by the simple act of listening to the sound of her husband's voice as he tells a joke, of feeling my fingers on her body, of sensing the animal presence of the three of us sharing the room, or even the pang of noticing her jealous state of mind. Now this kind of pang, of noticing that you have an ungenerous attitude, can actually be very sweet. It adds to the texture of your life. You begin to include the shadow in your life: your conscious life begins to be shaded and textured by your anguish and your petty little jealousies.

I pointed some of these things out to her. The next time I saw her she told me that after our session she had begun to be flooded with perceptions. She had noticed she had a very painful situation with her son which she immediately decided to take care of. She hadn't even noticed it before; she was just living with the pain of it. She had even enjoyed doing the dishes.

It seems to me that when we fall ill, we have an opportunity we may not have noticed when we were well, to demythologize the wisdom of the Buddhas, and to literally incorporate it, in-*corpor*-ate it, and to present it as our own body. I thank you very much.

This touching account by Mitsu Suzuki (Suzuki Roshi's wife) reveals her warm heart and strong determination. What an inspiration! For over twenty years after Suzuki Roshi's death, she lived at 300 Page Street, teaching tea and providing a shining presence to everyone. In 1993, she moved back to Shyouka, Japan where she now lives with her daughter.
—M.W.

Seventy-seven Years of My Life

Mitsu Suzuki

SPRING 1991

The best part of my life has been that I could experience love as a mother. Although I live in the United States, the thought that I have a daughter in Japan has always enriched my life.

I was raised without a mother, so I was hungry for a mother's love. As a child I had to take care of my clothes and everything myself. I was a determined and proud person, and I didn't like that part of myself; I wanted to be a warm-hearted person. I wanted to develop my spiritual life, so after I finished girl's high school I went to the Christian church and was baptized. My family members didn't like me going to church; they said if I became a Christian I'd have less chance to be married.

I got married in 1936. My husband was in the Navy-Air Force reconnaissance. Neither of us had any idea that the war between China and Japan was going to start. The next year, on the day of the Bon festival, July 13, the war broke out and he had to leave. He was stationed on a warship that carried seaplanes. I was pregnant at that time. Every day was a horrible experience, because the wives of other soldiers received telegrams that their husbands had been killed. There was news on the radio that they bombed some parts of China and two airplanes did not come back. I thought that one of them might be his airplane. Then my mother-in-law received a telegram that he had been killed.

One of my husband's jobs was to choose targets for bombs. When he was going on a mission to China I would write to him: "Please remember that these people in China also have wives and children; I would like you to target rice fields instead of cities and towns. Drop bombs to surprise the snails in the rice fields."

Mitsu Suzuki.

About three years ago we had a fifty years memorial service for him and I told this story to the friends who attended. Someone said, "Did you really write that kind of letter?" And I said, "Yes I did. The suffering of Chinese people would be the same as my suffering."

My first husband was a very cheerful and mature person. He was very thoughtful; for example, he took care of all the details when my father visited us. I wanted my daughter to be like him and not like me. When I was pregnant and he was away, I was sending messages to the child in my womb—sending my wish that this child would be like him. And I am blessed because actually Harumi's nature is similar to her father's, although she never met him.

Looking back on seventy-seven years of my life, my ideal was the life of marriage. Unfortunately I was only a wife for ten years altogether during my two marriages. But I feel fortunate; both of my husbands were very fine people.

I'm very grateful that while in America I have been living in a Buddhist temple. My friends tell me where I live is so special, not like typical American society. I don't know life outside this community and it's been wonderful to be here.

I could not really teach tea ceremony in a formal way—I didn't have the correct tea utensils or formal tea room. And I didn't have enough knowledge myself to teach formal tea ceremony. But because I was studying Zen, I wanted my students to grasp the heart of Zen. That is, in a very narrow space, a one mat room or two mat room, you establish a universe. Here there is harmony between host and guest. The host is always thoughtful of the guest, thinking how to create and serve delicious tea to the guest. The guest, instead of trying to look for the host's mistake, watches and wishes for the host to make delicious tea. So there is a real warm harmony; this is the spirit of tea ceremony. In this country, people tend to think of their own matters and not worry about others' business. I wanted people here to learn this spirit of harmony.

I'm very fortunate that my students are all Zen students. They probably understand the spirit of tea more than other Americans. Among tea teachers, even in Japan, few people want to study Zen, which is very strange because tea ceremony started from Zen practice. Dogen Zenji said, "Dignified bearing is itself Buddha Dharma." He taught that everything we do in our daily life—how we converse with each other and how we take meals, go to the bathroom, how we use water—all is Zen. Tea ceremony is just like that: however and wherever you meet someone else, being fully thoughtful of the other is most important. That is the mastery of tea ceremony.

My students have been studying, maybe harder than Japanese students, although they have many difficulties like pain in their legs sitting *seiza*. Because of his age, Issan (Issan Dorsey, late Abbot of Hartford Street Zen Center) would often forget the movements. I would just hit his hand to correct him, asking him what was next. He would say, "I don't know." So I would say "I've told you this a million times—please say you forgot, not that you don't know!" A Japanese student who spilled tea would say, "Oh, I'm extremely sorry, my mistake." Here I would just clean up for my students. They wouldn't even say thank you. They might have thought that this was some accident, not their mistake. I was often shocked with their reactions. If I asked them to say they were sorry, they would look puzzled, wondering why I'm asking them this.

One real challenge is that people here are not really trained from childhood in precise physical movements like using right hand or left hand. In American education you don't need to learn this. All movements in tea ceremony involve right and left. But my students are really open for suggestions and instructions, and they have been following my instructions in a faithful way.

I first asked Hojo (Shunryu Suzuki Roshi) what he would think of doing haiku when we were in Tassajara. It was about 1970, shortly before he died. He thought it was a wonderful idea. I started writing haiku and sent some to Japanese magazines, but then he became very sick and I could not do that.

Hojo had also originally encouraged me to study tea ceremony and bought me an issue of a magazine featuring the tea ceremony. I started after that. Hojo left me these two things: tea ceremony and haiku. These two arts have enriched my life and have also enabled me to stay here. Otherwise I would have had nothing to do and my life here would have been very difficult.

The best thing about haiku is that you see things clearly, and appreciate the wonder and beauty of nature. Gratitude for the air, sun and water comes from appreciation of nature. Being aware of how, in such a deep way, we are enriched by nature. You have to see things in nature in a very honest way, and you have to write in a direct straightforward way. To penetrate our self, and to cleanse our self—haiku has that function.

Normally in Japan there are leaders of haiku groups and you work together as a group. Since I'm here just by myself, I write haiku by myself. To send haiku to magazines to be evaluated is the usual way to write and develop your skill, but I started out when I was older, and I just write in my own way. I don't care about being accepted or having awards. I'm a very poor haiku student in that way.

For example, my haiku are appreciated by Eiheiji magazine, I guess because they're often Buddhist; but in haiku groups in San Francisco my poems are not selected so often. I'm not doing so well here.

Before Hojo died, when he was very sick, he asked me to go back to Japan. He wanted to be re-ordained, to renounce his life as a householder again. He wished to devote himself to his students twenty-four hours a day. I said, "Hojo-san, if you are getting well, I will respect your wish, but I cannot leave you here so sick. Who would cook Japanese meals for you?" I wrote to Hoichi (Hoitsu Suzuki Roshi, Shunryu Suzuki Roshi's son and Dharma heir) and asked for his opinion. He wrote, "Mother, please stay in America and take care of him." Hoichi wrote to both Hojo and me and said that I should stay. So Hojo gave up his idea. He didn't bring it up again.

I said to Hojo, "After you die, what shall I do?"

"Stay here and help these people."

"How can I help them? I've only been able to help them because I've been with you."

Hojo said, "You are an honest and fair person, so you can help them."

Even after twenty years, I feel grateful every day for his trust.

Hojo said to his American students, "It's all yours; American Zen is all yours," and I feel exactly that way. I have taught tea ceremony at Zen Center, but Zen Center has its own life and it's beyond my opinion. Here at Zen Center we see new people all the time. I feel that I am friends with the many people here even though I often don't know their names. People are coming from all over the world; lately we see more Asian people. When I see Tenshin-san and Mel-san, I ask them to take good care of Zen Center, that's all. And when I see Baker-san, I also say please take care. It is wonderful that people come from various countries looking for the Way.

By the end of March I will stop teaching tea, and pass my students on to other teachers. Students can choose their own teachers; some may choose not to continue. At that time I'll be withdrawing from any official position in the tea organization, and will continue as a member. In April, I will have no work and I will have to see how I feel and what I want to do. I've taken care of myself for seventy-seven years and I feel that is enough. My life has been good and it's all right if I don't wake up tomorrow morning.

I have had my full life so every day I pray to the Buddha that I will die without troubling others, while I can still take care of myself. It's a kind of responsibility of doctors, monks and lawyers to establish a system whereby one can choose the best time to end his or her life. I think this is a system that should be legalized. This may sound strange to young people, but this is how I really feel at this moment. So I tell Harumi all the time that if I don't wake up tomorrow morning, if she hears that news, please say "Hurray, mother." Even though Harumi and I have been separated, I've said everything I wanted to say, and done everything I wanted to do. She has hundreds of my letters and she feels that we are very close. She says, "Even after you go, I'll read all your letters, so we'll have a closer relationship." She is Zen, so she understands my feeling.

Tenshin-san said, "Please stay here, it will be helpful for many of us and for Zen Center." I am very grateful, but I have to think also of my own health. Most likely I'll go back to Japan. I'll be a grandmother and a great-grandmother, and become part of the family I left in Japan. I have two great-grandchildren. My daughter Harumi has visited Zen Center twice, and Hojo loved her and she enjoyed visiting here. I have a small room in Harumi's house in Japan. Harumi has two altars, one is for Hojo, and upstairs there is an altar for her father and the Matsuno family. (Harumi's husband took her father's name since she was the only child.)

First I felt very funny about coming to America. Americans and Japanese hated each other and fought each other. People in Japan expected to be killed during the war. It was strange when American people took care of us, I couldn't really understand. Of course now I feel very comfortable being here. Japanese people usually don't express their opinions so clearly. Probably I wouldn't have been able to stay here if I had been quiet and humble, a typical Japanese person. I'm very outspoken; in that way I'm like an American, and that's why I have been able to stay here among so many different kinds of people.

Translated by Kaz Tanahashi Sensei.

Zen and art are often linked together. In this 1991 interview, artist Gordon Onslow-Ford talks to his life, his work and his understanding. Gordon studied with Hodo Tobase, the priest at Sokoji temple before Suzuki Roshi came. –M.W.

Creation in the Instant: An Interview with Gordon Onslow-Ford

Michael Wenger and Kaz Tanahashi

FALL 1991

On May 13, 1991, Michael Wenger and Kaz Tanahashi met with Gordon Onslow-Ford. Discussion focused on the life and art of Hodo Tobase Roshi, who preceded Suzuki Roshi as Abbot of Sokoji. Tobase Roshi invited Suzuki Roshi to come to San Francisco in the 1950s. Gordon, born in 1912, studied calligraphy with Tobase for several years.

MICHAEL WENGER: We're in Gordon's studio in Inverness, the fire is going and we're talking about Gordon's work, about Hodo Tobase, and the relationship between them.

GORDON ONSLOW-FORD: I was very fond of Hodo Tobase. Fond isn't a strong enough word. I had a bond with him. Tobase was the fourth or fifth son of a farmer. The monastery of Eiheiji asked his father to give them a child, so Tobase was given to Eiheiji when he was eight or nine years old. He was looked after with great affection for four years and then he was entered into monastic training. He was really a child of the monastery. He had the greatest affection for it. It was his home.

After World War II, he was sent here by the Japanese Government to give consolation to all the Japanese-American farmers whose land had been taken away during the War. He arrived to a very sad situation. He was oriented entirely towards the Japanese-American community rather than towards the general public. He didn't speak English, although I have a feeling that he understood much more than he let on. Tobase wasn't a scholar in any way, he was a monk who had great wisdom about the mind. He knew about human beings. He wasn't particularly interested in politics or modern art.

He was perhaps five-foot-three and very robust. As well as being a calligrapher, he was a cook. He spent twelve years as a cook in his monastery. When we went to a Chinese or Japanese restaurant, he used to walk straight into the kitchen and talk to the chef. We had such dinners as I've never had, before or since. He was also a wrestler, which stood him in good stead once or twice defending his groceries on Bush Street.

MW: How did your interest in calligraphy start?

GOF: I met Saburo Hasegawa, a well-known Japanese painter and calligrapher, through Alan Watts. I took him for a walk in Muir Woods. Hasegawa was a man of Tea. He was dressed in an immaculate brown kimono. We walked for two hours and he didn't say anything and I didn't say anything. Afterwards we went to my studio, which at that time was on board the ferry boat, "Vallejo," moored in Sausalito. When we got on board, after looking around, he indicated that he would like to do some calligraphy. We cleared an area of paints and brushes and spread newspaper on the floor. Hasegawa took out of his sleeve two-hundred-year old ink wrapped in a brocade, an ink stone, a roll of paper and a brush. He placed the paper flat with small stones at each corner, ground the ink rhythmically and gently, and then was still for some time. It seemed that it had taken him the best part of the afternoon to prepare to write.

He made the character for infinity that contains all the brush strokes employed in square writing *(Kaisho)*. And then he made a one-two-three which is a test of the calligrapher's skill. The six lines have to be placed correctly on the paper; each line is given a different weight and the spacing between each line is different.

After my first calligraphy lesson, I was convinced that I was a barbarian and that I had to pursue this. The next day I invited a few friends, among them Lucienne Bloch, the painter, to the ferry.

Transmission outside
Scriptures
Not depending on words

Virtue

Calligraphy by Hodo Tobase.

In front of a blazing fire, Hasegawa gave us tea and made some calligraphy. When Hasegawa left after a week, he was in good shape and I was exhausted, but hooked on calligraphy. I sent him a haiku:

A sheet of paper
on the ferry deck
how white the mountain water.

Anyway, Lucienne Bloch was so impressed with Hasegawa that she went around Japantown looking for a calligraphy master who would teach. "No, no there's no one here, but there's that old monk Tobase in the Zen Temple on Bush Street and he may know something about calligraphy." So she went to Sokoji to ask Tobase if he would teach calligraphy and he said "Yes."I never heard Tobase say no; he always said yes. If someone asked him to do something: "Yes." Always yes. His affability was somewhat stern and people never dared to ask him to do something that was untoward.

Tobase's first few classes at the Asian Academy met in the subterranean kitchen/dining room on Monday nights after the students finished supper. Later he suggested that we meet at his temple, Sokoji, at 1881 Bush Street. This was in 1952. He had a wonderful kitchen. There was the big hall, the zendo, and behind that a spacious kitchen. We had the most friendly and enlightening meetings.

Tobase was a benevolent tyrant. He'd give us a tremendous amount of work. Just to study four characters a week, to be able to write them with a feeling of what they meant was enough, but there was always something else. I gave my best energies to calligraphy for five years and learned by leaps and bounds. It was just what I had been lacking. Because the Surrealists in Paris with whom I had grown up had made intuitively many of the discoveries of Zen but they didn't have any metaphysics; they didn't know how to talk about it. They were poets and painters and revolutionaries and they didn't have the wisdom of Buddhism behind them. So my calligraphy studies complemented my life as a painter.

I know that this was an enormous adventure for Tobase, too. He had no expectation of meeting the general American public, he was there to comfort the Japanese-American community. This calligraphy class was an unexpected encounter for him.

MW: Why is calligraphy so important? What did your relationship with Tobase Roshi bring to your life and to your work?

GOF: I had discovered that the line, the circle and the dot were the three elements at the root of art before I met Tobase Sensei. But I was making line, circle, dot elements in a rather mechanical way that did not have the blood and bones of calligraphy. After studying *Kaisho* and *Sosho* (square writing and grass writing), I continued working faster until grass writing became illegible and changed into painting. As the line speeds up, it moves from one world to another. The fastest lines possible are the line, the circle and the dot. When a meandering line changes its kind of motion, it slows up, but a circle can go round at full speed, a line can dash up and down at full speed and a dot can hit the paper with maximum intensity. This confirmed my conviction that line-circle-dot elements make up the "seed" world, that is, as far as art is concerned, the ground of existence within and without.

Little by little I discovered through my meetings with Tobase Sensei that calligraphy—not writing about something but expressing yourself in line—was the way of talking about the spirit. That gave a fluency and assurance to what I was doing. Western calligraphy is different. It's done with a rigid nib with a strong technique. It is done with the fingers and the wrist while Chinese and Japanese calligraphy is done with the whole body/mind.

My painting is a form of meditation. For a day to have depth I need to paint. It was working with Sensei that clarified this feeling. I wrote a book called *Painting in the Instant* in which I tried to make a synthesis between the automatism of Surrealism and the spirit of Zen in calligraphy. The book revolves about the Instant. You cannot think about the Instant any more than you can think about the Big Bang. They are beyond conception but they are present.

KT: How did Tobase teach—in what way?

GOF: He chose some saying—usually a Zen saying of four or five characters—and he wrote it. Then he made a small copy for everyone in the class. We had to study that in meaning and in brush stroke. We had to know it by the next time we came. We had to be able to do it in Kaisho and Sosho. He used to correct with a red ink brush on top of what we had done. If he liked it he put a red circle on the side; if he didn't, he indicated very boldly on top. This was so expressive, we could tell exactly the spirit of the character.

KT: When you were training as a painter, maybe you copied Western paintings

GOF: When I went to Paris in 1937 I did go to study with Andre L'Hote for six weeks and with Fernand Leger for four days, but I realized that my way was not to paint with a student mentality. Of course, I learned from Leger as he was a great painter. When I left his class he congratulated me and I went to see him from time to time in his studio. Right from the beginning I was involved in an adventure. I think it is true to say that I was original from the beginning; not very good, but I was on new territory.

The Surrealists were interested in dreams and myths and making a synthesis between the dream world and daily living. We got into terrible trouble—there weren't any gurus—and there were disasters in all directions. Matta [the seminal Surrealist artist] and I saw that the future of art lay in discovering the worlds beyond dreams. And we found a way to get in there.

KT: That was before World War II?

GOF: Yes. I started painting automatically. Automatic lines have their own reality and it soon became clear to me that I was in the inner world, beyond dreams. Once I discovered that, I had a direction which I have followed ever since.

MW: You had that in 1940?

GOF: In 1938. I started off as a good Surrealist being interested in dreams. I had a notebook and I tried to write down my dreams. If you make a drawing of a dream, you can suggest some episode but the rest disappears. Remembering a dream and then painting it is an illustration of a past event that misses the dream reality. I wanted to find a way of expressing the functioning of the mind directly as it happens.

The spiritual in art, as I see it, is a message from the invisible, intangible inner worlds. While painting it appears directly from mind to canvas. It awakens awe. The spiritual in art is always growing from the edge of the collective unconscious.

KT: Often people kind of mix up spiritual with religious.

GOF: I do not wish to try and speak for traditional religions. When asked what my religion is, I say I'm a painter.

KT: When you were copying the same thing over and over again, it was different from your own discipline—wasn't it confusing?

GOF: Learning Chinese calligraphy for me is more than copying. It is acquiring a new kind of sensitivity that increases my potential as a painter. With a knowledge of Japanese and Chinese calligraphy, additional accents—whiskers, tails—become available. I was fascinated with the Chinese and Japanese characters; it was like imprinting something on my memory. Just like the early landscapes I did served to imprint beauty on my memory, to give me a bank of beautiful memories. The symmetry and the beauty of the Chinese characters is a whole facet of existence; it gives you a whole aesthetic attitude toward life.

KT: Your own painting with oil or watercolor or using Chinese or Japanese brushes—How do you see the difference?

GOF: Studying Chinese calligraphy was something new for me. I never set out to become a Chinese calligrapher. I was always after my expression as a painter. My calligraphy studies led me to throwing paint in the air. Using the brush as a means to express a form or an object is using the brush with an ulterior motive. But in calligraphy, you are concentrating just on the line that you are making. When you have a character, you've got it in your soul: you've got the whole balance of it. That allows you to express how you feel about the character. Calligraphy, as I use it in painting, is a way of expression that happens as it is being made.

Wind Bell

Publication of Zen Center   Volume XXV, No. 2, Fall 1991

Fall 1991

Tobase Sensei said to me that if he saw a character written by a Zen monk over the last three hundred years, he could tell who wrote it and how he was feeling.

KT: Did you feel that you could understand the quality of Tobase's calligraphy when you were just beginning?

GOF: I felt every brush stroke that Tobase Sensei made from the very first. When he was writing he captured my full attention. Critical considerations never entered my mind. The more I got to know Tobase's calligraphy, the more I appreciated it. Hasegawa and Tobase Sensei were very different. Hasegawa's calligraphy was elegant, formal, and scholarly. Sensei's calligraphy was masterful, vigorous, lively.

MW: You studied some meditation with him. Did he suggest that as an adjunct to calligraphy or was calligraphy an adjunct to meditation or were they both their own thing?

GOF: We really only meditated occasionally and never when there was a full class. But sometimes when I was there with Tobase, he said, "Let's sit." He had wonderful advice about meditation, about how to breathe, how to bring the world in. I really have the impression that Tobase did his best to give me all that he could. I think he was a person who was genuinely loved by all his students. He was a ball of certainty—the kind of energy people could move around with a feeling of security.

KT: Would you tell a little about the exhibition of his calligraphy at the San Francisco Museum of Modern Art? When did it take place?

GOF: I was on good terms with the Director of the San Francisco Museum of Art (as it was called at that time), Dr. Grace McCann Morely. She had majored in Hindu Art at Berkeley and later became the first director of the National Museum of Indian Art in New Delhi. I said to her that there's a Zen master here who is a calligrapher, and she offered Tobase Sensei an exhibition. We were given a big gallery and the show was striking. It was a Zen manifesto for those who could read and for those who could not. Tobase Sensei's Mystery Elegance was a forward at the entrance and it remains an appropriate statement of priorities to this day.

KT: You see his pieces in an aesthetic way, in a spiritual way?

GOF: In a sentimental way, too.

MW: How would you describe how you took your study with him further?

GOF: I've taken calligraphy beyond Sosho, the grass writing. I work in the air. I don't work with a brush. I discovered that the speed with which you make a calligraphy determines the nature of the calligraphy. Basically, each inner world has a range of speeds within which it appears. The inner worlds appear faster than you can think. If you work spontaneously, you have a chance of catching them. You know it but you couldn't get it unless you could work faster than you could think. Once you've got it down, it's an inspiring and elating experience. You enter a kind of second childhood; you cast care aside. But you have to be able to cultivate the power of paying attention. That's really what great art is about: paying attention. Students often are distracted. A little part of their mind is wishing for or thinking of something else.

KT: You know if you study Oriental art, maybe one tendency will be to make your art look Oriental. For you the influence seems to be not superficial at all. You don't work on that level—to get influence. It seems to be more in your heart.

GOF: On the one hand, art has the flavor of the place where the painter lives. Where would my art be today without the sunshine in the fog? On the other hand it is an expression of one's state of awareness. I would like my painting to be a bridge between Europe and America, between America and the Orient. East and West are meeting around the Pacific. The art of our age now coming into focus points towards a one-world art.

I have been on my own for the past forty-five years and I'm just beginning. Honestly, I'm just beginning. But I hope that other people will be able to take what I've done and be able to grow from it. Art comes from the inside out. Art doesn't come from trying to depict something out there. It's what the mind awakens.

If you pay full attention to what you are doing, to what is happening, you will find something new. It is only when you are tired or thinking about something else that you do what you already know. Creation happens in the Instant. In the Instant everything is present, everything is fresh. All that there is, is in the Instant. It doesn't have anything to do with speed—you can paint slowly in the instant as well as you can paint fast. But you pay full attention. When it comes off, it's in the Instant.

Zen Center started what has become the Zen Hospice
Project in 1987. Merrill Collett in this 1993 article shares
excerpts from his journal on hospice work and how it
deepened his experience of life. Death reveals life, life reveals
death. –M.W.

Letting Go, Falling to Rest: Hospice Work and Zen Practice

Merrill Collett

FALL 1993

We need, in love, to practice only this:
letting each other go.
    –RAINER MARIE RILKE
    Requiem for a Friend
    (translated by Steven Mitchell)

In the course of my career as a journalist, most of the corpses I've seen have been badly damaged by car wrecks or gun shots, leading me to believe that death is ugly. But when I started going volunteer work at the Zen Hospice Project I learned that death could be beautiful.

Headquartered in an elegant Victorian located kitty-corner from the Zen Center on Page Street, the Zen Hospice Project recruits and trains volunteers to care for patients in a twenty-eight-bed AIDS and cancer ward in the city-owned Laguna Honda Hospital and in a four-bed unit on the second floor of the hospice head-quarters itself. This smaller unit is where I work five hours a week, doing everything from taking temperatures to taking out trash, from wiping bottoms to washing dead bodies. It is, as they say, a complete practice.

I became a hospice caregiver after family obligations forced me to abandon my plans to go to Tassajara for practice period, and I volunteered for hospice work as an alternative. This discovery

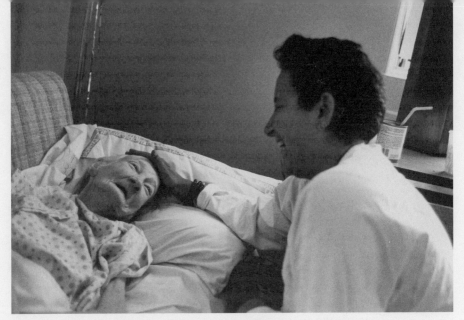

Alice Andrews with Zen Center Hospice volunteer Pam Weiss.

that death could be beautiful came soon after I finished the training program. I arrived for my shift and was told at the door that a new patient, a man I didn't know, had died, so I went upstairs to meet him. Lying on a bed in a bay window, he was bathed in a pool of soft morning light, his fine features and smooth skin marked only by two dainty, purple lesions of Kaposi's Sarcoma, a once rare form of cancer now common in AIDS victims. Completing the fragile, saintly tableau, someone had crossed his hands over a long-stemmed lavender rose. Seeing that all the miraculous forces animating both man and the flower had gone elsewhere, I was awed by the empty, terrible beauty of the scene. Later, with the deaths of patients who had become friends, death would not always seem so attractive. It hurts to let go. But it hurts more to hold on.

In teaching non-attachment, Buddhism encourages us to make death the mirror for life. Looking at life from the perspective of death, embracing our transience, we stop striving to make our moments more enjoyable and start savoring existence itself; it's a fruit of the practice. America's death-denying culture cuts us off from the liberating practice of contemplating our own mortality, but with the growth of the hospice movement, American Buddhists have a rich opportunity to deepen their lives.

In my case, although hospice work was my second choice after Tassajara, I see it now as my best choice. In eight months, I've undergone a simple but profound change in outlook. For example, of the days that end with a beautiful sunset and I have a backache, I now tend to pay more attention to the sunset than the backache! It's all a matter of not wasting my time. That's what the dying have taught me; that's why I owe them so much.

What follows are excerpts from the journal I've kept as a volunteer at the Zen Hospice project.

NOVEMBER 11: First training class. Just inside the door hangs the familiar picture of Suzuki Roshi quizzically arching one eyebrow. When I pass by he seems to give me a wink!

NOVEMBER 12: This work has its own language. There is the "dying process" and then there is the last stage—"active dying." Dr. Bob Brody describes it. Consciousness declines to the point of coma, and breathing becomes irregular; first shallow, then deep, then shallow, then deep. Strength slips away; the patient can't clear secretions and his coughs produce a rattle in the chest—the infamous "death rattle." Blood pressure declines. The skin becomes cold. The patient turns mottled and bluish.

One of my fellow volunteers witnessed active dying personally when he saw his lover "bleed out." Blood exuded from all orifices, including his penis, the volunteer says. His lover died peacefully in his arms.

NOVEMBER 14: Step-by-painful step, John and Stephen, two patients, come down to talk with us. They are lively men, and it pains me to see their lives ravaged. I leave the training deeply depressed. At home, in bed, I dream of snow. The next morning, during zazen, I fall against the wall in tears. No self-pity. Just good, cleansing tears.

NOVEMBER 29: When I arrive at the hospice for my first shift, I am handed a terse little list of duties:
–trash out
–waste baskets

–laundry
–diaper cart
–compost bucket
–water pitchers

Apparently hospice work is like everything else: mostly maintenance.

DECEMBER 9: Stephan has died and is gone. Harriet called me at home, but it's still a shock to arrive and find his bed empty. Just last week I had given him a bath. Slowly walking his stick-thin body to the bathroom, my arms around this dear, sweet man whom all of us loved, a man who never failed to thank us for minor kindness, holding this man close, hugging him, it occurred to me that the two of us, him gay and me straight, were doing an intimate little dance that our fathers could not have done. I felt grateful, and deeply reconciled.

DECEMBER 16: Stephen is gone but Leah has arrived, and boy do we know it. A former clothier of some success now in her late 70s and dying of lung cancer, Leah specializes in letting us know the ways in which we aren't doing the job to her standards. Every now and then she'll remind us of our inadequacies by saying things like, "Maybe I'll go to the Mayo Clinic." She rattles me, the new volunteer, but Harriet, who heads up the staff, is tickled pink to have a woman with gumption around. Harriet gets such genuine amusement out of Leah's performances that even Leah has to smile.

FEBRUARY 7: We have David now, and he's very demanding. Tall, gangly, gaunt, often moody, manipulative and highly theatrical, he favors black clothes and dramatic gestures. Our work is so pressing and practical—changing diapers, making meals, administering pain pills—we don't have much time for his flamboyance, but we do take his talk of suicide seriously. David does not handle pain very well. Today, as I help him ease his aching body into the bathtub, he is full of fear and remorse. "I had another life," he says. "It wasn't like this."

FEBRUARY 14: Leah's husband is ill so I sit with her, reading a book while holding her hand. Enfolded in gray winter light, the room is as quiet as a cathedral. After a while she asks me what I am reading. When I tell her it's a book of meditations, she turns away with a look of disgust, saying, "So you're one of those, too, huh?" I love this woman.

FEBRUARY 18: This morning, in the zendo, as I am hitting the bells for service, I am overcome by an inexplicable anguish. When I get home there is a message from the hospice: Leah died peacefully at 6:40 A.M., almost exactly the moment I was doing the bells.

Leah

The room is washed in winter light
And she is lost within it
Searching in the texture of her life
For the pattern of her pain
Angry at the Breath that makes her breathe,
The Heart that beats her heart,
Glaring with falcon eyes that seem to say
    you'll never know
I will.
I will.

MARCH 21: David works us hard with his moods and complaints, but his unceasing effort to experience himself fully to the last days of his life commands our total respect. David pulls himself up the hundred-foot pole hand-over-hand. He's putting out a personal newsletter, holding late-night salons with his friends and every now and then tottering down the hallway to visit other patients. Any day now he'll start a religion!

APRIL 18: We're busy assisting four demanding men dying of AIDS and bursting with needs. Victor, Armando and Michael are all interesting but David's transformation is stunning. His relentless self-searching had found expression in art. The walls of his room are covered with wavy, pastel drawings of crosses, flowers, humanoid figures, abstract designs. He sits at his window for hours, a sketchpad on his knees, his eyes illuminated by interior light.

APRIL 25: Michael is having a very hard time. Already so thin I can put my fingers around his limbs at any point, he hasn't eaten for two days. The little bit he managed to get down today went right through his bowels. But somewhere in that bag of skin and bones there's still room for generosity. When Armando, who occupies the other wing of the room, has a chill, Michael instantly offers his heater, reminding me of how much more I can do. These saints—have they no mercy?

MAY 9: Armando has died. I gratefully remember the time he confessed to me that he'd thought life was all about money, but dying had taught him otherwise. Thank you Armando. Standing by his empty bed, I recite the Heart Sutra and then do nine bows.

Perhaps because of Armando's death, David is needy today. He tries to draw me in with complaints but I'm not buying. So for a couple of hours he hides out in his strange, psychically driven drawings. Finally he asks my opinion. I rather like what he's working on; there is something both familiar and yet weirdly intriguing about the bulbous "Mr. Tomato Man," the tooth-shaped,

Fall 1993

faintly Asian "Chang," and the many-eared "Mr. Mousy." We talk about colors, about symbolism, about the names that he's given his characters. I suggest that he do a comic strip but he says he doesn't have the energy. Then it hits me. David is much weaker now; he won't last long. When my shift is over, I turn back from the door to have a look at him. He blesses me with a deep smile that says he's ready to die. I'm not ready to let him.

JUNE 13: I don't feel like writing, but I feel that I have to. The climate in the hospice has radically shifted from summer to winter. The four charmers are gone—first Armando, then Victor, then David, then Michael. The new crew is introspective, withdrawn. Time and people pass, leaving so little. The past, says William Mathews, is "the little we remember." I can't remember all the names of those who've died in the hospice. It troubles me. If I can't remember them, were they here? Was I?

JUNE 28: Louis, a very private man whose tragic life touched us all, dies abruptly. We are shocked. I get the word during dinner and immediately go to the hospice. Two other volunteers have also drifted in. We sit with him in the twilight, his small body floating in the bed's vast space. A young woman, a new volunteer, comes in crying and desperately throws herself down. I go to the kitchen and help prepare meals for patients. Others are on the phone, passing the word, passing the word.

My kitchen chores done, I light some candles and go back and spend some time alone with Louis, holding his hand. Although he has only been dead for two hours his skin is already cold. When I place a kiss on his forehead, my lips make a smacking sound in the stillness. Returning to Zen Center I sit in the dark courtyard wanting to cry—or something. Finally I go over and hug a rock bench as if it were Louis, or the earth, or myself. When I let go, I fall into rest.

AUGUST 2: Eight months after his death, Stephen's parents have sent us a card on his birthday saying how much they miss him, letting us know we are still a part of their lives. This work is such a privilege. How is it that in letting go we get so much?

I've taken a night shift now, and walking home from the hospice under a luminescent full moon, I think of these lines by the poet Tu Fu:

> No one knows your thoughts, master,
> And night is empty around us, silent.

Tassajara redwood cabins.

In 1993, when the US Navy proposed the installation of a stargazing interferometer on the peak of Chews Ridge next to the Ventana Wilderness in California, local environmentalists and Native American leaders were alarmed. Citing concerns that the project would lead to development of the mountain, they called for a meeting with representatives from the Navy and the U.S. Forest Service. In this essay, Teah Strozer, then director of Tassajara Zen Mountain Center, describes that powerful encounter. The Navy has not yet budgeted this project. –M.W.

Chews Ridge Ceremony

Teah Strozer

FALL 1993

We gathered in the Round House, a covered amphitheatre dug into the ground. We sat on dirt benches molded out of the earthen walls. Four huge tree trunks placed in a square in the middle of the room supported wooden beams making the roof which, like an earthen tee-pee, was open in the center to the sky. Beneath the opening burned a large fire. We sat and waited.

Tommy Little Bear, chief of the Esalen tribe, welcomed and purified us all with sage incense. He reached for the Two-Faced Talking Stick, one side a smiling face, painted white and decorated with feathers and ribbons, the other side a sorrowful face, painted black and hung with strips of leather and beads. He explained that whoever was holding the Talking Stick could speak uninterruptedly.

For hours the Talking Stick passed from person to person each one adding another heartfelt speech asking the Navy to leave the mountain untouched. But, as the room got smoky and the day grew long, I began to wonder if anything being said would make a difference.

Often during the talking I noticed an elderly Native American man and his son slowly and methodically putting on their traditional tribal dress. Quietly the father adjusted the son's feathered headdress. The son helped his father with a belt and skirt. When I looked over at them later on, they had removed their shirts to put on arm bracelets and paint. I became increasingly interested in what they might have to say.

Meanwhile, the Talking Stick continued to make its way around the room. I was becoming tired and uncomfortable and ready for a break. Then the father reached out and took the Talking Stick. He looked long at his son who was fully dressed, painted and sitting quietly, holding ceremonial objects in his hands as they rested on his knees. The father walked slowly to the fire and from the center of the room gazed at each person. He stood in his native dress, a feather fan in one hand, the Talking Stick in the other and said clearly and distinctly, "I think all white people should be killed."

He had our attention. He related a dream he'd had, in which all white people were put on ships and sent back to Europe. Their land was taken from them, their animals killed, and sickness and death spread through their people. He talked about what life was like for his ancestors before white people came with their guns and greed. He said that everybody thinks the first atomic bomb fell on the Japanese, but in reality it fell on the Native Americans who were downwind from the testing sites in New Mexico. Their land was poisoned. They suffer even now from high rates of cancer and other illnesses. He wanted us to understand how much he hated what had been done to his people, how hard he had struggled to understand the white culture's still insatiable desire to control and subdue the land his ancestors had lived with in harmony.

I found it difficult listening to him speak about the overwhelming suffering of his people, of the desecration of the land. But his voice—alternating quiet, even timid or sometimes loud and strong—was magnetic, his bearing confident and proud as he walked round and round the fire chanting this litany of sorrow and rage. He said that whites in power simply take whatever they want, and that protesting probably wouldn't stop them; but he still believed that we were all one people, that we needed to listen to each other and to the Great Spirit. Humbly, he asked the Great Spirit if he could offer his pain, the pain of his people, as well as the pain of all people and all living beings, in a prayer that we might hear each other and learn from the earth how to live in a balanced way.

Then he asked his son to come to his side and a man with a drum to begin playing. The drum began a steady, slow, hypnotic beat, BOOM, BOOM, BOOM, like the beating of my own heart. It sent shivers through my body. As the drum sounded the father explained that he was going to chant a song expressing an offering and a prayer. He faced the fire, held one arm up to the heavens, and began to chant. As he did this, his son unwrapped some objects from a ceremonial pouch. I could clearly see that one was a scalpel. With the utmost sensitivity and care, the son began to cut a piece of flesh from his father's arm, near the shoulder. The father never missed a word of the chant as his son cut into him. I made myself watch as the blood ran down his arm. Halfway through the cutting the father looked at the son with a calm and completely open face. The son looked up into his father's eyes. At that moment I saw a man pass on to his son, as his ancestors had passed on to him, the truth of the suffer-

Full moon at Tassajara.

ing of life, and teach that one could stand there in the middle of pain still open, with perfect equanimity and grace. When the son finally finished I felt limp, clear and empty, both physically and emotionally. At the last moment I would have given them anything.

The father motioned for his son to sit down and for the drummer to stop. He circled the fire again, letting his blood drip into it as he began to pray. He prayed for understanding of the interconnectedness of everything, and for the return of balance. As he gave his flesh to the fire, I believed that what he asked was possible. When he sat down the room went silent.

But after only a few minutes I could see as I looked around the room, that we were already putting ourselves together. We were insulating ourselves from the pain. The felt connection was dissipating as if the suffering we had witnessed wasn't our really our own.

Wendy Johnson's touching celebration of the passing of the Coast Live Oak tree that grew in front of the Green Gulch Farm office. This piece, like the previous one, is about death and continuity. –M.W.

Sitting Together Under a Dead Tree

Wendy Johnson

SUMMER 1996

There is a beautiful story about Shakyamuni Buddha that Katagiri Roshi told us which I cannot forget. There was a time in India, long ago, when diplomatic relations failed between the neighboring countries of Magadha and Kapilivatthu, where the Shakya clan of the Buddha lived.

When the Shakya people realized that the king of Magadha was planning to attack them, they implored the Buddha to step forward and make peace. The Buddha agreed. Although he proposed peace in many ways, the king of Magadha could not hear the Buddha. His mind would not stop burning and finally he decided to attack.

Shakyamuni Buddha went out by himself and sat in meditation under a dead tree on the side of the road leading to Kapilivatthu. The king of Magadha passed along the road with his army and saw the Buddha sitting under the dead tree in the full blast of the sun. So the king asked, "Why do you sit under this dead tree?" The Buddha answered the king very calmly, "I feel cool, even under this dead tree, because it is growing near my native country."

Summer 1996

The answer pierced the heart of the king and he returned to his country with his army. Later this same king was incited to war and his army destroyed Kapilivatthu. Shakyamuni Buddha stood by and watched his native land being destroyed.

There are two points to this story. First, real peace is not a matter of discussion. This is why Shakyamuni Buddha sat in meditation under the dead tree, thoroughly at peace, "merging with real peace beyond the idea of peace or no peace" as Katagiri Roshi used to say. The second point is that no matter how long we emphasize the need for real peace to all beings, not everyone will accept our peace. To approach real peace requires a strong vow, a vow with deep roots, a vow that cannot be shaken, like the dead tree under which the Buddha sat, no matter what.

Wendy Johnson.

This winter at Green Gulch Farm, we lost two of our great teachers, the Coast Live Oak tree that grew in front of the office and the giant Monterey Pine growing by the zendo door and shading our barn meditation hall. Both of these trees were weakened by damage and disease. During the winter Rohatsu sesshin, some of us practiced night sitting under the shelter of these deep-rooted ones, feeling the real peace that welled up from their dark pool of roots.

In 1990, to celebrate the twentieth anniversary of Earth Day, we had a special ceremony for our Coast Live Oak tree. Following an inspiration of the forest monks of Thailand who have given ordination to their oldest and most venerated trees to protect those trees from the devastation of clear-cutting, we had an ordination ceremony at Green Gulch for the Coast Live Oak. Tenshin Reb Anderson, as Abbot of Zen Center, ordained our cracked-open oak tree and gave it the Dharma name, "Great Bodhisattva Precepts Tree," while a group of a hundred or more of us joined in chanting and circumambulating the grand oak at the center of Green Gulch.

This spring the oak and the pine are gone from our landscape. The oak toppled over in the hurricane-force winds of early December that left west Marin without electrical power for more than a week. And the massive Monterey Pine by the back door of the meditation hall was removed this March, killed by bark beetles and other diseases.

We celebrated the passage of these noble ones with sadness and regret. When I walk to zazen in the early dawn, way before the rising of the light, I can still hear the voice of the oak tree in the sound of the ocean traveling across the swept open landscape of Green Gulch. And when we sit in the zendo in the early autumn, captive audience to the delighted cries and coos of the blue jays as they peck open the oil-rich seeds of the Monterey Pine on the old roof above our heads, I am sure that these seeds come from the roots of trees of real peace, from those trees that shelter and nourish our practice, lifetime after lifetime.

In the garden we have planted local acorns of the Coast Live Oak and some fat seeds of the zendo Monterey Pine. The oak seedling is eight inches high, covered with the downy bloom of vigor on its spring leaves. The pine is growing vigorously, waiting to be planted. I dream that as we work to plant the garden around the tea house, these new trees will stand sentry as the wild fringe where the cultivated field of our practice runs into the old landscape of real, inexhaustible peace.

Re-opening of Green Gulch zendo 1992.

Rachael Carr's "The Agony of Hate" is about repentance, compassion, and transformation. We all make mistakes, but what do we do about them? –M.W.

The Agony of Hate

Rachel Carr

SPRING 1998

Nothing endures but change.
  –HERACLITUS

My feelings for the Japanese people were sharply divided between hate and love. I had suffered greatly from starvation and cold in Shanghai when the Japanese occupied this city. In the 1950s when I made my home in Tokyo with my family, I agonized over how to rid myself of this hate. I began a serious study of the language and various cultural arts. Before long I was accepted in the warm embrace of my Japanese tutors and new friends.

I thought a great deal about finding a place where I could study the philosophy of Zen. Still, I wanted to make peace with the inner conflicts of my mind.

In one of my jaunts through the suburbs of Tokyo, I discovered a little-known temple that became a haven for me. As I approached the garden I was surprised to see a slender, tall Caucasian in his thirties, in Buddhist robes, raking the sand with a bamboo broom. In this small garden was the harmony of force, of nature, and of spirit. It was deceptively simple in design, but it is this very quality that gives it power. The rocks were so arranged in a sea of raked sand that some remained hidden from any vantage point, suggesting life's mysteries. The Zen masters believe that a spiritual garden of this kind speaks, but only to those who are willing to listen.

I approached the monk and asked if I could study Zen in the temple. He smiled and said in an American accent that I had come to the right place. In Japan it is customary to carry name cards, so I handed him one and followed him inside the temple. I wondered how this man with a shaved head had chosen a life of retreat in a foreign country. The mystery soon revealed itself.

"Please wait here," he said in a soft tone, "I will call Suzuki *Sensei* (teacher). He will be the newly appointed *hojo-san* (Abbot) of this temple."

The tiny waiting room was simply furnished. Nothing garish offended the eye. The bare walls were a soft beige enhanced by a polished bench and a dynamic calligraphic scroll that hung above two morning glories with their long, rhythmic tendrils peeking out of a slender bamboo vase. Printed by hand in small letters attached to the scroll was the English translation: "Lost in the beauty of nature."

"*Irrashai* (welcome)," a melodious voice greeted me. It was the new Abbot, a man of slender build and medium height with unusually expressive eyes. I apologized for the intrusion.

"*Iye! Iye!* (no! no!)" he said with a broad smile. Breaking into fluent English he added, "It's a pleasure to meet you. I understand you want to study Zen."

"Yes," I nodded, and went on to explain to him my distress and the almost insurmountable difficulty I anticipated in resolving it.

The young Abbot listened sympathetically and nodded as if he understood the depth of my anguish. "The only way to find your inner peace," he said, "is by knowing that others have suffered in similar ways and how they have transcended agonizing barriers."

"You are perhaps wondering what the gentle, tall *gaijin* (foreigner) you have just met is doing in my temple. Shigeru is his Japanese name given to him by our revered Roshi. He has abandoned his worldly cares and shares a life of serenity and peace with us here.

"I will tell you how we met. It is not an easy story to relate. When Tokyo was bombed by American planes during the Second World War, I lost my entire family. I was wandering in a daze among the ruins when the Roshi of this temple found me. I have lived with him since. He is now a man of advanced age, and that's the reason I will become the new Abbot, which is most unusual at my age of 45. All through those years I had been sheltered in this temple, protected by compassion and dedicated only to a spiritual existence. Though I loved the Roshi I could not understand how he was able to forgive the enemy who exploded two atomic bombs on innocent Japanese. I find it difficult to admit that years of daily meditation did not erase this deep-seated hate. That was the time when Shigeru came to this temple for instruction in zazen (meditation) and was a faithful student for a long time. Whenever I saw him, I was stirred with mounting fury.

Stone Buddha head at Hiroshima Museum. Burn scars on stone!

"On the day I was to be installed as the Abbot, I was so unsettled inside myself. Was I really capable of taking over the mantle from the Roshi? He was the personification of compassion and forgiveness: I was the one plagued with hate and revenge!"

The Abbot described this memorable day in detail. He was accustomed to rising at dawn. On hearing the sounds of the drum that broke the early morning stillness in the temple, he quickly slipped into his Buddhist robes and strode barefoot across the flagstones to draw water from the well, rinsing his hands and mouth as a daily purification ritual. He lingered in the garden. He knew it well. Every day he scrubbed and swept it, sprinkling water on the winding paths of flagstones and on the soft velvet moss. He raked the bed of white gravel into artful symmetry around a grouping of rocks to simulate an island. He knew it well and spoke of this spiritual sanctuary with passion. It was here that the monks, invited by the Roshi for this auspicious day, chanted the Buddhist Sutras. He lit an incense stick and planted it in the ashes of the porcelain brazier. Facing the bronze statue of Buddha, he placed a zabuton (square cushion) in front of it and made his prostration, then knelt on the zabuton and lowered his head to the polished floor, his hands, palms up. His limber legs folded easily into the lotus pose. Eyes half-closed, he drew long breaths, focusing his mind on its rhythmic flow. He chanted the Sutras in a deep baritone. He thought of the Roshi who loved his voice and listened to his chanting every day.

Somehow he could not anchor his concentration. He was unable to find his path to the level of serenity where all extremes disappear. The flow of boundless thoughts and images paraded through his mind. One quotation was particularly persistent, and he recited it carefully, pronouncing each meaningful word:

"No gate stands on public roads. There are paths of various kinds. Those who pass this barrier walk freely throughout the universe."

He knew of his weakness. He was unable to pass this barrier and walk freely throughout the universe. In his mind he could hear the Roshi's voice assuring him that there are times when one must use continued gentle persuasion eventually to reach the depth of stillness. Hard as he tried, only his body was in repose.

Spring 1998

His mind was unbearably painful. So many memories inflicted themselves on his need to bring about inner calm. His anger soared whenever he thought of the gaijin—mostly Americans who came to the temple for instruction in zazen. Did they really understand zazen and the total devotion that one must have to achieve any degree of serenity? He had failed. How could they succeed? Deep in his heart he had qualms about his capability of assuming the role of an Abbot.

On his way to the Roshi's chambers he heard a familiar voice laughing. "No, it couldn't be!" he thought with a shudder. His heart pounded when he heard the resonant laughter again. He feared the worst. On entering the chambers he saw Shigeru sitting awkwardly on a zabuton. His long legs were loosely crossed and he was chatting amiably to the Roshi in a mixture of Japanese and English. The Roshi smiled at the Abbot's arrival, then suddenly excused himself and withdrew from the room, followed by the monks in attendance. The two young men, now left alone, faced each other.

The Abbot bowed to break the silence.

"I am humbled by your presence," he told Shigeru.

"And I, yours," Shigeru bowed lower to express humility. "I have heard that your parents and three brothers were killed in the war. I suppose you feel that we Americans killed your family with our bombs. Remember, Japan started the war!"

The Abbot felt as if a dagger had pierced his heart when Shigeru laughed: "Ah that clever old Roshi. He had reasons for bringing us together on this auspicious day, challenging you to the edge! You see, my father was killed by the Japanese gendarme in China. I was a teenager then. My mother died soon after from grief."

"Was your father a spy?" the Abbot asked, gritting his teeth.

"No, just a simple devoted missionary who loved the Chinese, but the Japanese were convinced that he was engaged in some kind of espionage. He was tortured and died in a concentration camp."

Shigeru was now caught up in his own bitterness.

"You see, I didn't choose to come to your country, I was sent here by my company. The reason I have been coming to the temple for study in zazen is to rid myself of the hate I harbor for the Japanese, except the Roshi. I love him. He is like a father to me."

The Abbot's heart was racing. "That makes us brothers!" he thought, suppressing his emotions.

"Tell me," Shigeru asked, "Why do you refer to me as the gaijin?"

"That is what you are. A foreigner. All non-Japanese are gaijin to us."

"And where did you learn to speak such fluent English?"

"At school, and I read a lot."

"Perhaps I have no right to ask this," Shigeru said, "It's rather personal. How long did it take you to rise above anger and hate?"

It was then that the young Abbot searched his conscience for an honest answer.

"Only now," he admitted. With this confession he felt a sudden release from his tortured soul and a strange rising warmth for Shigeru. He burst into uncontrollable laughter.

"What's so funny?"

"You!" the Abbot said. "You really look ridiculous trying to meditate with those long legs that refuse to bend. I've watched you many times struggling with yourself."

"I must have been quite a sight!"

The Abbot could no longer restrain the surge of affection he felt for the American. He reached out and clasped Shigeru's hand.

"Since we both look upon the Roshi as our father, that does make us brothers."

"Indeed!" Shigeru agreed.

The old Roshi had an uncanny sense of timing. When he entered the room he was pleased to see the two men in a warm embrace. He reminded them that the ceremony was about to begin.

"Are you ready?" he asked.

The young Abbot smiled with tears in his eyes.

"Yes, now I can truly say that I am!"

"Then it is time for you to be installed as hojo-san of this temple."

◈

After hearing this moving story I found it incredible that the three of us were caught in the same web of hate. Eventually I also came to terms with my own agony. I learned to forgive and forget. While living in Japan I developed a love for that country.

The Zen masters with whom I have studied in later years taught me that the spirit of Zen is feeling life, and that Zen has no doctrinal teaching, no formal program of spiritual development. Its philosophy develops a sense of clarity that permits one to absorb the sufferings of one's life. I have learned that we are the possessors of special perceptions and ability. We can, with the proper use of will and mind, come to understand just who and where we are in the scheme of things.

The Roshi died in 1975, followed by the Abbot in 1987. Shigeru is living somewhere in the United States as a Zen monk. The calligraphic scroll that I saw when I first came to the temple was given to me, and now graces my home.

This article about Tassajara's response to a large fire shows
something about Tassajara community life as well as the
large-scale drama of fire in the forest.

Fire Comes to Tassajara

Gaelyn Godwin

FALL 1999

On September 8, 1999, a lightning storm in the Ventana
Wilderness started at least ten small fires. The small fires
grew slowly and joined to become two huge fires, named the
Tassajara/Five Fire and the Kirk/Hare Fire. The Tassajara/
Five Fire encroached on the Tassajara watershed. Here are
some excerpts from notes kept by Gaelyn Godwin as the fire
moved closer to Tassajara Zen Mountain Center.

On Wednesday, September 15, I drove up the road in the Tassajara pickup to make a quick trip to Salinas for building
materials. I had just about reached the bathtub near the ridge when
the first of a long phalanx of fire vehicles stopped me. Captain
Jamie Copple, in command of the operation, asked me to pull over
to let the wide engines proceed—they were on their way to evac-
uate Tassajara. I asked if I could turn my truck around and return
to Tassajara. When I got back, far in advance of the slow parade
of engines, most people were still at lunch but Leslie James, the
director, and several others came outside to meet the fire chief
before he entered the gate. Jamie informed us that fire was racing
up the ridge to the southwest, behind the Tony Trail, and was
expected to reach Tassajara within hours. They wanted all but a
small group evacuated within half an hour. The huge engines waited
outside the gates, engines thrumming, while we took this in. Then
we went to work: a group of volunteers gathered in the courtyard
and twenty-eight people were allowed to stay. Most of them were
sent to secure the buildings, some were sent to help the evacuees

Clouds and smoke at Tassajara.

move and to make sure the activity in the parking lot proceeded smoothly.

By the time the evacuation was complete the fire had reached the ridge and was flaming over the top, backing down the steep sides of the ridge that looms high above the Tony Trail. The flames were large. Later we would be able to see that the entire east facing slope of the Tassajara watershed was burned to the ground, but for now just the crescent shaped piece of the ridge was clearly on fire.

The firefighters positioned their engines throughout Tassajara, in an array that Jamie had designed after his earlier inspection visit. Now eighty-four firefighters were spreading out through Tassajara: three engines in the flats, two near the bathhouse, two near the stone rooms, one next to the zendo, two near the dining room, two near the shop and the propane tanks. Long lines of fire hose snaked through Tassajara, all of it charged with water and ready to go.

Meanwhile, the remaining Tassajara residents along with several work period volunteers were taking care of Tassajara: closing down all the buildings, removing small wooden altars, bringing the wooden objects down from the memorial site, cutting fire lines around the stupas and the photovoltaic panels, setting the sprinkler systems going on the wood shingled kitchen and on the propane tanks, filling in ditches that had been dug for projects but which would now be hazardous for the fire fighters.

Once our tasks were completed, our job was to wait until the fire got close enough so that Tassajara could be set afire all around us. Since the fire was approaching so fast from so many directions the plan was to wait until it was approximately 100 feet above us and then set "back fires" at Tassajara that would be drawn up to the main fires, thus exhausting the fuel around Tassajara and allowing the main fire to move elsewhere. After this, the plan was to spend however much time it required to clean things up and to extinguish falling embers. The fire teams expected the road to be closed by fire immediately and were planning to spend many weeks at Tassajara if necessary.

We established teams to keep the fire pumps going to provide continuous water to the engines. As evening approached, we established a communications network because the fire was still hovering outside of the back fire border and would slow down as night fell. Next on our agenda, dinner. Kathy Egan and Linda Macalwee organized the kitchen and cooked for 112 people. The firefighters pretty much kept to themselves at first, remaining alert and eating in shifts so that the engines were all kept ready, but they were quite pleased and surprised that we provided food for them. As the evening wore on, we knew we needed to rest, so, as the fire teams kept watch, the Tassajara residents moved into rooms very close to the center and went to sleep.

September 17, 1999

We spent yesterday waiting for the fire on the ridge to reach us. We learned much more about fire behavior and about each other. Today, three days into the fire here, the captains in charge of the inmates' team approach me to ask if the inmates can use the showers. As far as I can tell none of the firefighters have ventured into the bathhouse, and the inmates' captains are the first to ask. There are thirty-two inmates, and they use both the men's and women's sides. They haven't had a chance to bathe in days and they emerge looking good. They wear orange clothes while the regular fire fighters wear yellow fire shirts. They are camping out past the flats; they've discovered the free weights out there, and they are getting a little antsy with the lack of activity.

Actually all of the crews are beginning to notice that they have time on their hands and they begin to look around for ways to help. The afternoon kitchen is now staffed by Forest Service people in blue tee-shirts; they are strong, physically adept people, very calm in their movements. Engine Crew 27 takes on finishing up the repairs to Cabin 4 and then they move to help shop member Sarah Emerson finish installing the plywood to cover the insulation under the dining room. They are skilled and handy, accustomed to doing the repairs around their own station houses. Judith Keenan supervises firefighters all over the place: she has anybody with any time and moderate skill at work. They are beginning to show signs of merging with the Tassajara residents. There are often comments now about how special the place and the people are, about how unusually kind things seem here.

The Forest Service catering service insists on sending down meals for the firefighters, which they do not want, preferring our food. Jamie does everything he can to prevent this calamity. Nevertheless, buckets of heavy, meaty, high protein products arrive, and we do our best by putting out two long tables in the dining room with firefighter food on one and Tassajara cuisine on the other. One door is marked "Chicken"; the other door is marked "Not Chicken". Most firefighters select from both tables; some firefighters remain vegetarian for their entire stay. We end up sending a truckload of fresh leftovers to the homeless shelter in Salinas.

The road remains closed except for accompanied trips. The fire has reached the road in several places; back burning is taking place in others. I drive up the road several days in a row, following Jamie, to keep up with developments. Some days it's like driving through a burning forest—it is driving through a burning forest; other days the fire is down in the valleys.

Someone suggests that we have an evening Dharma event, a simple question-and-answer for the firefighters. I assume that there are only three or four who are interested in the practice we are doing, yet, surprisingly, when Luminous Owl Charlie Henkel and

I arrive to do the answer part of the question-and-answer, the room is full. About half of the firefighters have come, along with most of the Tassajara people. In the middle of it, Jeff, a firefighter from Los Angeles, asks how to start a meditation practice and we move casually into basic zazen instruction right there and then, on our dining room chairs. As the group sits upright, gathering their attention, straightening up, relaxing their shoulders, the whole room becomes gently quiet and still. The first stillness since the fire reached us.

The next day several of the firefighters seek out the ino for further instruction. When I walked through the upper garden and around the side of the zendo I glanced up to see that the zendo shoe rack was full of firefighter boots—large heavy leather boots with many hooks for laces. It was a wonderful sight, touching me somehow more than any other single impression during the fire. I have seen many wonderful things at Tassajara, and the rows of well-worn firefighter boots on the zendo racks will remain emblematic for me.

Fire trucks at Tassajra.

They've all fallen under the spell of Tassajara now. No hesitation now in going to the bathhouse. Some of them have made a few gentle bows as they leave the kitchen. They smile openly and explore the cookbooks, the bookstore, making themselves at home in the kitchen, in the shop, some even in the zendo.

They know they are the envy of other crews in the forest. Word is out that something curious is going on here. Reporters have begun to arrive. Teasing is happening after an article appeared describing the firefighters' proximity to the famous Tassajara Hot Springs and bathhouse.

The fire is still burning just out of reach and the valley fills with smoke each evening. The firefighters have fixed practically everything we were working on when work period came to its abrupt end; the inmate crews have even cleared a fire line along the length of the phone cable and an area fifty feet around the phone transmitter. This was a difficult task and they are justifiably proud of their work. We won't lose the phone after all. They have now begun to dig a new septic line for us.

September 21, 1999

Tonight is quiet and we're all sensing that our paradise is coming to an end. The decision makers at the higher level won't let two strike teams (ten engine crews of five people each) stay to protect Tassajara forever. Besides, we've got forty people outside, somewhere, wanting to come in to begin practice period. Tonight, heavy rain is predicted and the fire crews have accepted our offer of rooms; many of them sleep inside Tassajara guest rooms this night. Not a few choose to remain in tents near their engines.

Rain arrived, along with lightning. Not enough rain to douse fires lurking under trees. Rain and large flakes of ash fall at the same time. Ashes have been falling throughout the event, of course, some are incinerated leaves—exact shadows of their formerly green selves. It is more humid now, but once the humidity lifts and the day heats up as predicted it will be a dangerous situation again, they all say. But, in truth, they seem to want it to heat up; this is, after all, their chosen line of work. They like forest fires and they like Tassajara. At breakfast this morning one captain, when told

Gaelyn Godwin.

that it might rain again reacts with disappointment, "They said it was going to be hot and dry today, not raining!"

September 22, 1999

Suddenly, at 11:30 A.M., Jamie returns to order all the engine crews to pack up and move. It is the moment we've all dreaded—the end of paradise. The bustle of activity masks the emotions and keeps the farewells short and hurried. But we postpone the ending, and decide to have a final lunch together, spending one last boisterous half hour in the dining room. Then the parade begins. The residents line the road waving goodbye as each huge engine pulls toward the gate, all the lights flashing and swirling in farewell. Some firefighters put their hands in gassho as they drive out. The final two vehicles contain the inmate fire crews and they also smile their thanks to us and put up V for victory or, hopefully, for peace, as they leave.

The fires are still burning, but Tassajara is not in immediate danger. Jamie will return with two new crews tonight. The two crews had been stationed at Church Ranch and had protected it, enduring several days of heavy smoke in the valley, trapped by the fire on the Church Road before they could get out. Jamie leads the new crews around Tassajara himself, pointing out the important landmarks. The one feature of which he is most proud is our fire standpipe system. All the firefighters have been impressed with the prominent yellow standpipes lining Tassajara.

September 23, 1999

This morning the air is extremely humid and, even though there were lightning strikes last night, the fire in our area seems quiet. For the first time in two weeks we have permission to run on the trails and, from the top of the Horse Pasture Trail near the Tassajara cut-off, we can see how extensive the fire was in the Tassajara watershed. We were lucky, very lucky. Back at Tassajara we learn that the remaining two crews are being pulled out and assigned to duties on the northern end of the fire. Jamie returns to take his laundry off the line and to say goodbye; he will be transferred, helicoptered in to another hot situation on the other side of the forest but he is proud of the friendships that were nurtured here.

Later on in the afternoon another news crew drops in with Forest Service guides. The focus of their interest is the remarkable story of the bond that developed between the fire crews and the Tassajara monks. Apparently legends are growing about this event at Tassajara—on the one side, the legendary kindness and hospitality of the twenty-eight Tassajara residents, and on the other, the legendary receptivity, professionalism and kindness of the eighty-four firefighters.

✦

The fire is quiet around us but huge helicopters pass overhead throughout the following days, approaching the fire directly now that the perimeter has been established. Fires are still burning to the north and west, but the road is open and Tassajara residents have begun to return. Preparations for practice period are under way again. We are prepared to continue to live in this wilderness. As one fire captain said, "If you want to live here you'd better learn to live with fire." And we are learning.

In the Spring of 2000, I taught a class on the oxherding pictures and asked students to submit their own versions of the well-known scenes, depicting the path of Zen. –M.W.

The Oxherding Pictures
Robert Dodge
SUMMER 2000

Searching for the Ox

all alone
something missing
everything shifting
and unsteady

Seeing the Traces

what's this?
something flashes
startling
right under his nose

Seeing the Ox

sudden insight
overwhelming
unexpected
in his face

The Ox Forgotten

the dream is over
but something lingers
safe, content
he floats

Herding the Ox

dropped away
too much to handle
just observing
looks OK

Catching the Ox

chaos!
nowhere to stand
attachment, aversion
clinging in fear

The Ox and Boy Both Gone

through the window
moonlight streaming
floods everything
all disolves

Returning to the Origin

morning sunlight
restores the world
so familiar
ever new

Coming Home on the Ox's Back

strong and steady
marching homeward
now is found
what was not lost

Entering the Market with
Bliss-Bearing Hands

life goes on
moment by moment
his delight
shows the way

This confrontation between Abbot Sojun Weitsman and Mitsuzen Lou Hartman took place on January 29, 1997 on the occasion of Sojun stepping down as Abbott of the San Francisco Zen Center. It is a moment in a thirty-year discussion between two practitioners of The Way. Dogen once said life is one continuous mistake. Dear reader, continue on! –M.W.

Mondo (Dharma Dialogue)
Mel Weitsman and Lou Hartman
SUMMER 1997

MITSUZEN LOU HARTMAN: One third of my life has been spent in this practice and you were my first teacher. I can still remember your original teaching. One morning I ran into your old house on Dwight Way, waving Daisetz Suzuki's *No Mind* and saying, "I just have to talk to you about this book!" And you said "*I* don't have to talk with you about that book. But if you want to go up to the zendo and sit, that's fine with me."

Well, I didn't realize it at the time, but that was my first step away from practice "based on intellectual understanding." Now it's twenty-seven years later and not only don't I talk about books anymore, I don't *write* books anymore, and I don't even *read* them. So I'll tell you something—your advice was a big mistake. [laughter] So what do you have to say to me *now?*

SOJUN MEL WEITSMAN [without a pause]: Make the best of a bad mistake.

Unless otherwise indicated, images are courtesy of San Francisco Zen Center. The editor gratefully acknowledges the following individuals for use of their work as either cover art for Wind Bell, separate photographs, or drawings:

Minoru Aoki: p. 8; Morley Baer: p. 19; Butch Baluyut: pp. 69, 96; Robert Boni: pp. 129, 161, 180, 238; Dhyana Carbarga: p. 252; Francis Checkley: p. 88; Sterling Doghty: p. 307; Lyn Flitton: p. 308; John Gruenwald: p. 42; Karen Hamilton: p. 34 (drawing); Heather Hiett: pp. 242, 301; Chris Honeysett: p. 250; Dan Howe: pp. 72, 262, 296; Judith Keenan: pp. 312, 315; Rob Lee: p. 81; Martina Lutz: p. 294; Mayumi Oda: p. 28; Robert Quagliata: pp. 166, 216, 270; Paul Reps: p. 265; Gib Robertson: p. 145; Michael Sawyer: p. 153; Hoitsu Suzuki: p. 101; Mitsu Suzuki: p. 37 (calligraphy); Kaz Tanahashi: p. 142; Katharine Thanas: p. 31; Hodo Tobase: p. 281; Dan Welch: p. 78; Barbara Wenger: pp. 44, 65, 115, 248, 304; William Williams: p. 286.